ILLUSTRATED COURSE GUIDES

Microsoft® Excel® 2010

Intermediate

ILLUSTRATED COURSE GUIDES

Microsoft® Excel® 2010

Intermediate

Lynn Wermers

Australia • Brazil • Japan • Korea • Mexico • Singapore • Spain • United Kingdom • United States

COURSE TECHNOLOGY
CENGAGE Learning™

Illustrated Course Guide: Microsoft® Excel® 2010 Intermediate

Lynn Wermers

Vice President, Publisher: Nicole Jones Pinard

Executive Editor: Marjorie Hunt

Associate Acquisitions Editor: Brandi Shailer

Senior Product Manager: Christina Kling Garrett

Associate Product Manager: Michelle Camisa

Editorial Assistant: Kim Klasner

Director of Marketing: Cheryl Costantini

Senior Marketing Manager: Ryan DeGrote

Marketing Coordinator: Kristen Panciocco

Contributing Author: Carol Cram

Developmental Editor: Barbara Clemens

Content Project Manager: Danielle Chouhan

Copy Editor: Mark Goodin

Proofreader: Vicki Zimmer

Indexer: BIM Indexing and Proofreading Services

QA Manuscript Reviewers: Nicole Ashton, John Frietas, Serge Palladino, Susan Pedicini, Jeff Schwartz, Danielle Shaw, Marianne Snow

Print Buyer: Fola Orekoya

Cover Designer: GEX Publishing Services

Cover Artist: Mark Hunt

Composition: GEX Publishing Services

Trademarks:

Some of the product names and company names used in this book have been used for identification purposes only and may be trademarks or registered trademarks of their respective manufacturers and sellers.

Microsoft and the Office logo are either registered trademarks or trademarks of Microsoft Corporation in the United States and/or other countries. Course Technology, Cengage Learning is an independent entity from Microsoft Corporation, and not affiliated with Microsoft in any manner.

Library of Congress Control Number: 2010938582

ISBN-13: 978-0-538-74837-7
ISBN-10: 0-538-74837-0

Course Technology
20 Channel Center Street
Boston, MA 02210
USA

Cengage Learning is a leading provider of customized learning solutions with office locations around the globe, including Singapore, the United Kingdom, Australia, Mexico, Brazil, and Japan. Locate your local office at:
international.cengage.com/region

Cengage Learning products are represented in Canada by Nelson Education, Ltd.

To learn more about Course Technology, visit **www.cengage.com/coursetechnology**

To learn more about Cengage Learning, visit **www.cengage.com**

Purchase any of our products at your local college store or at our preferred online store **www.cengagebrain.com**

Printed in the United States of America
2 3 4 5 6 7 8 9 18 17 16 15 14 13 12 11

Brief Contents

Contents

Preface

Welcome to *Illustrated Course Guide: Microsoft® Excel® 2010 Intermediate*. If this is your first experience with the Illustrated Course Guides, you'll see that this book has a unique design: each skill is presented on two facing pages, with steps on the left and screens on the right. The layout makes it easy to learn a skill without having to read a lot of text and flip pages to see an illustration.

This book is an ideal learning tool for a wide range of learners—the "rookies" will find the clean design easy to follow and focused with only essential information presented, and the "hotshots" will appreciate being able to move quickly through the lessons to find the information they need without reading a lot of text. The design also makes this a great reference after the course is over! See the illustration on the right to learn more about the pedagogical and design elements of a typical lesson.

What's New In This Edition

- **Fully Updated.** Highlights the new features of Microsoft Excel 2010 including creating sparklines, using Paste Preview, and the new Backstage view.

- **Maps to SAM 2010.** This book is designed to work with SAM (Skills Assessment Manager) 2010. SAM Assessment contains performance-based, hands-on SAM exams for each unit of this book, and SAM Training provides hands-on training for skills covered in the book. Some exercises are available in SAM Projects, which is auto-grading software that provides both learners and instructors with immediate, detailed feedback (SAM sold separately.) See page xii for more information on SAM.

Each two-page spread focuses on a single skill.

Introduction briefly explains why the lesson skill is important.

A case scenario motivates the the steps and puts learning in context.

UNIT
E
Excel 2010

Checking Formulas for Errors

When formulas result in errors, Excel displays an error value based on the error type. See Table E-1 for a description of the error types and error codes that might appear in worksheets. One way to check formulas in a worksheet for errors is to display the formulas on the worksheet rather than the formula results. You can also check for errors when entering formulas by using the IFERROR function. The IFERROR function simplifies the error-checking process for your worksheets. This function displays a message or value that you specify, rather than the one automatically generated by Excel, if there is an error in a formula. Kate asks you to use formulas to compare the tour revenues for January. You will use the IFERROR function to help catch formula errors.

STEPS

1. **Click cell B11, click the Formulas tab, click the AutoSum button in the Function Library group, then click the Enter button ✓ on the formula bar**
   The number of tours sold, 60, appears in cell B11.

2. **Drag the fill handle to copy the formula in cell B11 into cell C11, click the Auto Fill options list arrow, then click the Fill Without Formatting option button**
   The tour revenue total of $77,352 appears in cell C11. You decide to enter a formula to calculate the percentage of revenue the Pacific Odyssey tour represents by dividing the individual tour revenue figures by the total revenue figure. To help with error checking, you decide to enter the formula using the IFERROR function.

3. **Click cell D7, click the Logical button in the Function Library group, click IFERROR, with the insertion point in the Value text box, click cell C7, type /, click cell C11, press [Tab], in the Value_if_error text box, type ERROR, then click OK**
   The Pacific Odyssey tour revenue percentage of 19.75% appears in cell D7. You want to be sure that your error message will be displayed properly, so you decide to test it by intentionally creating an error. You copy and paste the formula—which has a relative address in the denominator, where an absolute address should be used.

   TROUBLE
   You will fix the ERROR codes in cells D8:D10 in the next step.

4. **Drag the fill handle to copy the formula in cell D7 into the range D8:D10**
   The ERROR value appears in cells D8:D10, as shown in Figure E-9. The errors are a result of the relative address for C11 in the denominator of the copied formula. Changing the relative address of C11 in the copied formula to an absolute address of $C$11 will correct the errors.

   QUICK TIP
   You can also check formulas for errors using the buttons in the Formula Auditing group on the Formulas tab.

5. **Double-click cell D7, select C11 in the formula, press [F4], then click ✓ on the formula bar**
   The formula now contains an absolute reference to cell C11.

6. **Copy the corrected formula in cell D7 into the range D8:D10**
   The tour revenue percentages now appear in all four cells, without error messages, as shown in Figure E-10. You want to check all of your worksheet formulas by displaying them on the worksheet.

   QUICK TIP
   You can also display worksheet formulas by holding [Ctrl] and pressing [`].

7. **Click the Show Formulas button in the Formula Auditing group**
   The formulas appear in columns B, C, and D. You want to display the formula results again. The Show Formulas button works as a toggle, turning the feature on and off with each click.

8. **Click the Show Formulas button in the Formula Auditing group**
   The formula results appear on the worksheet.

9. **Add your name to the center section of the footer, save the workbook, preview the worksheet, close the workbook, then submit the workbook to your instructor**

Excel 112   Analyzing Data Using Formulas

Tips and troubleshooting advice, right where you need it—next to the step itself.

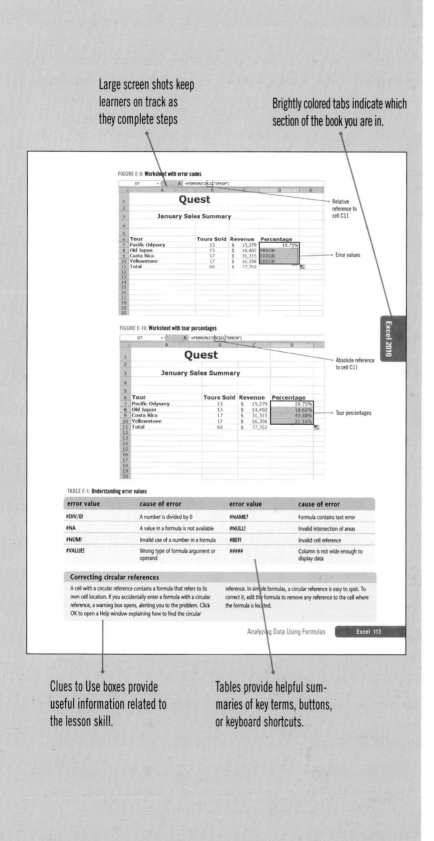

Large screen shots keep learners on track as they complete steps

Brightly colored tabs indicate which section of the book you are in.

FIGURE E-9: Worksheet with error codes

Quest

January Sales Summary

Tour	Tours Sold	Revenue	Percentage
Pacific Odyssey	13	$ 15,279	19.75%
Old Japan	13	$ 14,402	ERROR
Costa Rica	17	$ 31,315	ERROR
Yellowstone	17	$ 16,356	ERROR
Total	60	$ 77,352	

Relative reference to cell C11

Error values

FIGURE E-10: Worksheet with tour percentages

Quest

January Sales Summary

Tour	Tours Sold	Revenue	Percentage
Pacific Odyssey	13	$ 15,279	19.75%
Old Japan	13	$ 14,402	18.62%
Costa Rica	17	$ 31,315	40.48%
Yellowstone	17	$ 16,356	21.14%
Total	60	$ 77,352	

Absolute reference to cell C11

Tour percentages

TABLE E-1: Understanding error values

error value	cause of error	error value	cause of error
#DIV/0!	A number is divided by 0	#NAME?	Formula contains text error
#NA	A value in a formula is not available	#NULL!	Invalid intersection of areas
#NUM!	Invalid use of a number in a formula	#REF!	Invalid cell reference
#VALUE!	Wrong type of formula argument or operand	#####	Column is not wide enough to display data

Correcting circular references

A cell with a circular reference contains a formula that refers to its own cell location. If you accidentally enter a formula with a circular reference, a warning box opens, alerting you to the problem. Click OK to open a Help window explaining how to find the circular reference. In simple formulas, a circular reference is easy to spot. To correct it, edit the formula to remove any reference to the cell where the formula is located.

Analyzing Data Using Formulas   Excel 113

Excel 2010

Clues to Use boxes provide useful information related to the lesson skill.

Tables provide helpful summaries of key terms, buttons, or keyboard shortcuts.

Assignments

The lessons use Quest Specialty Travel, a fictional adventure travel company, as the case study. The assignments on the light yellow pages at the end of each unit increase in difficulty. Assignments include:

- **Concepts Review** consist of multiple choice, matching, and screen identification questions.
- **Skills Reviews** are hands-on, step-by-step exercises that review the skills covered in each lesson in the unit.
- **Independent Challenges** are case projects requiring critical thinking and application of the unit skills. The Independent Challenges increase in difficulty, with the first one in each unit being the easiest. Independent Challenges 2 and 3 become increasingly open-ended, requiring more independent problem solving.
- **Real Life Independent Challenges** are practical exercises in which learners create documents to help them with their every day lives.
- **Advanced Challenge Exercises** set within the Independent Challenges provide optional steps for more advanced learners.
- **Visual Workshops** are practical, self-graded capstone projects that require independent problem solving.

About SAM

SAM is the premier proficiency-based assessment and training environment for Microsoft Office. Web-based software along with an inviting user interface provide maximum teaching and learning flexibility. SAM builds learners' skills and confidence with a variety of real-life simulations, and SAM Projects' assignments prepare learners for today's workplace.

The SAM system includes Assessment, Training, and Projects, featuring page references and remediation for this book as well as Course Technology's Microsoft Office textbooks. With SAM, instructors can enjoy the flexibility of creating assignments based on content from their favorite Microsoft Office books or based on specific course objectives. Instructors appreciate the scheduling and reporting options that have made SAM the market-leading online testing and training software for over a decade. Over 2,000 performance-based questions and matching Training simulations, as well as tens of thousands of objective-based questions from many Course Technology texts, provide instructors with a variety of choices across multiple applications. SAM Projects is auto-grading software that lets learners complete projects using Microsoft Office and then receive detailed feedback on their finished projects. (SAM sold separately.)

SAM Assessment

- Content for these hands-on, performance-based tasks includes Word, Excel, Access, PowerPoint, Internet Explorer, Outlook, and Windows. Includes tens of thousands of objective-based questions from many Course Technology texts.

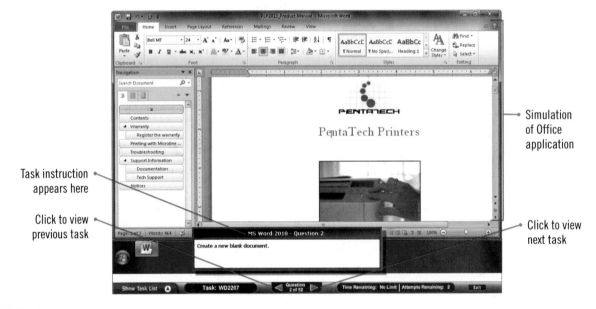

SAM Training

- Observe mode allows the learners to watch and listen to a task as it is being completed.
- Practice mode allows the learner to follow guided arrows and hear audio prompts to help visual learners know how to complete a task.
- Apply mode allows the learner to prove what they've learned by completing a project using on-screen instructions.

SAM Projects

- Live-in-the-application assignments in Word, Excel, Access and PowerPoint allow learners to create a project using the Microsoft Office software and then receive immediate, detailed feedback on their completed project.
- Learners receive detailed feedback on their project within minutes.
- Unique anti-cheating detection feature is encrypted into the data files to ensure learners complete their own assignments.

Instructor Resources

The Instructor Resources CD is Course Technology's way of putting the resources and information needed to teach and learn effectively into your hands. With an integrated array of teaching and learning tools that offer you and your learners a broad range of technology-based instructional options, we believe this CD represents the highest quality and most cutting edge resources available to instructors today. The resources available with this book are:

• **Instructor's Manual**—Available as an electronic file, the Instructor's Manual includes detailed lecture topics with teaching tips for each unit.

• **Sample Syllabus**—Prepare and customize your course easily using this sample course outline.

• **PowerPoint Presentations**—Each unit has a corresponding PowerPoint presentation that you can use in lecture, distribute to your learners, or customize to suit your course.

• **Figure Files**—The figures in the text are provided on the Instructor Resources CD to help you illustrate key topics or concepts. You can create traditional overhead transparencies by printing the figure files. Or you can create electronic slide shows by using the figures in a presentation program such as PowerPoint.

• **Solutions to Exercises**—Solutions to Exercises contains every file learners are asked to create or modify in the lessons and end-of-unit material. Also provided in this section, there is a document outlining the solutions for the end-of-unit Concepts Review, Skills Review, and Independent Challenges. An Annotated Solution File and Grading Rubric accompany each file and can be used together for quick and easy grading.

• **Data Files for Learners**—To complete most of the units in this book, learners will need Data Files. You can post the Data Files on a file server for learners to copy. The Data Files are available on the Instructor Resources CD-ROM, the Review Pack, and can also be downloaded from cengagebrain.com. For more information on how to download the Data Files, see the inside back cover.

Instruct learners to use the Data Files List included on the Review Pack and the Instructor Resources CD. This list gives instructions on copying and organizing files.

• **ExamView**—ExamView is a powerful testing software package that allows you to create and administer printed, computer (LAN-based), and Internet exams. ExamView includes hundreds of questions that correspond to the topics covered in this text, enabling learners to generate detailed study guides that include page references for further review. The computer-based and Internet testing components allow learners to take exams at their computers, and also saves you time by grading each exam automatically.

Content for Online Learning.

Course Technology has partnered with the leading distance learning solution providers and class-management platforms today. To access this material, visit www.cengage.com/webtutor and search for your title. Instructor resources include the following: additional case projects, sample syllabi, PowerPoint presentations, and more. For additional information, please contact your sales representative. For learners to access this material, they must have purchased a WebTutor PIN-code specific to this title and your campus platform. The resources for learners might include (based on instructor preferences): topic reviews, review questions, practice tests, and more.

Acknowledgements

Instructor Advisory Board

We thank our Instructor Advisory Board who gave us their opinions and guided our decisions as we updated our texts for Microsoft Office 2010. They are as follows:

Terri Helfand, Chaffey Community College

Barbara Comfort, J. Sargeant Reynolds Community College

Brenda Nielsen, Mesa Community College

Sharon Cotman, Thomas Nelson Community College

Marian Meyer, Central New Mexico Community College

Audrey Styer, Morton College

Richard Alexander, Heald College

Xiaodong Qiao, Heald College

Student Advisory Board

We also thank our Student Advisory Board members, who shared their experiences using the book and offered suggestions to make it better: **Latasha Jefferson**, Thomas Nelson Community College, **Gary Williams**, Thomas Nelson Community College, **Stephanie Miller**, J. Sargeant Reynolds Community College, **Sarah Styer**, Morton Community College, **Missy Marino**, Chaffey College

Author Acknowledgements

Lynn Wermers Thanks to Barbara Clemens for her insightful contributions, invaluable feedback, great humor, and patience. Thanks also to Christina Kling Garrett for her encouragement and support in guiding and managing this project.

Read This Before You Begin

Frequently Asked Questions

What are Data Files?

A Data File is a partially completed Excel spreadsheet or another type of file that you use to complete the steps in the units and exercises to create the final document that you submit to your instructor. Each unit opener page lists the Data Files that you need for that unit.

Where are the Data Files?

Your instructor will provide the Data Files to you or direct you to a location on a network drive from which you can download them. For information on how to download the Data Files from cengagebrain.com, see the inside back cover.

What software was used to write and test this book?

This book was written and tested using a typical installation of Microsoft Office 2010 Professional Plus on a computer with a typical installation of Microsoft Windows 7 Ultimate.

The browser used for any Web-dependent steps is Internet Explorer 8.

Do I need to be connected to the Internet to complete the steps and exercises in this book?

Some of the exercises in this book require that your computer be connected to the Internet. If you are not connected to the Internet, see your instructor for information on how to complete the exercises.

What do I do if my screen is different from the figures shown in this book?

This book was written and tested on computers with monitors set at a resolution of 1024 × 768. If your screen shows more or less information than the figures in the book, your monitor is probably set at a higher or lower resolution. If you don't see something on your screen, you might have to scroll down or up to see the object identified in the figures.

The Ribbon—the blue area at the top of the screen—in Microsoft Office 2010 adapts to different resolutions. If your monitor is set at a lower resolution than 1024 × 768, you might not see all of the buttons shown in the figures. The groups of buttons will always appear, but the entire group might be condensed into a single button that you need to click to access the buttons described in the instructions.

COURSECASTS Learning on the Go. Always Available...Always Relevant.

Our fast-paced world is driven by technology. You know because you are an active participant—always on the go, always keeping up with technological trends, and always learning new ways to embrace technology to power your life. Let CourseCasts, hosted by Ken Baldauf of Florida State University, be your guide into weekly updates in this ever-changing space. These timely, relevant podcasts are produced weekly and are available for download at http://coursecasts.course.com or directly from iTunes (search by CourseCasts). CourseCasts are a perfect solution to getting learners (and even instructors) to learn on the go!

Managing Workbook Data

As you analyze data using Excel, you will find that your worksheets and workbooks become more complex. In this unit, you will learn several Excel features to help you manage workbook data. In addition, you will want to share workbooks with coworkers, but you need to ensure that they can view your data while preventing unwarranted changes. You will learn how to save workbooks in different formats and how to prepare workbooks for distribution. Kate Morgan, the vice president of sales at Quest Specialty Travel, asks for your help in analyzing yearly sales data from the Canadian branches. When the analysis is complete, she will distribute the workbook for branch managers to review.

OBJECTIVES

View and arrange worksheets

Protect worksheets and workbooks

Save custom views of a worksheet

Add a worksheet background

Prepare a workbook for distribution

Insert hyperlinks

Save a workbook for distribution

Group worksheets

Viewing and Arranging Worksheets

As you work with workbooks made up of multiple worksheets, you might need to compare data in the various sheets. To do this, you can view each worksheet in its own workbook window, called an **instance**, and display the windows in an arrangement that makes it easy to compare data. When you work with worksheets in separate windows, you are working with different views of the same workbook; the data itself remains in one file. ▰▰▰ Kate asks you to compare the monthly store sales totals for the Toronto and Vancouver branches. Because the sales totals are on different worksheets, you want to arrange the worksheets side by side in separate windows.

STEPS

1. **Start Excel, open the file EX F-1.xlsx from the drive and folder where you store your Data Files, then save it as EX F-Store Sales**

2. **With the Toronto sheet active, click the View tab, then click the New Window button in the Window group**

   There are now two instances of the Store Sales workbook open. You can see them when you place the mouse pointer over the Excel icon on the task bar: EX F-Store Sales.xlsx:1 and EX F-Store Sales.xlsx:2. The Store Sales.xlsx:2 window is active—you can see its name on the title bar.

3. **Click the Vancouver sheet tab, click the Switch Windows button in the Window group, then click EX F-Store Sales.xlsx:1**

   The EX F-Store Sales.xlsx:1 instance is active. The Toronto sheet is active in the EX F-Store Sales.xlsx:1 workbook, and the Vancouver sheet is active in the EX F-Store Sales.xlsx:2 workbook.

4. **Click the Arrange All button in the Window group**

   The Arrange Windows dialog box, shown in Figure F-1, lets you choose how to display the instances. You want to view the workbooks next to each other.

5. **Click the Vertical option button to select it, then click OK**

   The windows are arranged next to each other, as shown in Figure F-2. You can activate a workbook by clicking one of its cells. You can also view only one of the workbooks by hiding the one you do not wish to see.

6. **Scroll horizontally to view the data in the EX F-Store Sales.xlsx:1 workbook, click anywhere in the EX F-Store Sales.xlsx:2 workbook, scroll horizontally to view the data in the EX F-Store Sales.xlsx:2 workbook, then click the Hide button in the Window group**

   When you hide the second instance, only the EX F-Store Sales.xlsx:1 workbook is visible.

7. **Click the Unhide button in the Window group; click EX F-Store Sales.xlsx:2, if necessary, in the Unhide dialog box; then click OK**

   The EX F-Store Sales.xlsx:2 book reappears.

8. **Close the EX F-Store Sales.xlsx:2 instance, then maximize the Toronto worksheet in the EX F-Store Sales.xlsx workbook**

   Closing the EX F-Store Sales.xlsx:2 instance leaves only the first instance open. Its name in the title bar returns to EX F-Store Sales.xlsx.

Managing Workbook Data

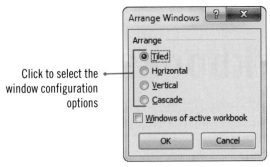
FIGURE F-1: **Arrange Windows dialog box**

Click to select the
window configuration
options

FIGURE F-2: **Windows displayed vertically**

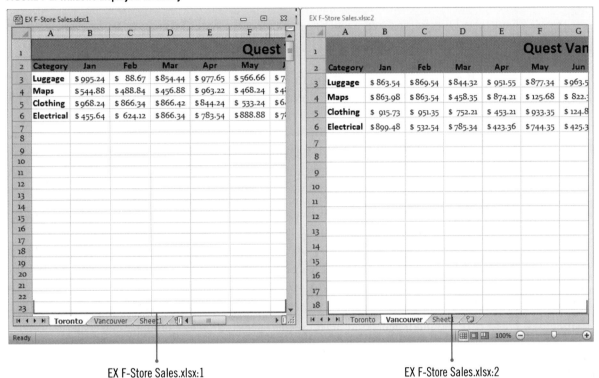

EX F-Store Sales.xlsx:1   EX F-Store Sales.xlsx:2

Splitting the worksheet into multiple panes

Excel lets you split the worksheet area into vertical and/or horizontal panes, so that you can click inside any one pane and scroll to locate information in that pane while the other panes remain in place, as shown in Figure F-3. To split a worksheet area into multiple panes, drag a split box (the small box at the top of the vertical scroll bar or at the right end of the horizontal scroll bar) in the direction you want the split to appear. To remove the split, move the pointer over the split until the pointer changes to a double-headed arrow, then double-click.

FIGURE F-3: **Worksheet split into two horizontal and two vertical panes**

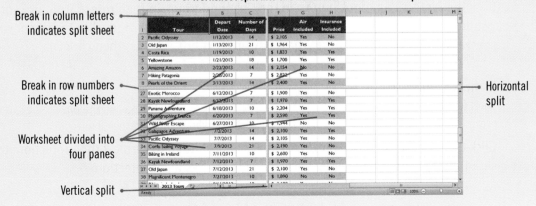

Break in column letters indicates split sheet

Break in row numbers indicates split sheet

Worksheet divided into four panes

Vertical split

Horizontal split

Excel 2010

Protecting Worksheets and Workbooks

To protect sensitive information, Excel lets you **lock** one or more cells so that other people can view the values and formulas in those cells, but not change it. Excel locks all cells by default, but this locking does not take effect until you activate the protection feature. A common worksheet protection strategy is to unlock cells in which data will be changed, sometimes called the **data entry area**, and to lock cells in which the data should not be changed. Then, when you protect the worksheet, the unlocked areas can still be changed. ▰▰▰▰ Because the Toronto sales figures for January through March have been finalized, Kate asks you to protect that worksheet area. That way, users cannot change the figures for those months.

STEPS

1. **On the Toronto sheet, select the range E3:M6, click the Home tab, click the Format button in the Cells group, click Format Cells, then in the Format Cells dialog box click the Protection tab**

   The Locked check box in the Protection tab is already checked, as shown in Figure F-4. All the cells in a new workbook start out locked. The protection feature is inactive by default. Because the April through December sales figures have not yet been confirmed as final and may need to be changed, you do not want those cells to be locked when the protection feature is activated. You decide to unlock the cell range and protect the worksheet.

2. **Click the Locked check box to deselect it, click OK, click the Review tab, then click the Protect Sheet button in the Changes group**

   The Protect Sheet dialog box opens, as shown in Figure F-5. In the "Allow users of this worksheet to" list, you can select the actions that you want your worksheet users to be able to perform. The default options protect the worksheet while allowing users to select locked or unlocked cells only. You choose not to use a password.

3. **Verify that Protect worksheet and contents of locked cells is checked, that the password text box is blank, and that Select locked cells and Select unlocked cells are checked, then click OK**

   You are ready to test the new worksheet protection.

4. **In cell B3, type 1 to confirm that locked cells cannot be changed, click OK, click cell F3, type 1, notice that Excel lets you begin the entry, press [Esc] to cancel the entry, then save your work**

   When you try change a locked cell, a dialog box, shown in Figure F-6, reminds you of the protected cell's read-only status. **Read-only format** means that users can view but not change the data. Because you unlocked the cells in columns E through M before you protected the worksheet, you can change these cells. You decide to protect the workbook from these changes to the workbook's structure, but decide not to require a password.

5. **Click the Protect Workbook button in the Changes group, in the Protect Structure and Windows dialog box, make sure the Structure check box is selected, click the Windows check box to select it, verify that the password text box is blank, then click OK**

   You are ready to test the new workbook protection.

6. **Right-click the Toronto sheet tab**

   The Insert, Delete, Rename, Move or Copy, Tab Color, Hide, and Unhide menu options are not available because the sheet is protected. You decide to remove the workbook and worksheet protections.

7. **Click the Protect Workbook button in the Changes group to turn off the protection, then click the Unprotect Sheet button to remove the worksheet protection**

FIGURE F-4: **Protection tab in Format Cells dialog box**

Click to remove check mark

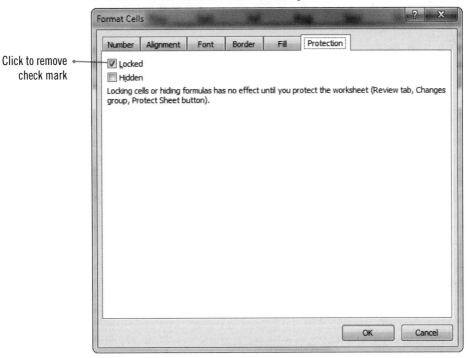

FIGURE F-5: **Protect Sheet dialog box**

Protects locked cells from changes

Allows users to select worksheet cells

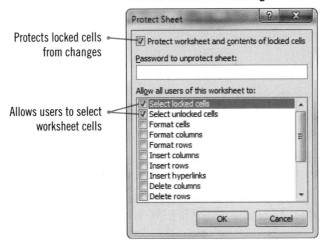

FIGURE F-6: **Reminder of protected cell's read-only status**

Freezing rows and columns

As the rows and columns of a worksheet fill up with data, you might need to scroll through the worksheet to add, delete, change, and view information. You can temporarily freeze columns and rows so you can keep column or row labels in view as you scroll. **Panes** are the columns and rows that **freeze**, or remain in place, while you scroll through your worksheet. To freeze panes, click the first cell in the area you want to scroll, click the View tab, click the Freeze Panes button in the Window group, then click Freeze Panes. Excel freezes the columns to the left and the rows above the selected cell. You can also select Freeze Top Row or Freeze First Column to freeze the top row or left worksheet column.

Saving Custom Views of a Worksheet

A **view** is a set of display and/or print settings that you can name and save, then access at a later time. By using the Excel Custom Views feature, you can create several different views of a worksheet without having to create separate sheets. For example, if you often hide columns in a worksheet, you can create two views, one that displays all of the columns and another with the columns hidden. You set the worksheet display first, then name the view. ⬛⬛⬛ Because Kate wants to generate a sales report from the final sales data for January through March, she asks you to save the first-quarter sales data as a custom view. You begin by creating a view showing all of the worksheet data.

STEPS

1. **With the Toronto sheet active, click the** View tab, **then click the** Custom Views button **in the Workbook Views group**

   The Custom Views dialog box opens. Any previously defined views for the active worksheet appear in the Views box. No views are defined for the Toronto worksheet. You decide to add a named view for the current view, which shows all the worksheet columns. That way, you can easily return to it from any other views you create.

   > **QUICK TIP**
   > To delete views from the active worksheet, select the view in the Custom Views dialog box, then click Delete.

2. **Click** Add

   The Add View dialog box opens, as shown in Figure F-7. Here, you enter a name for the view and decide whether to include print settings and hidden rows, columns, and filter settings. You want to include the selected options.

3. **In the Name box, type** Year Sales, **then click** OK

   You have created a view called Year Sales that shows all the worksheet columns. You want to set up another view that will hide the April through December columns.

4. **Drag across the column headings to select columns** E through M, **right-click the selected area, then click** Hide **on the shortcut menu**

   You are ready to create a custom view of the January through March sales data.

5. **Click cell** A1, **click the** Custom Views button **in the Workbook Views group, click** Add, **in the Name box type** First Quarter, **then click** OK

   You are ready to test the two custom views.

   > **TROUBLE**
   > If you receive the message "Some view settings could not be applied", turn off worksheet protection by clicking the Unprotect Sheet button in the Changes group of the Review tab.

6. **Click the** Custom Views button **in the Workbook Views group, click** Year Sales **in the Views list, then click** Show

   The Year Sales custom view displays all of the months' sales data. Now you are ready to test the First Quarter custom view.

7. **Click the** Custom Views button **in the Workbook Views group, then with** First Quarter **in the Custom Views dialog box selected, click** Show

   Only the January through March sales figures appear on the screen, as shown in Figure F-8.

8. **Return to the Year Sales view, then save your work**

FIGURE F-7: **Add View dialog box**

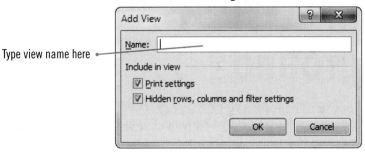

Type view name here →

FIGURE F-8: **First Quarter view**

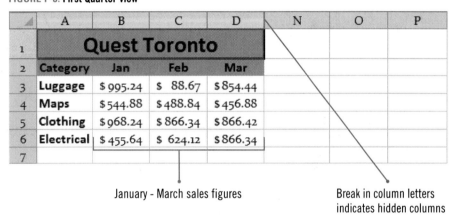

January - March sales figures

Break in column letters indicates hidden columns

Using Page Break Preview

The vertical and horizontal dashed lines in the Normal view of worksheets represent page breaks. Excel automatically inserts a page break when your worksheet data doesn't fit on one page. These page breaks are **dynamic**, which means they adjust automatically when you insert or delete rows and columns and when you change column widths or row heights. Everything to the left of the first vertical dashed line and above the first horizontal dashed line is printed on the first page. You can manually add or remove page breaks by clicking the Page Layout tab, clicking the Breaks button in the Page Setup group, then clicking the appropriate command. You can also view and change page breaks manually by clicking the View tab, then clicking the Page Break Preview button in the Workbook Views group, or by clicking the Page Break Preview button 🖳 on the status bar, then clicking OK. You can drag the blue page break lines to the desired location, as shown in Figure F-9. Some cells may temporarily display ##### while you are in Page Break Preview. If you drag a page break to the right to include more data on a page, Excel shrinks the type to fit the data on that page. To exit Page Break Preview, click the Normal button in the Workbook Views group.

FIGURE F-9: **Page Break Preview window**

Drag blue page break lines to change page breaks

	A	B	C	D	E	F	G	H	I	J	K	L	M
1						Quest Toronto							
2	Category	Jan	Feb	Mar	Apr	May	Jun	Jul	Aug	Sep	Oct	Nov	Dec
3	Luggage	$995.24	$88.67	$854.44	$977.65	$566.66	$745.23	$995.32	$546.33	$299.32	$855.14	$963.42	$785.33
4	Maps	$544.88	$488.84	$456.88	$963.22	$468.24	$482.42	$844.62	$245.88	$445.88	$445.68	$458.66	$288.88
5	Clothing	$968.24	$866.34	$866.42	$844.24	$533.24	$644.22	$983.65	$648.44	$893.24	$542.98	$877.95	$963.57
6	Electrical	$455.64	$624.12	$866.34	$783.54	$888.88	$783.24	$983.24	$842.56	$236.54	$865.22	$888.88	$893.24
7													

Adding a Worksheet Background

In addition to using a theme's font colors and fills, you can make your Excel data more attractive on the screen by adding a picture to the worksheet background. Companies often use their logo as a worksheet background. A worksheet background will be displayed on the screen but will not print with the worksheet. If you want to add a worksheet background that appears on printouts, you can add a **watermark**, a translucent background design that prints behind your data. To add a watermark, you add the image to the worksheet header or footer. ▩▩▩ Kate asks you to add the Quest logo to the printed background of the Toronto worksheet. But first she wants to see it as a nonprinting background.

STEPS

1. **With the Toronto sheet active, click the Page Layout tab, then click the Background button in the Page Setup group**

   The Sheet Background dialog box opens.

2. **Navigate to the drive and folder where you store your Data Files, click EX F-Logo.gif, then click Insert**

   The Quest logo appears behind the worksheet data. It appears twice because the graphic is **tiled**, or repeated, to fill the background.

3. **Click the File tab, click Print, view the preview of the Toronto worksheet, then click the Page Layout tab**

   Because the logo is only for display purposes, it will not print with the worksheet, so is not visible in the Print preview. You want the logo to print with the worksheet, so you decide to remove the background and add the logo to the worksheet header.

4. **Click the Delete Background button in the Page Setup group, click the Insert tab, then click the Header & Footer button in the Text group**

   The Header & Footer Tools Design tab appears, as shown in Figure F-10. The Header & Footer group buttons add preformatted headers and footers to a worksheet. The Header & Footer Elements buttons let you add page numbers, the date, the time, the file location, names, and pictures to the header or footer. The Navigation group buttons move the insertion point from the header to the footer and back. You want to add a picture to the header.

5. **With the insertion point in the center section of the header, click the Picture button in the Header & Footer Elements group, navigate to the drive and folder where you store your Data Files, click EX F-Logo.gif, then click Insert**

   A code representing a picture, "&[Picture]", appears in the center of the header.

6. **Click cell A1, then click the Normal button ▦ on the Status Bar**

   You want to scale the worksheet data to print on one page.

7. **Click the Page Layout tab, click the Width list arrow in the Scale to Fit group, click 1 page, click the Height list arrow in the Scale to Fit group, click 1 page, then preview the worksheet**

   Your worksheet should look like Figure F-11.

8. **Click the Home tab, then save the workbook**

FIGURE F-10: Design tab of the Header & Footer tools

Click these
buttons to
customize
the header
and footer

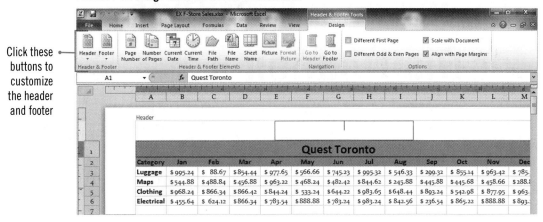

FIGURE F-11: Preview of Toronto worksheet with logo in the background

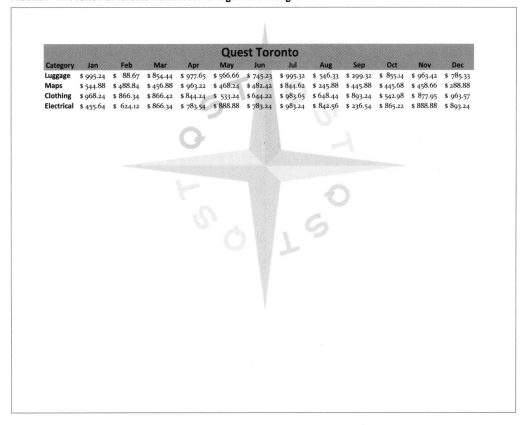

Clipping Screens in Excel

You can paste an image of an open file into an Excel workbook or another Office document. This pastes the screenshot into your document as an image that you can move, copy, or edit. To insert a screenshot, click the Insert tab, click the Screenshot button in the Illustrations group, then click on one of the available windows in the gallery. This pastes a screen shot of the window you clicked into the current Excel document. You can also click the Screen Clipping button in the gallery to select and paste an area from an open window.

After you paste an image on your worksheet, you can also cut or copy and paste in another program or in an e-mail. In addition to pasting screenshots from other windows into Excel, you can use the Screenshot feature to paste Excel screens into other programs such as Word, PowerPoint, and Outlook. This is helpful if you are having a problem with an Excel worksheet and want to e-mail your screen image to a Help Desk.

Preparing a Workbook for Distribution

If you are collaborating with others and want to share a workbook with them, you might want to remove sensitive information before distributing the file. Sensitive information can include headers, footers, or hidden elements. You can use Backstage view in Excel to open the Document Inspector, which finds hidden data and personal information in your workbooks and helps you remove it. On the other hand, you might want to add helpful information, called **properties**, to a file to help others identify, understand, and locate it. Properties might include keywords, the author's name, a title, the status, and comments. **Keywords** are terms users can search for that will help them locate your workbook. Properties are a form of **metadata**, information that describes data and is used in Microsoft Windows document searches. You enter properties in the Document Properties Panel. In addition, to ensure that others do not make unauthorized changes to your workbook, you can mark a file as final. This makes it a read-only file, which others can open but not change. ░░░░ Kate wants you to protect the workbook and prepare it for distribution.

STEPS

1. **Click the File tab**

   Backstage view opens, with the Info tab in front. It shows you a preview of your printed worksheet and information about your file. This information includes who has permission to open, copy, or change your workbook. It also includes tools you can use to check for security issues.

2. **Click the Check for Issues button in the Prepare for Sharing area, then click Inspect Document**

   The Document Inspector dialog box opens, as shown in Figure F-12. It lists items from which you can have Excel evaluate hidden or personal information. All the options are selected by default.

3. **Click Inspect**

   After inspecting your document, the inspector displays its results. Areas with personal information have a "!" in front of them. Headers and footers is also flagged. You want to keep the file's header and footer and remove personal information.

4. **Click Remove All next to Document Properties and Personal Information, then click Close**

   You decide to add keywords to help the sales managers find the worksheet. The search words "Toronto" or "Vancouver" would be good keywords for this workbook.

5. **Click the Properties list arrow on the right side of Backstage view, then click Show Document Panel**

   The Document Properties Panel appears at the top of the worksheet, as shown in Figure F-13. You decide to add a title, status, keywords, and comments.

6. **In the Title text box type Store Sales, in the Keywords text box type Toronto Vancouver store sales, in the Status text box type DRAFT, then in the Comments text box type The first-quarter figures are final., then click the Close button on the Document Properties Panel**

   You are ready to mark the workbook as final.

7. **Click the File tab, click the Protect Workbook button in the Permissions area, click Mark as Final, click OK, then click OK again**

   "[Read-Only]" appears in the title bar indicating the workbook is saved as a read-only file.

8. **Click the Home tab, click cell B3, type 1 to confirm that the cell cannot be changed, then click the Edit Anyway button above the formula bar**

   Marking a workbook as final is not a strong form of workbook protection because a workbook recipient can remove this Final status. Removing the read-only status makes it editable again.

FIGURE F-12: Document Inspector dialog box

Items you can inspect for personal information

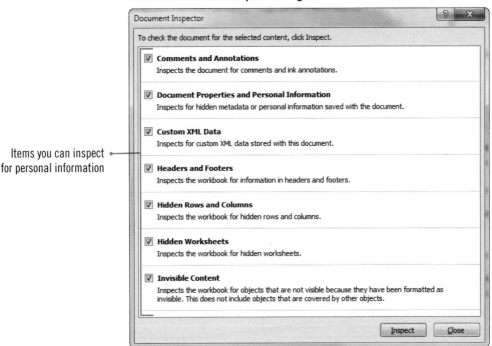

FIGURE F-13: Document Properties panel

Add file information in text boxes

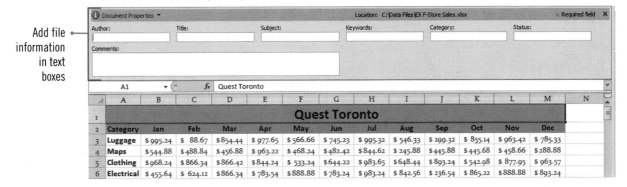

Sharing a workbook

You can make an Excel file a **shared workbook** so that several users can open and modify it at the same time. Click the Review tab, click the Share Workbook button in the Changes group, then on the Editing tab of the Share Workbook dialog box click "Allow changes by more than one user at the same time. This also allows workbook merging.", then click OK. If you get an error that the workbook cannot be shared because privacy is enabled, click the File tab, click Options in the left section, click the Trust Center category on the left side of the dialog box, click Trust Center Settings, click Privacy Options in the list on the left, click the "Remove personal information from file properties on save" check box to deselect it, then click OK twice. When you share workbooks, it is often helpful to **track**

modifications, or identify who made which changes. You can track all changes to a workbook by clicking the Track Changes button in the Changes group, and then clicking Highlight Changes. To view all changes that have been tracked in a workbook, click the Review tab, click the Track Changes button in the Changes group, click Highlight Changes, select the When check box in the Highlight Changes dialog box, click the When text box list arrow, then select All in the list. To resolve the tracked changes in a workbook, click the Track Changes button, then click Accept/Reject Changes. The changes are displayed one by one. You can accept the change or, if you disagree with any of the changes, you can reject them.

Managing Workbook Data

Excel 2010

Inserting Hyperlinks

As you manage the content and appearance of your workbooks, you might want the workbook user to view information that exists in another location. It might be nonessential information or data that is too detailed to place in the workbook itself. In these cases, you can create a hyperlink. A **hyperlink** is an object (a file-name, word, phrase, or graphic) in a worksheet that, when you click it, displays, or "jumps to," another location, called the **target**. The target can also be a worksheet, another document, or a site on the World Wide Web. For example, in a worksheet that lists customer invoices, at each customer's name, you might create a hyperlink to an Excel file containing payment terms for each customer. 🔲🔲🔲 Kate wants managers who view the Store Sales workbook to be able to view the item totals for each sales category in the Toronto sheet. She asks you to create a hyperlink at the Category heading so that users can click the hyperlink to view the items for each category.

STEPS

1. **Click cell A2 on the Toronto worksheet**

2. **Click the Insert tab, then click the Hyperlink button in the Links group**

   The Insert Hyperlink dialog box opens, as shown in Figure F-14. The icons under "Link to" on the left side of the dialog box let you select the type of location to where you want the link jump: an existing file or Web page, a place in the same document, a new document, or an e-mail address. Because you want the link to display an already-existing document, the selected first icon, Existing File or Web Page, is correct, so you won't have to change it.

3. **Click the Look in list arrow, navigate to the location where you store your Data Files if necessary, then click EX F-Toronto Sales.xlsx in the file list**

   The filename you selected and its path appear in the Address text box. This is the document users will see when they click the hyperlink. You can also specify the ScreenTip that users see when they hold the pointer over the hyperlink.

   > **QUICK TIP**
   > To remove a hyper-link or change its target, right-click it, then click Remove Hyperlink or Edit Hyperlink.

4. **Click the ScreenTip button, type Items in each category, click OK, then click OK again**

   Cell A2 now contains underlined yellow text, indicating that it is a hyperlink. The color of a hyperlink depends on the worksheet theme colors. You need to change the text color of the hyperlink text so it is visible on the dark background. After you create a hyperlink, you should check it to make sure that it jumps to the correct destination.

   > **QUICK TIP**
   > If you link to a Web page, you must be connected to the Internet to test the link.

5. **Click the Home tab, click the Font Color list arrow 🅰️▾ in the Font group, click the White, Background 1 color (first color in the Theme Colors), move the pointer over the Category text, view the ScreenTip, then click once**

   After you click, the EX F-Toronto Sales workbook opens, displaying the Sales sheet, as shown in Figure F-15.

6. **Close the EX F-Toronto Sales workbook, click Don't Save, then save the EX F-Store Sales workbook**

Returning to your document

After you click a hyperlink and view the destination document, you will often want to return to your original document that contains the hyperlink. To do this, you can add the Back button to the Quick Access toolbar. However, the Back button does not appear in the Quick Access toolbar by default; you need to customize the toolbar. (If you are using a computer in a lab, check with your system administrator to see if you have permission to do this.) To custom-ize the Quick Access toolbar, click the Customize Quick Access Toolbar arrow, click More Commands, click the Choose Commands from list arrow, select All Commands, scroll down, click the Back button, click Add, then click OK.

FIGURE F-14: Insert Hyperlink dialog box

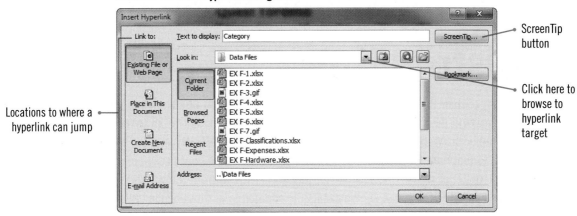

Locations to where a hyperlink can jump

ScreenTip button

Click here to browse to hyperlink target

FIGURE F-15: Target document

	A	B	C
1	**Quest Toronto**		
2	**Travel Store Sales**		
3	**Item**	**Total Sales**	**Category**
4	PopOut Maps	$ 1,619.81	Maps
5	Smart Packing Books	$ 3,934.77	Maps
6	Airport Guides	$ 4,941.61	Maps
7	Pack It Guides	$ 1,114.65	Maps
8	Computer Case	$ 1,855.65	Luggage
9	Backpack	$ 1,836.91	Luggage
10	Plane Slippers	$ 1,099.15	Clothing
11	Travel Socks	$ 1,108.16	Clothing
12	Men's Sandals	$ 1,103.14	Clothing
13	Women's Sandals	$ 1,954.19	Clothing
14	Hats	$ 975.44	Clothing
15	Men's T-Shirts	$ 3,111.76	Clothing
16	Women's T-Shirts	$ 1,108.41	Clothing
17	Converter	$ 1,798.53	Electrical
18	Phone Charger	$ 1,108.41	Electrical
19			
20			
21			
22			

Sales / Sheet2 / Sheet3

Ready

Using research tools

You can access resources online and locally on your computer using the Research task pane. To open the Research task pane, click the Review tab, then click the Research button in the Proofing group. The Search for text box in the Research pane lets you specify a research topic. The Research pane has a drop-down list of the resources available to search for your topic. You can use this list to access resources such as a thesaurus, a dictionary, financial web sites, and research web sites. You can also quickly access the thesaurus in the Research task pane using the Thesaurus button on the Review tab in the Proofing group.

Excel 2010

Saving a Workbook for Distribution

One way to share Excel data is to place, or **publish**, the data on a network or on the Web so that others can access it using their Web browsers. To publish an Excel document to an **intranet** (a company's internal Web site) or the Web, you can save it in an HTML format. **HTML (Hypertext Markup Language)**, is the coding format used for all Web documents. You can also save your Excel file as a **single-file Web page** that integrates all of the worksheets and graphical elements from the workbook into a single file. This file format is called MHTML, also known as MHT. In addition to distributing files on the Web, you might need to distribute your files to people working with an earlier version of Excel. You can do this by saving your files as Excel 97-2003 workbooks. See Table F-1 for a list of the most popular formats. ░░░░░ Kate asks you to create a workbook version that managers running an earlier Excel version can use. She also asks you to save the EX F-Store Sales workbook in MHT format so she can publish it on the Quest intranet.

STEPS

1. **Click the File tab, click Save As, click the Save as type list arrow in the Save As dialog box, click Excel 97-2003 Workbook (*.xls), navigate to the drive and folder where you store your Data Files if necessary, then click Save**

   The Compatibility Checker dialog box opens. It alerts you to the features that will be lost or converted by saving in the earlier format. Some Excel 2010 features are not available in earlier versions of Excel.

   QUICK TIP

   To ensure that your workbook is displayed the same way on different computer platforms and screen settings, you can publish it in PDF format.

2. **Click Continue, close the workbook, then reopen the EX F-Store Sales.xls workbook**

   "[Compatibility Mode]" appears in the title bar, as shown in Figure F-16. Compatibility mode prevents you from including Excel features in your workbook that are not supported in Excel 97-2003 workbooks. To exit compatibility mode, you need to save your file in one of the Excel 2010 formats and reopen the file.

3. **Click the File tab, click Save As, click the Save as type list arrow in the Save As dialog box, click Excel Workbook (*.xlsx); if necessary, navigate to the drive and folder where you store your Data Files, click Save, then click Yes when you are asked if you want to replace the existing file**

   "[Compatibility Mode]" remains displayed in the title bar. You decide to close the file and reopen it to exit compatibility mode.

   QUICK TIP

   You can convert an .xls file to an .xlsx file when opening it in Excel 2010 by clicking the File tab and clicking Convert in the information pane. Note that this deletes the original .xls file.

4. **Close the workbook, then reopen the EX F-Store Sales.xlsx workbook**

   The title bar no longer displays "[Compatibility mode]". You still need to save the file for Web distribution.

5. **Click the File tab, click Save As, in the Save As dialog box navigate to the drive and folder where you store your Data Files if necessary, change the filename to sales, then click the Save as type list arrow and click Single File Web Page (*.mht, *.mhtml)**

   The Save as type list box indicates that the workbook is to be saved as a Single File Web Page, which is in MHTML or MHT format. To avoid problems when publishing your pages to a Web server, it is best to use lowercase characters, omit special characters and spaces, and limit your filename to eight characters with an additional three-character extension.

   TROUBLE

   The message above your workbook in the browser tells you that active content is restricted. Active content is interactive and usually in the form of small programs. These programs can present a security threat, and you should allow the active content only if you trust the source of the file.

6. **Click Save, then click Yes**

   The dialog box indicated that some features may not be retained in the Web page file. Excel saves the workbook as an MHT file in the location you specified. The MHT file is open on your screen. See Figure F-17. It's a good idea to open an MHT file in your browser to see how it will look to viewers.

7. **Close the sales.mht file in Excel, start your browser, open the sales.mht file by double-clicking it in the folder where you store your Data Files, click the Vancouver sheet tab, then close your browser window**

FIGURE F-16: Workbook in compatibility mode

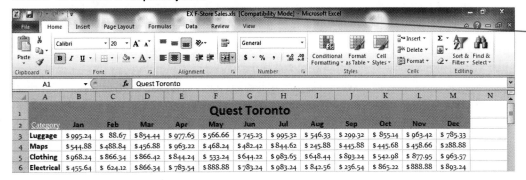

File is marked as using compatibility mode

FIGURE F-17: Workbook saved as a single file Web page

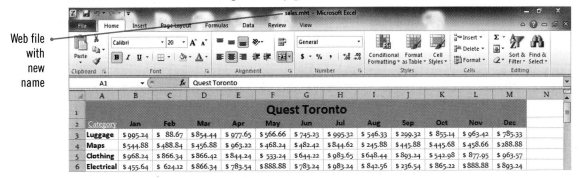

Web file with new name

TABLE F-1: Workbook formats

type of file	file extension(s)	used for
Macro-enabled workbook	.xlsm	Files that contain macros
Excel 97 – 2003 workbook	.xls	Working with people using older versions of Excel
Single file Web page	.mht, .mhtml	Web sites with multiple pages and graphics
Web page	.htm, .html	Simple single-page Web sites
Excel template	.xltx	Excel files that will be reused with small changes
Excel macro-enabled template	.xltm	Excel files that will be used again and contain macros
Portable document format	.pdf	Files with formatting that needs to be preserved
XML paper specification	.xps	Files with formatting that needs to be preserved and files that need to be shared
OpenDocument spreadsheet	.ods	Files created with OpenOffice

Understanding Excel file formats

The default file format for Excel 2010 files is the Office Open XML format, which supports all Excel features. This has been the default file format of Office files since Microsoft Office 2007. This format stores Excel files in small XML components that are zipped for compression making the files smaller. The most often used format, .xlsx, does not support macros. **Macros**, programmed instructions that perform tasks, can be a security risk. If your worksheet contains macros, you need to save it with an extension of .xlsm so the macros can function in the workbook. If you use a workbook's text and formats repeatedly, you might want to save it as a template with the extension .xltx. If your template contains macros, you need to save it with the .xltm extension.

Grouping Worksheets

You can group worksheets to work on them as a collection. When you enter data into one worksheet, that data is also automatically entered into all of the worksheets in the group. This is useful for data that is common to every sheet of a workbook, such as headers and footers, or for column headings that will apply to all monthly worksheets in a yearly summary. Grouping worksheets can also be used to print multiple worksheets at one time. ████ Kate asks you to add the text "Quest" to the footer of both the Toronto and Vancouver worksheets. You will also add 1-inch margins to the top of both worksheets.

STEPS

1. **Open the** EX F-Store Sales.xlsx **file from the drive and folder where you store your Data Files**

QUICK TIP

You can group non-contiguous worksheets by pressing and holding [Ctrl] while clicking the sheet tabs that you want to group.

2. **With the Toronto sheet active, press and hold** [Shift], **click the** Vancouver sheet, **then release** [Shift]

   Both sheet tabs are selected, and the title bar now contains "[Group]", indicating that the worksheets are grouped together. Now any changes you make to the Toronto sheet will also be made to the Vancouver sheet.

3. **Click the** Insert tab, **then click the** Header & Footer button **in the Text group**

4. **On the Header & Footer Tools Design tab, click the** Go to Footer button **in the Navigation group, type** Quest **in the center section of the footer, enter your name in the left section of the footer, click cell** A1, **then click the** Normal button ▦ **on the Status Bar**

   You decide to check the footers in Print Preview.

5. **With the worksheets still grouped, click the** File tab, **click** Print, **preview the first page, then click the** Next Page button ▶ **to preview the second page**

   Because the worksheets are grouped, both pages contain the footer with "Quest" and your name. The worksheets would look better with a wider top margin.

6. **Click the** Normal Margins list arrow, **click** Custom Margins, **in the Top text box on the Margins tab of the Page Setup dialog box type** 1, **then click** OK

   You decide to ungroup the worksheets.

7. **Click the** Home tab, **right-click the** Toronto worksheet sheet tab, **then click** Ungroup Sheets

8. **Save and close the workbook, exit Excel, then submit the workbook to your instructor**

9. **The completed worksheets are shown in Figures F-18 and F-19.**

Adding a digital signature to a workbook

You can digitally sign a workbook to establish its validity and prevent it from being changed. You can obtain a valid certificate from a certificate authority to authenticate the workbook or you can create your own digital signature. To add a signature line in a workbook, click the Insert tab, click the Signature Line button in the Text group, then click OK. In the Signature Setup dialog box, enter information about the signer of the worksheet and then click OK. To add a signature, double-click the signature line, click OK; if prompted, in the Get a Digital ID dialog box, click the Create your own digital ID option button, then click OK. Click Create, in the Sign dialog box, click Select Image next to the sign box, browse to the location where your signature is saved, click Sign, then click OK. To add the certificate authenticating the workbook, click the File tab, click the Protect Workbook button, click Add a Digital Signature, then click OK. In the Sign dialog box click Sign, then click OK. The workbook will be saved as read-only, and it will not be able to be changed by other users.

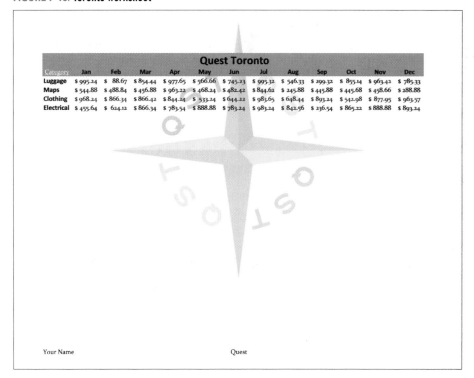

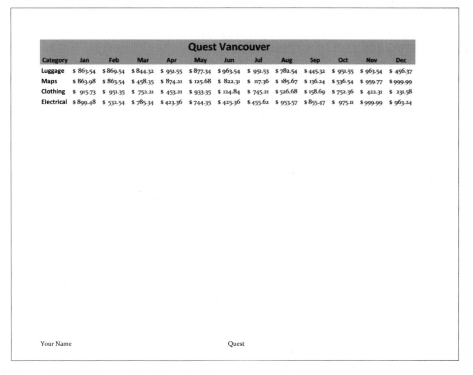

Creating a workspace

If you work with several workbooks at a time in a particular arrangement on the screen, you can group them so that you can open them in one step by creating a workspace. A **workspace** is a file with an .xlw extension. Then, instead of opening each workbook individually, you can open the workspace. To create a workspace, open the workbooks you wish to group, then position and size them as you would like them to appear. Click the View tab, click the Save Workspace button in the Window group, type a name for the workspace file, navigate to the location where you want to store it, then click Save. The workspace file does not contain the workbooks themselves, however. You still have to save any changes you make to the original workbook files. If you work at another computer, you need to have the workspace file and all of the workbook files that are part of the workspace.

Practice

Concepts Review

FIGURE F-20

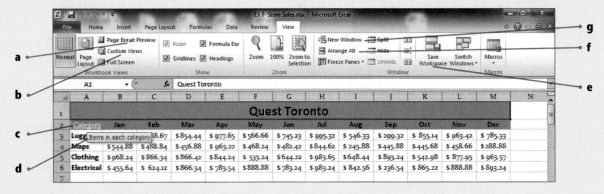

1. Which element do you click to view and change the way worksheet data is distributed on printed pages?
2. Which element do you click to group workbooks so that they open together as a unit?
3. Which element do you click to name and save a set of display and/or print settings?
4. Which element do you click to open the active worksheet in a new window?
5. Which element points to a hyperlink?
6. Which element points to a ScreenTip for a hyperlink?
7. Which element do you click to organize windows in a specific configuration?

Match each term with the statement that best describes it.

8. Dynamic page breaks
9. HTML
10. Watermark
11. Hyperlink
12. Data entry area

a. Web page format
b. Portion of a worksheet that can be changed
c. Translucent background design on a printed worksheet
d. An object that when clicked displays another worksheet or a Web page
e. Adjusted automatically when rows and columns are inserted or deleted

Select the best answer from the list of choices.

13. You can establish the validity of a workbook by adding a:
    a. Template.
    c. Custom View.
    b. Digital signature.
    d. Keyword.

14. So that they can be opened together rather than individually, you can group several workbooks in a:
    a. Workspace.
    c. Workgroup.
    b. Consolidated workbook.
    d. Work unit.

Skills Review

1. **View and arrange worksheets.**
    a. Start Excel, open the file EX F-2.xlsx from the drive and folder where you store your Data Files, then save it as **EX F-Dolce**.
    b. Activate the 2013 sheet if necessary, then open the 2014 sheet in a new window.
    c. Activate the 2013 sheet in the EX F-Dolce.xlsx:1 workbook. Activate the 2014 sheet in the EX F-Dolce.xlsx:2 workbook.
    d. View the EX F-Dolce.xlsx:1 and EX F-Dolce.xlsx:2 workbooks tiled horizontally. View the workbooks in a vertical arrangement.
    e. Hide the EX F-Dolce.xlsx:2 instance, then unhide the instance. Close the EX F-Dolce.xlsx:2 instance, and maximize the EX F-Dolce.xlsx workbook.
    f. Split the 2013 sheet into two horizontal panes. (*Hint*: Drag the Horizontal split box.) Remove the split by double-clicking it, then save your work.

2. **Protect worksheets and workbooks.**
    a. On the 2013 sheet, unlock the expense data in the range B12:F19.
    b. Protect the sheet without using a password.
    c. To make sure the other cells are locked, attempt to make an entry in cell D4 and verify that you receive an error message.
    d. Change the first-quarter mortgage expense in cell B12 to 5500.
    e. Protect the workbook's structure and windows without applying a password. Right-click the 2013 and 2014 sheet tabs to verify that you cannot insert, delete, rename, move, copy, hide, or unhide the sheets, or change their tab color.
    f. Unprotect the workbook. Unprotect the 2013 worksheet.
    g. Save the workbook.

3. **Save custom views of a worksheet**
    a. Using the 2013 sheet, create a custom view of the entire worksheet called **Entire 2013 Budget**.
    b. Hide rows 10 through 23, then create a new view called **Income** showing only the income data.
    c. Use the Custom Views dialog box to display all of the data on the 2013 worksheet.
    d. Use the Custom Views dialog box to display only the income data on the 2013 worksheet.
    e. Use the Custom Views dialog box to return to the Entire 2013 Budget view.
    f. Save the workbook.

4. **Add a worksheet background.**
    a. Use EX F-3.gif as a worksheet background for the 2013 sheet, then delete it.
    b. Add EX F-3.gif to the 2013 header, then preview the sheet to verify that the background will print.
    c. Add your name to the center section of the 2013 worksheet footer, then save the workbook.

5. **Prepare a workbook for distribution.**
    a. Inspect the workbook and remove any properties, personal data, and header and footer information.
    b. Use the Document Properties Panel to add a title of **Quarterly Budget** and the keywords **dolce** and **coffee**.
    c. Mark the workbook as final and verify that "[Read-Only]" is in the title bar.
    d. Remove the final status, then save the workbook.

6. **Insert hyperlinks.**
    a. On the 2013 worksheet, make cell A11 a hyperlink to the file **EX F-Expenses.xlsx** in your Data Files folder.
    b. Test the link and verify that Sheet1 of the target file displays expense details.

Skills Review (continued)

    c. Return to the EX F-Dolce.xlsx workbook, edit the hyperlink in cell A11, adding a ScreenTip that reads **Expense Details**, then verify that the ScreenTip appears.

    d. On the 2014 worksheet, enter the text **Based on 2013 budget** in cell A25.

    e. Make the text in cell A25 a hyperlink to cell A1 in the 2013 worksheet. (*Hint*: Use the Place in This Document button and note the cell reference in the Type the cell reference text box.)

    f. Test the hyperlink. Remove the hyperlink in cell A25 of the 2014 worksheet, then save the workbook.

7. Save a workbook for distribution.

    a. Save the EX F-Dolce.xlsx workbook as a single file Web page with the name **dolce.mht**. Close the dolce.mht file that is open in Excel, then open the dolce.mht file in your Web browser. (The Information bar at the top of the Web page notifies you about blocked content. Your Web page doesn't contain any scripts that need to run so you can ignore the Information bar.) Close your browser window, and reopen EX F-Dolce.xlsx.

    b. Save the EX F-Dolce.xlsx workbook with the 2013 sheet active as a PDF file. Close the file EX F-Dolce.pdf.

    c. Save the EX F-Dolce workbook as an Excel 97-2003 workbook, and review the results of the Compatibility Checker.

    d. Close the EX F-Dolce.xls file, and reopen the EX F-Dolce.xlsx file.

    e. Save the workbook as a macro-enabled template in the drive and folder where you store your Data Files. (*Hint*: Select the type Excel Macro-Enabled Template (*.xltm) in the Save as type list.)

    f. Close the template file, then reopen the EX F-Dolce.xlsx file.

8. Grouping worksheets.

    a. Group the 2013 and 2014 worksheets, then add your name to the center footer section of the worksheets.

    b. Save the workbook, preview both sheets, comparing your worksheets to Figure F-21, then ungroup the sheets.

    c. Submit your EX F-Dolce.xlsx workbook to your instructor, close all open files, and exit Excel.

FIGURE F-21

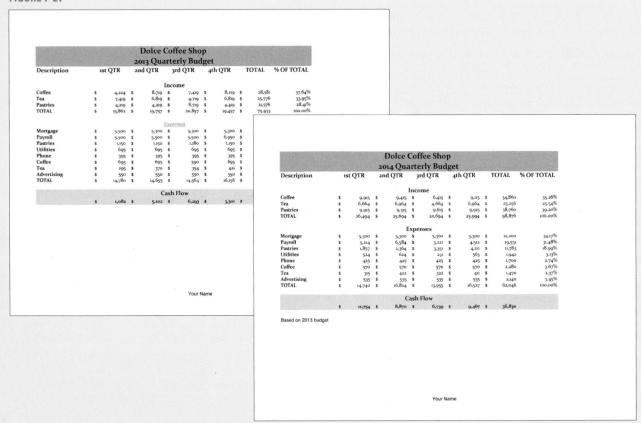

Independent Challenge 1

You manage Shore Road Rugs, a wholesale supplier to retail stores. You are organizing your first-quarter sales in an Excel worksheet. Because the sheet for the month of January includes the same type of information you need for February and March, you decide to enter the headings for all of the first-quarter months at the same time. You use a separate worksheet for each month and create data for 3 months.

a. Start Excel, then save the workbook as **EX F-Rug Sales.xlsx** in the drive and folder where you store your Data Files.

b. Name the first sheet **January**, name the second sheet **February**, and name the third sheet **March**.

c. Group the worksheets.

d. With the worksheets grouped, add the title **Shore Road Rugs** centered across cells A1 and B1. Enter the label **Sales** in cell B2. Enter rug labels in column A beginning in cell A3 and ending in cell A9. Use the following rug types in the range A3:A9: **Wool**, **Custom**, **Antique**, **Commercial**, **Cotton**, **Indoor/Outdoor**, and **Runners**. Add the label **TOTAL** in cell A10. Enter your own sales data in the range B3:B9.

e. Enter the formula to sum the Amount column in cell B10. Ungroup the worksheets, and enter your own data for each of the sales categories in the January, February, and March sheets.

f. Display each worksheet in its own window, then arrange the three sheets vertically.

g. Hide the window displaying the March sheet. Unhide the March sheet window.

h. Split the March window into two panes: the upper pane displaying rows 1 through 5, and the lower pane displaying rows 6 through 10. Scroll through the data in each pane, then remove the split.

i. Close the windows displaying EX F-Rug Sales.xlsx:2 and EX F-Rug Sales.xlsx:3, then maximize the EX F-Rug Sales.xlsx workbook.

j. Add the keywords **rugs custom** to your workbook, using the Document Properties Panel.

k. Group the worksheets again.

l. Add headers to all three worksheets that include your name in the left section and the sheet name in the center section.

m. With the worksheets still grouped, format the worksheets appropriately.

n. Ungroup the worksheets, then mark the workbook status as final. Close the workbook, reopen the workbook, and enable editing.

o. Save the workbook, submit the workbook to your instructor, then exit Excel.

Independent Challenge 2

As the payroll manager at New Media, a Web Development firm, you decide to organize the weekly timecard data using Excel worksheets. You use a separate worksheet for each week and track the hours for employees with different job classifications. A hyperlink in the worksheet provides pay rates for each classification, and custom views limit the information that is displayed.

a. Start Excel, open the file EX F-4.xlsx from the drive and folder where you store your Data Files, then save it as **EX F-Timesheets**.

b. Compare the data in the workbook by arranging the Week 1, Week 2, and Week 3 sheets horizontally.

c. Maximize the Week 1 window. Unlock the hours data in the Week 1 sheet and protect the worksheet. Verify that the employee names, numbers, and classifications cannot be changed. Verify that the total hours data can be changed, but do not change the data.

d. Unprotect the Week 1 sheet, and create a custom view called **Complete Worksheet** that displays all the data.

e. Hide column E and create a custom view of the data in the range A1:D22. Name the view **Employee Classifications**. Display each view, then return to the Complete Worksheet view.

f. Add a page break between columns D and E so that the Total Hours data prints on a second page. Preview the worksheet, then remove the page break. (*Hint*: Use the Breaks button on the Page Layout tab.)

Independent Challenge 2 (continued)

g. Add a hyperlink to the Classification heading in cell D1 that links to the file EX F-Classifications.xlsx. Add a ScreenTip that reads Pay rates, then test the hyperlink. Compare your screen to Figure F-22.

FIGURE F-22

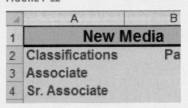

h. Save the EX F-Classifications workbook as an Excel 97-2003 workbook, reviewing the Compatibility Checker information. Close the EX F-Classifications.xls file.

i. Group the three worksheets in the EX F-Timesheets.xlsx workbook, and add your name to the center footer section.

j. Save the workbook, then preview the grouped worksheets.

k. Ungroup the worksheets, and add 2-inch top and left margins to the Week 1 worksheet.

l. Hide the Week 2 and Week 3 worksheets, inspect the file and remove all document properties, personal information, and hidden worksheets. Do not remove header and footer information.

m. Add the keyword **hours** to the workbook, save the workbook, then mark it as final.

Advanced Challenge Exercise

■ Remove the final status from the workbook.

■ If you have access to an Information Rights Management server, restrict the permissions to the workbook by granting only yourself permission to change the workbook.

■ If you have a valid certificate authority, add a digital signature to the workbook.

■ Delete the hours data in the worksheet, and save the workbook as an Excel template.

n. Submit the workbook to your instructor, close the workbook, and exit Excel.

Independent Challenge 3

One of your responsibilities as the office manager at Chicago Management Consultants is to track supplies for the home office. You decide to create a spreadsheet to track these orders, placing each month's orders on its own sheet. You create custom views that will focus on the categories of supplies. A hyperlink will provide the supplier's contact information.

a. Start Excel, open the file EX F-5.xlsx from the drive and folder where you store your Data Files, then save it as **EX F-Supplies**.

b. Arrange the sheets for the 3 months horizontally to compare expenses, then close the extra workbook windows and maximize the remaining window.

c. Create a custom view of the entire January worksheet named **All Supplies**. Hide the paper, pens, and miscellaneous supply data, and create a custom view displaying only the hardware supplies. Call the view **Hardware**.

d. Display the All Supplies view, group the worksheets, and create a total for the total costs in cell D32 on each month's sheet. Use the Format Painter to copy the format from cell D31 to cell D32.

e. With the sheets grouped, add the sheet name to the center section of each sheet's header and your name to the center section of each sheet's footer.

f. Ungroup the sheets and use the Compatibility Checker to view the features that are unsupported in earlier Excel formats.

g. Add a hyperlink in cell A1 of the January sheet that opens the file EX F-Hardware.xlsx. Add a ScreenTip of **Hardware Supplier**. Test the link, viewing the ScreenTip, then return to the EX F-Supplies.xlsx workbook without closing the EX F-Hardware.xlsx workbook. Save the EX F-Supplies.xlsx workbook.

h. Create a workspace that includes the workbooks EX F-Supplies.xlsx and EX F-Hardware.xlsx in the tiled layout. Name the workspace **EX F-Office Supplies**. (*Hint*: Save Workspace is a button on the View tab in the Window group.)

i. Hide the EX F-Hardware.xlsx workbook, then unhide it.

j. Close the EX F-Hardware.xlsx file, and maximize the EX F-Supplies.xlsx worksheet.

k. Save the EX F-Supplies workbook as a macro-enabled workbook. Close the workbook, submit the workbook to your instructor, then exit Excel.

Real Life Independent Challenge

Homework A6 Due midnight 10/9

Excel can be a useful tool in tracking expenses for volunteering or service learning activities. Whether you are volunteering at an organization now or will be in the future, you can use Excel to enter and organize your volunteer expenses. After your data is entered, you create custom views of the data, add a hyperlink and keywords, and save the file in an earlier version of Excel.

a. Start Excel, save the new workbook as **EX F-Volunteer Expenses** in the drive and folder where you store your Data Files.

b. Enter the label Volunteer Activity in cell A1 and Expenses in cell A2. Center each label across columns A and B. Enter the labels **Category** in cell A4 and **Amount** in cell B4. Enter your expenses in column A. Examples of expenses might be **Supplies**, **Printing**, **Postage**, **Workshops**, **Reference Materials**, **Transportation**, **Mileage**, and **Meals**. Add the corresponding expense amounts in column B.

c. Add a hyperlink to cell A1 that links to a Web page with information about your volunteer activity. If you don't have a volunteer activity, link to a volunteer organization that interests you. If necessary, adjust the formatting for cell A1 so the label is visible in the cell. (*Hint*: In the Insert Hyperlink dialog box, click the Existing File or Web Page button, and enter the address of the Web page in the Address text box.)

d. Create a custom view called **All Expenses** that displays all of the budget information. Create a custom view named **Transportation** that displays only the transportation data. Check each view, then display the All Expenses view.

e. Using the Document Panel, add your name in the Author text box, add **volunteer** in the Subject text box, and add the keywords **expenses** and **volunteer**.

f. Add a footer that includes your name on the left side of the printout. Preview the worksheet.

g. Unlock the expense amounts in the worksheet. Protect the worksheet without using a password.

h. Remove the worksheet protection, then save the workbook.

i. Save the workbook in Excel 97-2003 format, then close the EX F-Volunteer Expenses.xls file.

Advanced Challenge Exercise

- Open the EX F-Volunteer Expenses.xlsx file and verify the worksheet is not protected.
- Enable the workbook to be changed by multiple people simultaneously.
- Set up the shared workbook so that all future changes will be tracked, then change the data for two of your dollar amounts.
- Review the tracked changes, and accept the first change and reject the second change.
- Save and close the workbook.

j. Submit the workbook to your instructor. Exit Excel.

Visual Workshop

Start Excel, open the file EX F-6.xlsx from the drive and folder where you store your Data Files, then save it as **EX F-Ocean View**. Make your worksheet look like the one shown in Figure F-23. The text in cell A4 is a hyperlink to the EX F-Price Information workbook, and it has been formatted in the standard color of green. The worksheet background is the Data File EX F-7.gif. Enter your name in the footer, preview the worksheet, then submit the worksheet to your instructor.

FIGURE F-23

	A	B	C	D	E	F	G	H	I	J
1			Ocean View Realty							
2			Seasonal Rentals							
3	Listing Number	Location	Type	Bed	Bath	Pets				
4	1025	Waterfront	Condominium	2	1	No				
5	1564	Village	House	4	2	No				
6	1999	1 block from water	House	4	2	Yes				
7	1485	1 mile from water	Condominium	2	2	No				
8	1324	Waterfront	Condominium	4	2	No				
9	1524	Village	House	2	1	No				
10	1332	Waterfront	House	3	1	Yes				
11	1563	Village	Condominium	3	2	No				
12	1966	1 block from water	House	4	2	Yes				
13	1458	1 mile from water	Condominium	2	2	No				
14	1221	Waterfront	House	4	2	No				
15	1469	Village	House	2	1	No				

Managing Workbook Data

Managing Data Using Tables

Files You Will Need:

EX G-1.xlsx
EX G-2.xlsx
EX G-3.xlsx
EX G-4.xlsx
EX G-5.xlsx

In addition to using Excel spreadsheet features, you can analyze and manipulate data in a table structure. An Excel **table** is an organized collection of rows and columns of similarly structured worksheet data. For example, a table might contain customer information, with a different customer in each row, with columns holding address, phone, and sales data for each customer. You can use a table to work with data independently of other data on your worksheet. When you designate a particular range of worksheet data as a table and format it, Excel automatically extends its formatting to adjacent cells when you add data. In addition, all table formulas are updated to include the new data. Without a table, you would have to manually adjust formatting and formulas every time you add data to a range. A table lets you easily change the order of information while keeping all row information together. You can also use a table to show and perform calculations on only the type of data you need, making it easier to understand large lists of data. In this unit, you'll learn how to plan and create a table; add, change, find, and delete table information; and then sort table data, perform table calculations, and print a table. Quest uses tables to analyze tour data. The vice president of sales, Kate Morgan, asks you to help her build and manage a table of 2013 tour information.

OBJECTIVES

Plan a table

Create and format a table

Add table data

Find and replace table data

Delete table data

Sort table data

Use formulas in a table

Print a table

Planning a Table

Tables are a convenient way to understand and manage large amounts of information. When planning a table, consider what information you want your table to contain and how you want to work with the data, now and in the future. As you plan a table, you should understand its most important components. A table is organized into rows called records. A **record** is a table row that contains data about an object, person, or other item. Records are composed of fields. **Fields** are columns in the table; each field describes a characteristic of the record, such as a customer's last name or street address. Each field has a **field name**, which is a column label, such as "Address," that describes its contents. Tables usually have a **header row** as the first row that contains the field names. To plan your table, use the steps below. ▓▓▓▓ Kate asks you to compile a table of the 2013 tours. Before entering the tour data into an Excel worksheet, you plan the table contents.

DETAILS

As you plan your table, use the following guidelines:

*   **Identify the purpose of the table**

    The purpose of the table determines the kind of information the table should contain. You want to use the tours table to find all departure dates for a particular tour and to display the tours in order of departure date. You also want to quickly calculate the number of available seats for a tour.

*   **Plan the structure of the table**

    In designing your table's structure, determine the fields (the table columns) you need to achieve the table's purpose. You have worked with the sales department to learn the type of information they need for each tour. Figure G-1 shows a layout sketch for the table. Each row will contain one tour record. The columns represent fields that contain pieces of descriptive information you will enter for each tour, such as the name, departure date, and duration.

*   **Plan your row and column structure**

    You can create a table from any contiguous range of cells on your worksheet. Plan and design your table so that all rows have similar types of information in the same column. A table should not have any blank rows or columns. Instead of using blank rows to separate table headings from data, use a table style, which will use formatting to make column labels stand out from your table data. Figure G-2 shows a table, populated with data, that has been formatted using a table style.

*   **Document the table design**

    In addition to your table sketch, you should make a list of the field names to document the type of data and any special number formatting required for each field. Field names should be as short as possible while still accurately describing the column information. When naming fields it is important to use text rather than numbers because Excel could interpret numbers as parts of formulas. Your field names should be unique and not easily confused with cell addresses, such as the name D2. You want your tours table to contain eight field names, each one corresponding to the major characteristics of the 2013 tours. Table G-1 shows the documentation of the field names in your table.

FIGURE G-1: Table layout sketch

2013 Quest Tours							
Tour	Depart Date	Number of Days	Seat Capacity	Seats Reserved	Price	Air Included	Insurance Included

→ Header row will contain field names

→ Each tour will be placed in a table row

FIGURE G-2: Formatted table with data

	A	B	C	D	E	F	G	H
1	Tour	Depart Date	Number of Days	Seat Capacity	Seats Reserved	Price	Air Included	Insurance Included
2	Pacific Odyssey	1/12/2013	14	50	50	$ 2,105	Yes	No
3	Old Japan	1/13/2013	21	46	41	$ 1,964	Yes	No
4	Costa Rica	1/19/2013	10	31	28	$ 1,833	Yes	Yes
5	Yellowstone	1/21/2013	18	50	40	$ 1,700	Yes	Yes
6	Yellowstone	1/31/2013	18	20	0	$ 1,005	Yes	Yes
7	Amazing Amazon	2/22/2013	14	44	38	$ 2,154	No	No
8	Hiking Patagonia	2/28/2013	7	20	15	$ 2,822	Yes	No
9	Pearls of the Orient	3/13/2013	14	45	15	$ 2,400	Yes	No
10	Silk Road Travels	3/19/2013	18	23	19	$ 2,031	Yes	Yes
11	Photographing France	3/20/2013	7	20	20	$ 1,541	Yes	Yes
12	Green Adventures in Ecuador	3/23/2013	18	25	22	$ 2,450	No	No
13	African National Parks	4/8/2013	30	12	10	$ 3,115	Yes	Yes
14	Experience Cambodia	4/11/2013	12	35	21	$ 2,441	Yes	No
15	Old Japan	4/15/2013	21	47	30	$ 1,900	Yes	No
16	Costa Rica	4/18/2013	10	30	20	$ 2,800	Yes	Yes
17	Yellowstone	4/20/2013	18	51	31	$ 1,652	Yes	Yes
18	Amazing Amazon	4/23/2013	14	43	30	$ 2,133	No	No
19	Catalonia Adventure	5/9/2013	14	51	30	$ 2,587	Yes	No
20	Treasures of Ethiopia	5/18/2013	10	41	15	$ 1,638	Yes	Yes

TABLE G-1: Table documentation

field name	type of data	description of data
Tour	Text	Name of tour
Depart Date	Date	Date tour departs
Number of Days	Number with 0 decimal places	Duration of the tour
Seat Capacity	Number with 0 decimal places	Maximum number of people the tour can accommodate
Seats Reserved	Number with 0 decimal places	Number of reservations for the tour
Price	Accounting with 0 decimal places and $ symbol	Tour price (This price is not guaranteed until a 30% deposit is received)
Air Included	Text	Yes: Airfare is included in the price No: Airfare is not included in the price
Insurance Included	Text	Yes: Insurance is included in the price No: Insurance is not included in the price

Creating and Formatting a Table

Once you have planned the table structure, the sequence of fields, and appropriate data types, you are ready to create the table in Excel. After you create a table, a Table Tools Design tab appears, containing a gallery of table styles. **Table styles** allow you to easily add formatting to your table by using preset formatting combinations of fill color, borders, type style, and type color. ⬛⬛⬛ Kate asks you to build a table with the 2013 tour data. You begin by entering the field names. Then you enter the tour data that corresponds to each field name, create the table, and format the data using a table style.

STEPS

TROUBLE
Don't worry if your field names are wider than the cells; you will fix this later.

1. **Start Excel, open the file EX G-1.xlsx from the drive and folder where you store your Data Files, then save it as EX G-2013 Tours**

2. **Beginning in cell A1 of the Practice sheet, enter each field name in a separate column, as shown in Figure G-3**

   Field names are usually in the first row of the table.

QUICK TIP
Do not insert extra spaces at the beginning of a cell because it can affect sorting and finding data in a table.

3. **Enter the information from Figure G-4 in the rows immediately below the field names, leaving no blank rows**

   The data appears in columns organized by field name.

4. **Select the range A1:H4, click the Format button in the Cells group, click AutoFit Column Width, then click cell A1**

   Resizing the column widths this way is faster than double-clicking the column divider lines.

QUICK TIP
You can also create a table using the shortcut key combination [Ctrl] + T.

5. **With cell A1 selected, click the Insert tab, click the Table button in the Tables group, in the Create Table dialog box verify that your table data is in the range $A$1:$H$4, and make sure My table has headers is checked as shown in Figure G-5, then click OK**

   The data range is now defined as a table. **Filter list arrows**, which let you display portions of your data, now appear next to each column header. When you create a table, Excel automatically applies a table style. The default table style has a dark blue header row and alternating gray and white data rows. The Table Tools Design tab appears, and the Table Styles group displays a gallery of table formatting options. You decide to choose a different table style from the gallery.

6. **Click the Table Styles More button ▾, scroll to view all of the table styles, then move the mouse pointer over several styles without clicking**

   The Table Styles gallery on the Table Tools Design tab has three style categories: Light, Medium, and Dark. Each category has numerous design types; for example, in some of the designs, the header row and total row are darker and the rows alternate colors. The available table designs use the current workbook theme colors so the table coordinates with your existing workbook content. If you select a different workbook theme and color scheme in the Themes group on the Page Layout tab, the Table Styles gallery uses those colors. As you point to each table style, Live Preview shows you what your table will look like with the style applied. However, you only see a preview of each style; you need to click a style to apply it.

7. **Click the Table Style Medium 21 to apply it to your table, then click cell A1**

   Compare your table to Figure G-6.

Managing Data Using Tables

FIGURE G-3: Field names entered in row 1

	A	B	C	D	E	F	G	H
1	Tour	Depart Date	Number of Days	Seat Capacity	Seats Reserved	Price	Air Included	Insurance Included

FIGURE G-4: Three records entered in the worksheet

	A	B	C	D	E	F	G	H
1	Tour	Depart Date	Number of Days	Seat Capacity	Seats Reserved	Price	Air Included	Insurance Included
2	Pacific Odyssey	1/12/2013	14	50	50	2105	Yes	No
3	Old Japan	1/13/2013	21	46	41	1964	Yes	No
4	Costa Rica	1/19/2013	10	31	28	1833	Yes	Yes
5								

FIGURE G-5: Insert Table dialog box

Table range →

Verify that this box is checked →

FIGURE G-6: Formatted table with three records

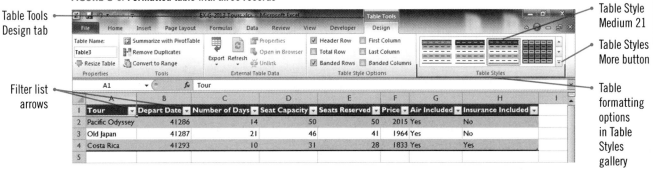

Table Tools Design tab

Filter list arrows

Table Style Medium 21

Table Styles More button

Table formatting options in Table Styles gallery

Changing table style options

You can change a table's appearance by using the check boxes in the Table Styles Options group on the Table Tools Design tab. For example, you can turn on or turn off the following options: **banding**, which creates different formatting for adjacent rows and columns; special formatting for first and last columns; Total Row, which calculates totals for each column; and Header Row, which displays or hides the header row. Use these options to modify a table's appearance either before or after applying a table style. For example, if your table has banded rows, you can select the Banded Columns check box to change the table to be displayed with banded columns. Also, you may want to deselect the Header Row check box to

hide a table's header row if a table will be included in a presentation. Figure G-7 shows the available table style options.

You can also create your own table style by clicking the Table Styles More button, then at the bottom of the Table Styles Gallery, clicking New Table Style. In the New Table Quick Style dialog box, name the style in the Name text box, click a table element, then format selected table elements by clicking Format. You can also set a custom style as the default style for your tables by checking the Set as default table quick style for this document check box. You can click Clear at the bottom of the Table Styles gallery if you want to clear a table style.

FIGURE G-7: Table Styles Options

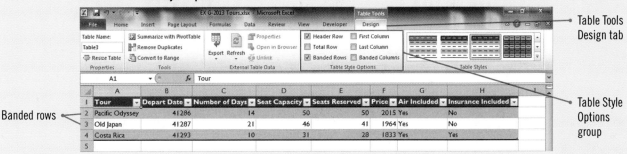

Banded rows

Table Tools Design tab

Table Style Options group

Adding Table Data

You can add records to a table by typing data directly below the last row of the table. After you press [Enter], the new row becomes part of the table and the table formatting extends to the new data. When the active cell is the last cell of a table, you can add a new row by pressing [Tab]. You can also insert rows in any table location. If you decide you need additional data fields, you can add new columns to a table. You can also expand a table by dragging the sizing handle in a table's lower-right corner; drag down to add rows and drag to the right to add columns. ▰▰▰▰ After entering all of the 2013 tour data, Kate decides to offer two additional tours. She also wants the table to display the number of available seats for each tour and whether visas are required for the destination.

STEPS

1. **Click the 2013 Tours sheet tab**

   The 2013 sheet containing the 2013 tour data becomes active.

2. **Scroll down to the last table row, click cell A65 in the table, enter the data for the new Costa Rica tour, as shown in Figure G-8, then press [Enter]**

   As you scroll down, the table headers are visible at the top of the table as long as the active cell is inside the table. The new Costa Rica tour is part of the table. You want to enter a record about a new January tour above row 6.

3. **Scroll up to and click the inside left edge of cell A6 to select the table row data, click the Insert list arrow in the Cells group, then click Insert Table Rows Above**

   Clicking the left edge of the first cell in a table row selects the entire table row, rather than the entire worksheet row. A new blank row 6 is available to enter the new record.

4. **Click cell A6, then enter the Yellowstone record, as shown in Figure G-9**

   The new Yellowstone tour is part of the table. You want to add a new field that displays the number of available seats for each tour.

5. **Click cell I1, enter the field name Seats Available, then press [Enter]**

   The new field becomes part of the table, and the header formatting extends to the new field. The AutoCorrect menu allows you to undo or stop the automatic table expansion, but in this case you decide to leave this feature on. You want to add another new field to the table to display tours that require visas, but this time you will add the new field by resizing the table.

QUICK TIP
You can also resize a table by clicking the Table Tools Design tab, clicking the Resize Table button in the Properties group, selecting the new data range for the table, then clicking OK.

6. **Scroll down until cell I66 is visible, drag the sizing handle in the table's lower-right corner one column to the right to add column J to the table, as shown in Figure G-10**

   The table range is now A1:J66, and the new field name is Column1.

7. **Scroll up to and click cell J1, enter Visa Required, then press [Enter]**

8. **Click the Insert tab, click the Header & Footer button in the Text group, enter your name in the center header text box, click cell A1, click the Normal button ▦ in the status bar, then save the workbook**

Managing Data Using Tables

FIGURE G-8: New record in row 65

62	Pacific Odyssey	12/21/2013	14	50	10	$ 2,105	Yes	No
63	Yellowstone	12/30/2013	18	51	15	$ 2,922	Yes	Yes
64	Old Japan	12/31/2013	21	47	4	$ 2,100	Yes	No
65	Costa Rica	1/30/2013	7	20	0	$ 1,927	Yes	Yes
66								
67								
68								

New record in row 65

FIGURE G-9: New record in row 6

	A	B	C	D	E	F	G	H
1	Tour	Depart Date	Number of Days	Seat Capacity	Seats Reserved	Price	Air Included	Insurance Included
2	Pacific Odyssey	1/12/2013	14	50	50	$ 2,105	Yes	No
3	Old Japan	1/13/2013	21	46	41	$ 1,964	Yes	No
4	Costa Rica	1/19/2013	10	31	28	$ 1,833	Yes	Yes
5	Yellowstone	1/21/2013	18	50	40	$ 1,700	Yes	Yes
6	Yellowstone	1/31/2013	18	20	0	$ 1,005	Yes	Yes
7	Amazing Amazon	2/22/2013	14	44	38	$ 2,154	No	No
8	Hiking Patagonia	2/28/2013	7	20	15	$ 2,822	Yes	No
9	Pearls of the Orient	3/13/2013	14	45	15	$ 2,400	Yes	No
10	Silk Road Travels	3/19/2013	18	23	19	$ 2,031	Yes	Yes

New record in row 6

FIGURE G-10: Resizing a table using the resizing handles

56	Exotic Morocco	10/31/2013	7	38	15	$ 1,900	Yes	No
57	Experience Cambodia	10/31/2013	12	40	2	$ 2,908	Yes	No
58	Treasures of Ethiopia	11/18/2013	10	41	12	$ 2,200	Yes	Yes
59	Panama Adventure	12/18/2013	10	50	21	$ 2,204	Yes	Yes
60	Panama Adventure	12/18/2013	10	50	21	$ 2,204	Yes	Yes
61	Galapagos Adventure	12/20/2013	14	15	1	$ 2,100	Yes	Yes
62	Galapagos Adventure	12/20/2013	14	15	1	$ 2,100	Yes	Yes
63	Pacific Odyssey	12/21/2013	14	50	10	$ 2,105	Yes	No
64	Yellowstone	12/30/2013	18	51	15	$ 2,922	Yes	Yes
65	Old Japan	12/31/2013	21	47	4	$ 2,100	Yes	No
66	Costa Rica	1/30/2013	7	20	0	$ 1,927	Yes	Yes
67								

Drag sizing handle to add column J

Selecting table elements

When working with tables you often need to select rows, columns, and even the entire table. Clicking to the right of a row number, inside column A, selects the entire table row. You can select a table column by clicking the top edge of the header. Be careful not to click a column letter or row number, however, because this selects the entire worksheet row or column. You can select the table data by clicking the upper-left corner of the first table cell. When selecting a column or a table, the first click selects only the data in the column or table. If you click a second time, you add the headers to the selection.

Excel 2010

Finding and Replacing Table Data

From time to time, you need to locate specific records in your table. You can use the Excel Find feature to search your table for the information you need. You can also use the Replace feature to locate and replace existing entries or portions of entries with information you specify. If you don't know the exact spelling of the text you are searching for, you can use wildcards to help locate the records. **Wildcards** are special symbols that substitute for unknown characters. ▓▓▓▓▓ In response to a change in the bike trip from Ireland to Scotland, Kate needs to replace "Ireland" with "Scotland" in all of the tour names. She also wants to know how many Pacific Odyssey tours are scheduled for the year. You begin by searching for records with the text "Pacific Odyssey".

STEPS

1. **Click cell A1 if necessary, click the Home tab, click the Find & Select button in the Editing group, then click Find**

   The Find and Replace dialog box opens, as shown in Figure G-11. In this dialog box, you enter criteria that specify the records you want to find in the Find what text box. You want to search for records whose Tour field contains the label "Pacific Odyssey".

2. **Type Pacific Odyssey in the Find what text box, then click Find Next**

   A2 is the active cell because it is the first instance of Pacific Odyssey in the table.

3. **Click Find Next and examine the record for each Pacific Odyssey tour found until no more matching cells are found in the table and the active cell is A2 again, then click Close**

   There are four Pacific Odyssey tours.

4. **Return to cell A1, click the Find & Select button in the Editing group, then click Replace**

   The Find and Replace dialog box opens with the Replace tab selected and "Pacific Odyssey" in the Find what text box, as shown in Figure G-12. You will search for entries containing "Ireland" and replace them with "Scotland". To save time, you will use the (*) wildcard to help you locate the records containing Ireland.

5. **Delete the text in the Find what text box, type Ir* in the Find what text box, click the Replace with text box, then type Scotland**

   The asterisk (*) wildcard stands for one or more characters, meaning that the search text "Ir*" will find words such as "iron", "hair", and "bird". Because you notice that there are other table entries containing the text "ir" with a lowercase "i" (in the Air Included column heading), you need to make sure that only capitalized instances of the letter "I" are replaced.

6. **Click Options >>, click the Match case check box to select it, click Options <<, then click Find Next**

   Excel moves the cell pointer to the cell containing the first occurrence of "Ireland".

7. **Click Replace All, click OK, then click Close**

   The dialog box closes. Excel made three replacements, in cells A27, A36, and A40. The Air Included field heading remains unchanged because the "ir" in "Air" is lowercase.

8. **Save the workbook**

FIGURE G-11: Find and Replace dialog box

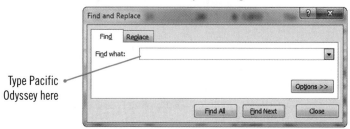

Type Pacific
Odyssey here

FIGURE G-12: The Replace tab in the Find and Replace dialog box

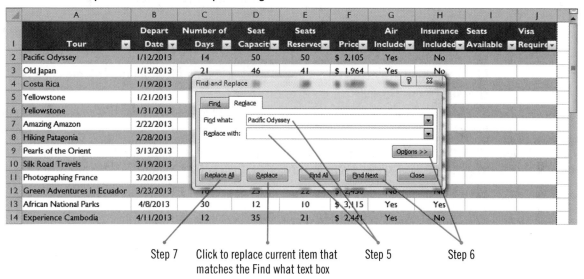

Step 7   Click to replace current item that   Step 5   Step 6
          matches the Find what text box

Using Find and Select features

You can also use the Find feature to navigate to a specific place in a workbook by clicking the Find & Select button in the Editing group, clicking Go To, typing a cell address, then clicking OK. Clicking the Find & Select button also allows you to find comments and conditional formatting in a worksheet. You can use the Go to Special dialog box to select cells that contain different types of formulas or objects. Some Go to Special commands also appear on the Find & Select menu. Using this menu, you can also change the mouse pointer shape to the Select Objects pointer so you can quickly select drawing objects when necessary. To return to the standard Excel pointer, press [Esc].

Deleting Table Data

To keep a table up to date, you need to be able to periodically remove records. You may even need to remove fields if the information stored in a field becomes unnecessary. You can delete table data using the Delete button in the Cells group or by dragging the sizing handle at the table's lower-right corner. You can also easily delete duplicate records from a table. ▄▄▟▟ Kate is canceling the Old Japan tour that departs on 1/13/2013 and asks you to delete the record from the table. You will also remove any duplicate records from the table. Because the visa requirements are difficult to keep up with, Kate asks you to delete the field with visa information.

STEPS

1. **Click the left edge of cell A3 to select the table row data, click the Delete button list arrow in the Cells group, then click Delete Table Rows**

   The Old Japan tour is deleted, and the Costa Rica tour moves up to row 3, as shown in Figure G-13. You can also delete a table row or a column using the Resize Table button in the Properties group of the Table Tools Design tab, or by right-clicking the row or column, pointing to Delete on the shortcut menu, then clicking Table Columns or Table Rows. You decide to check the table for duplicate records.

QUICK TIP
You can also remove duplicates from worksheet data by clicking the Data tab, then clicking the Remove Duplicates button in the Data Tools group.

2. **Click the Table Tools Design tab, then click the Remove Duplicates button in the Tools group**

   The Remove Duplicates dialog box opens, as shown in Figure G-14. You need to select the columns that will be used to evaluate duplicates. Because you don't want to delete tours with the same destination but different departure dates, you will look for duplicate data in all of the columns.

3. **Make sure that "My data has headers" is checked and that all the columns headers are checked, then click OK**

   Two duplicate records are found and removed, leaving 62 records of data and a total of 63 rows in the table, including the header row. You want to remove the last column, which contains space for visa information.

4. **Click OK, scroll down until cell J63 is visible, drag the sizing handle of the table's lower-right corner one column to the left to remove column J from the table**

   The table range is now A1:I63, and the Visa Required field no longer appears in the table.

5. **Delete the contents of cell J1, return to cell A1, then save the workbook**

FIGURE G-13: Table with row deleted

	Tour	Depart Date	Number of Days	Seat Capacity	Seats Reserved	Price	Air Included	Insurance Included	Seats Available
2	Pacific Odyssey	1/12/2013	14	50	50	$ 2,105	Yes	No	
3	Costa Rica	1/19/2013	10	31	28	$ 1,833	Yes	Yes	
4	Yellowstone	1/21/2013	18	50	40	$ 1,700	Yes	Yes	
5	Yellowstone	1/31/2013	18	20	0	$ 1,005	Yes	Yes	
6	Amazing Amazon	2/22/2013	14	44	38	$ 2,154	No	No	
7	Hiking Patagonia	2/28/2013	7	20	15	$ 2,822	Yes	No	
8	Pearls of the Orient	3/13/2013	14	45	15	$ 2,400	Yes	No	
9	Silk Road Travels	3/19/2013	18	23	19	$ 2,031	Yes	Yes	
10	Photographing France	3/20/2013	7	20	20	$ 1,541	Yes	Yes	
11	Green Adventures in Ecuador	3/23/2013	18	25	22	$ 2,450	No	No	
12	African National Parks	4/8/2013	30	12	10	$ 3,115	Yes	Yes	
13	Experience Cambodia	4/11/2013	12	35	21	$ 2,441	Yes	No	
14	Old Japan	4/15/2013	21	47	30	$ 1,900	Yes	No	
15	Costa Rica	4/18/2013	10	30	20	$ 2,800	Yes	Yes	
16	Yellowstone	4/20/2013	18	51	31	$ 1,652	Yes	Yes	
17	Amazing Amazon	4/23/2013	14	43	30	$ 2,133	No	No	
18	Catalonia Adventure	5/9/2013	14	51	30	$ 2,587	Yes	No	
19	Treasures of Ethiopia	5/18/2013	10	41	15	$ 1,638	Yes	Yes	
20	Monasteries of Bulgaria	5/20/2013	7	19	11	$ 1,663	Yes	Yes	
21	Biking in France	5/23/2013	7	12	10	$ 1,635	No	No	

Row is deleted and tours move up one row

H ◀ ▶ H   Practice   **2013 Tours**   Sheet2

FIGURE G-14: Remove Duplicates dialog box

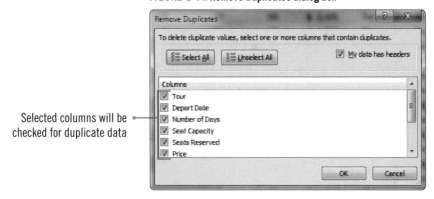

Selected columns will be checked for duplicate data

Sorting Table Data

Usually, you enter table records in the order in which you receive information, rather than in alphabetical or numerical order. When you add records to a table, you usually enter them at the end of the table. You can change the order of the records any time using the Excel **sort** feature. Because the data is structured as a table, Excel changes the order of the records while keeping each record, or row of information, together. You can sort a table in ascending or descending order on one field using the filter list arrows next to the field name. In **ascending order**, the lowest value (the beginning of the alphabet or the earliest date) appears at the top of the table. In a field containing labels and numbers, numbers appear first in the sorted list. In **descending order**, the highest value (the end of the alphabet or the latest date) appears at the top of the table. In a field containing labels and numbers, labels appear first. Table G-2 provides examples of ascending and descending sorts. ▆▆▆▆▆ Kate wants the tour data sorted by departure date, displaying tours that depart the soonest at the top of the table.

STEPS

1. **Click the Depart Date filter list arrow, then click Sort Oldest to Newest**

   Excel rearranges the records in ascending order by departure date, as shown in Figure G-15. The Depart Date filter list arrow has an upward pointing arrow indicating the ascending sort in the field. You can also sort the table on one field using the Sort & Filter button.

2. **Click the Home tab, click any cell in the Price column, click the Sort & Filter button in the Editing group, then click Sort Largest to Smallest**

   Excel sorts the table, placing those records with the higher price at the top. The Price filter list arrow now has a downward pointing arrow next to the filter list arrow, indicating the descending sort order. You can also rearrange the table data using a **multilevel sort**. This type of sort rearranges the table data using more than one field, where each field is a different level, based on its importance in the sort. If you use two sort levels, the data is sorted by the first field, and the second field is sorted within each grouping of the first field. Since you have many groups of tours with different departure dates, you want to use a multilevel sort to arrange the table data by tours and then by departure dates within each tour.

3. **Click the Sort & Filter button in the Editing group, then click Custom Sort**

   The Sort dialog box opens, as shown in Figure G-16.

4. **Click the Sort by list arrow, click Tour, click the Order list arrow, click A to Z, click Add Level, click the Then by list arrow, click Depart Date, click the second Order list arrow, click Oldest to Newest if necessary, then click OK**

   Figure G-17 shows the table sorted alphabetically in ascending order (A–Z) by Tour and, within each tour grouping, in ascending order by the Depart Date.

5. **Save the workbook**

Sorting a table using conditional formatting

If conditional formats have been applied to a table, you can sort the table using conditional formatting to arrange the rows. For example, if cells are conditionally formatted with color, you can sort a field on Cell Color, using the color with the order of On Top or On Bottom in the Sort dialog box.

Managing Data Using Tables

FIGURE G-15: Table sorted by departure date

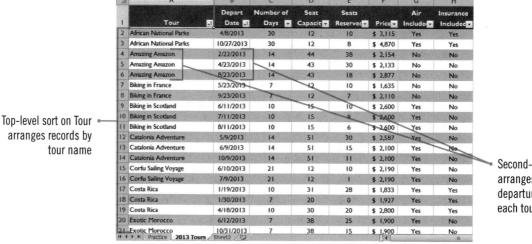

Up arrow indicates ascending sort in the field

FIGURE G-16: Sort dialog box

Click to add additional sort levels

Click to delete sort levels

Click to display fields

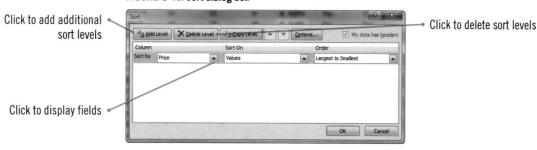

FIGURE G-17: Table sorted using two levels

Top-level sort on Tour arranges records by tour name

Second-level sort arranges records by departure date within each tour grouping

TABLE G-2: Sort order options and examples

option	alphabetic	numeric	date	alphanumeric
Ascending	A, B, C	7, 8, 9	1/1, 2/1, 3/1	12A, 99B, DX8, QT7
Descending	C, B, A	9, 8, 7	3/1, 2/1, 1/1	QT7, DX8, 99B, 12A

Specifying a custom sort order

You can identify a custom sort order for the field selected in the Sort by box. Click the Order list arrow in the Sort dialog box, click Custom List, then click the desired custom order. Commonly used custom sort orders are days of the week (Sun, Mon, Tues, Wed, etc.) and months (Jan, Feb, Mar, etc.); alphabetic sorts do not sort these items properly.

Using Formulas in a Table

Many tables are large, making it difficult to know from viewing them the "story" the table tells. The Excel table calculation features help you summarize table data so you can see important trends. After you enter a single formula into a table cell, the **calculated columns** feature fills in the remaining cells with the formula's results. The column continues to fill with the formula results as you enter rows in the table. This makes it easy to update your formulas because you only need to edit the formula once, and the change will fill in to the other column cells. The **structured reference** feature allows your formulas to refer to table columns by names that are automatically generated when you create the table. These names automatically adjust as you add or delete table fields. An example of a table reference is =[Sales]–[Costs], where Sales and Costs are field names in the table. Tables also have a specific area at the bottom called the **table total row** for calculations using the data in the table columns. The cells in this row contain a dropdown list of functions that can be used for the column calculation. The table total row adapts to any changes in the table size. ![icon] Kate wants you to use a formula to calculate the number of available seats for each tour. You will also add summary information to the end of the table.

STEPS

1. **Click cell I2, then type =[**
   A list of the table field names appears, as shown in Figure G-18. Structured referencing allows you to use the names that Excel created when you defined your table to reference fields in a formula. You can choose a field by clicking it and pressing [TAB] or by double-clicking the field name.

2. **Click [Seat Capacity], press [Tab], then type]**
   Excel begins the formula, placing [Seat Capacity] in the cell in blue and framing the Seat Capacity data in a blue border.

3. **Type -[, double-click [Seats Reserved], then type]**
   Excel places [Seats Reserved] in the cell in green and outlines the Seats Reserved data in a green border.

4. **Press [Enter]**
   The formula result, 2, is displayed in cell I2. The table column also fills with the formula displaying the number of available seats for each tour.

> **QUICK TIP**
> You can undo the calculated column results by clicking Undo Calculated Column in the AutoCorrect Options list. You can turn off the Calculated Columns feature by clicking Stop Automatically Creating Calculated Columns in the AutoCorrect Options list.

5. **Click the AutoCorrect Options list arrow** ![icon]
   Because the calculated columns option saves time, you decide to leave the feature on. You want to display the total number of available seats on all of the tours.

6. **Click any cell inside the table if necessary, click the Table Tools Design tab, then click the Total Row check box in the Table Style Options group to select it**
   A total row appears at the bottom of the table, and the sum of the available seats, 1028, is displayed in cell I64. You can select other formulas in the total row.

7. **Click cell C64, then click the cell list arrow on the right side of the cell**
   The list of available functions appears, as shown in Figure G-19. You want to find the average tour length.

8. **Click Average, then save your workbook**
   The average tour length, 13 days, appears in cell C64.

FIGURE G-18: Table field names

	A	B	C	D	E	F	G	H	I	J
1	Tour	Depart Date	Number of Days	Seat Capacity	Seats Reserved	Price	Air Included	Insurance Included	Seats Available	
2	African National Parks	4/8/2013	30	12	10	$ 3,115	Yes	Yes	=[	
3	African National Parks	10/27/2013	30	12	8	$ 4,870	Yes	Yes		
4	Amazing Amazon	2/22/2013	14	44	38	$ 2,154	No	No		
5	Amazing Amazon	4/23/2013	14	43	30	$ 2,133	No	No		
6	Amazing Amazon	8/23/2013	14	43	18	$ 2,877	No	No		
7	Biking in France	5/23/2013	7	12	10	$ 1,635	No	No		
8	Biking in France	9/23/2013	7	12	7	$ 2,110	No	No		
9	Biking in Scotland	6/11/2013	10	15	10	$ 2,600	Yes	No		
10	Biking in Scotland	7/11/2013	10	15	9	$ 2,600	Yes	No		
11	Biking in Scotland	8/11/2013	10	15	6	$ 2,600	Yes	No		
12	Catalonia Adventure	5/9/2013	14	51	30	$ 2,587	Yes	No		
13	Catalonia Adventure	6/9/2013	14	51	15	$ 2,100	Yes	No		
14	Catalonia Adventure	10/9/2013	14	51	11	$ 2,100	Yes	No		
15	Corfu Sailing Voyage	6/10/2013	21	12	10	$ 2,190	Yes	No		
16	Corfu Sailing Voyage	7/9/2013	21	12	1	$ 2,190	Yes	No		

Drop-down list: Tour, Depart Date, Number of Days, Seat Capacity, Seats Reserved, Price, Air Included, Insurance Included, Seats Available

Table field names

FIGURE G-19: Functions in the Total Row

	Tour	Depart Date	Number of	Seat Capac	Seats Reser	Price	Air Includ	Insurance I	Seats
54	Treasures of Ethiopia	5/18/2013	10	41	15	$ 1,638	Yes	Yes	
55	Treasures of Ethiopia	11/18/2013	10	41	12	$ 2,200	Yes	Yes	
56	Wild River Escape	6/27/2013	10	21	21	$ 1,944	No	No	
57	Wild River Escape	8/27/2013	10	21	11	$ 1,944	No	No	
58	Yellowstone	1/21/2013	18	50	40	$ 1,700	Yes	Yes	
59	Yellowstone	1/31/2013	18	20	0	$ 1,005	Yes	Yes	
60	Yellowstone	4/20/2013	18	51	31	$ 1,652	Yes	Yes	
61	Yellowstone	8/20/2013	18	51	20	$ 2,922	Yes	Yes	
62	Yellowstone	9/11/2013	18	51	20	$ 2,922	Yes	Yes	
63	Yellowstone	12/30/2013	18	51	15	$ 2,922	Yes	Yes	
64	Total								
65									
66									
67									
68									
69									
70									
71									

Drop-down list: None, Average, Count, Count Numbers, Max, Min, Sum, StdDev, Var, More Functions...

Functions available in the Total Row

Using structured references

When you create a table from worksheet data, Excel creates a default table name such as Table1. This table name appears in structured references. Structured references make it easier to work with formulas that use table data. You can reference the entire table, columns in the table, or specific data. Structured references are especially helpful to use in formulas because they automatically adjust as data ranges change in a table, so you don't need to edit formulas.

Printing a Table

You can determine the way a table will print using the Page Layout tab. Because tables often have more rows than can fit on a page, you can define the first row of the table (containing the field names) as the **print title**, which prints at the top of every page. Most tables do not have any descriptive information above the field names on the worksheet, so to augment the field name information, you can use headers and footers to add identifying text, such as the table title or the report date. ⬛⬛⬛ Kate asks you for a printout of the tour information. You begin by previewing the table.

STEPS

1. **Click the File tab, click Print, then view the table preview**

   Below the table you see 1 of 3.

2. **In the Preview window, click the Next Page button ▶ in the Preview area to view the second page, then click ▶ again to view the third page**

   All of the field names in the table fit across the width of the page. Because the records on pages 2 and 3 appear without column headings, you want to set up the first row of the table, which contains the field names, as a repeating print title.

   QUICK TIP

   You can hide or print headings and gridlines using the check boxes in the Sheet Options group on the Page Layout tab. You might want to hide a worksheet's headings if it will be displayed in a presentation.

3. **Click the Page Layout tab, click the Print Titles button in the Page Setup group, click inside the Rows to repeat at top text box under Print titles, scroll up to row 1 if necessary, click any cell in row 1 on the table, then compare your Page Setup dialog box to Figure G-20**

   When you select row 1 as a print title, Excel automatically inserts an absolute reference to the row that will repeat at the top of each page.

4. **Click the Print Preview button in the Page Setup dialog box, click ▶ in the preview window to view the second page, then click ▶ again to view the third page**

   Setting up a print title to repeat row 1 causes the field names to appear at the top of each printed page. The printout would be more informative with a header to identify the table information.

   QUICK TIP

   You can also add a header or a footer by clicking the Page Layout View in the status bar and clicking in the header or footer area.

5. **Click the Insert tab, click the Header & Footer button in the Text group, click the left header section text box, then type 2013 Tours**

6. **Select the left header section information, click the Home tab, click the Increase Font Size button A̅ in the Font group twice to change the font size to 14, click the Bold button B in the Font group, click any cell in the table, then click the Normal button ▦ in the status bar**

7. **Save the table, preview it, close the workbook, exit Excel, then submit the workbook to your instructor**

   Compare your printed table with Figure G-21.

FIGURE G-20: Page Setup dialog box

Print title is set to row 1

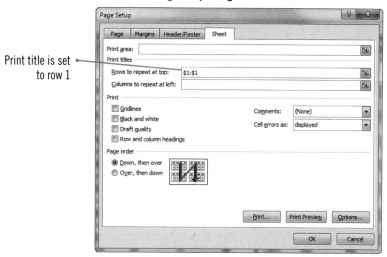

FIGURE G-21: Printed table

Tour	Depart Date	Number of Days	Seat Capacity	Seats Reserved	Price	Air Included	Insurance Included	Seats Available
African National Parks	4/8/2013	30	12	10	$ 3,115	Yes	Yes	2
African National Parks	10/27/2013	30	12	8	$ 4,870	Yes	Yes	4
Amazing Amazon	2/22/2013	14	44	38	$ 2,154	No	No	6
Amazing Amazon	4/23/2013	14	43	30	$ 2,133	No	No	13
Amazing Amazon	8/23/2013	14	43	18	$ 2,877	No	No	25
Biking in France	5/23/2013	7	12	10	$ 1,635	No	No	2
Biking in France	9/23/2013	7	12	7	$ 2,110	No	No	5
Biking in Scotland	6/11/2013	10	15	10	$ 2,600	Yes	No	5
Biking in Scotland	7/11/2013	10	15	9	$ 2,600	Yes	No	6
Biking in Scotland	8/11/2013	10	15	6	$ 2,600	Yes	No	9
Catalonia Adventure	5/9/2013	14	51	30	$ 2,587	Yes	No	21
Catalonia Adventure	6/9/2013	14	51	15	$ 2,100	Yes	No	36
Catalonia Adventure	10/9/2013	14	51	11	$ 2,100	Yes	No	40
Corfu Sailing Voyage	6/10/2013	21	12	10	$ 2,190	Yes	No	2
Corfu Sailing Voyage	7/9/2013	21	12	1	$ 2,190	Yes	No	11
Costa Rica	1/19/2013	10	31	28	$ 1,833	Yes	Yes	3
Costa Rica	1/30/2013	7	20	0	$ 1,927	Yes	Yes	20
Costa Rica	4/18/2013	10	30	20	$ 2,800	Yes	Yes	10
Exotic Morocco	6/12/2013	7	38	25	$ 1,900	Yes	No	13
Exotic Morocco	10/31/2013	7	38	15	$ 1,900	Yes	No	23
Experience Cambodia	4/11/2013	12	35	21	$ 2,441	Yes	No	14
Experience Cambodia	10/31/2013	12	40	2	$ 2,908	Yes	No	38
Galapagos Adventure	7/2/2013	14	15	12	$ 2,100	Yes	Yes	3
Galapagos Adventure	12/20/2013	14	15	1	$ 2,100	Yes	Yes	14
Green Adventures in Ecuador	3/23/2013	18	25	22	$ 2,450	No	No	3
Green Adventures in Ecuador	10/23/2013	18	25	12	$ 2,450	No	No	13
Photographing France	3/20/2013	7	20	20	$ 1,541	Yes	Yes	0
Photographing France	6/20/2013	7	20	2	$ 2,590	Yes	Yes	18
Silk Road Travels	3/19/2013	18	23	19	$ 2,031	Yes	Yes	4
Silk Road Travels	9/18/2013	18	25	9	$ 2,190	Yes	Yes	16

Setting a print area

Sometimes you will want to print only part of a worksheet. To do this, select any worksheet range, click the File tab, click Print, click the Print Active Sheets list arrow, then click Print Selection. If you want to print a selected area repeatedly, it's best to define a **print area**, the area of the worksheet that previews and prints when you use the Print command in Backstage view. To set a print area, select the range of data on the worksheet that you want to print, click the Page Layout tab, click the Print Area button in the Page Setup group, then click Set Print Area. You can add to the print area by selecting a range, clicking the Print Area button, then clicking Add to Print Area. A print area can consist of one contiguous range of cells, or multiple areas in different parts of a worksheet.

Practice

Concepts Review

For current SAM information, including versions and content details, visit SAM Central (http://www.cengage.com/samcentral). If you have a SAM user profile, you may have access to hands-on instruction, practice, and assessment of the skills covered in this unit. Since various versions of SAM are supported throughout the life of this text, check with your instructor for the correct instructions and URL/Web site for accessing assignments.

FIGURE G-22

Tour	Depart Date	Number of Days	Seat Capacity	Seats Reserved	Price	Air Included	Insurance Included	Seats Available
African National Parks	4/8/2013	30	12	10	$ 3,115	Yes	Yes	2
African National Parks	10/27/2013	30	12	8	$ 4,870	Yes	Yes	4
Amazing Amazon	2/22/2013	14	44	38	$ 2,154	No	No	6
Amazing Amazon	4/23/2013	14	43	30	$ 2,133	No	No	13
Amazing Amazon	8/23/2013	14	43	18	$ 2,877	No	No	25
Biking in France	5/23/2013	7	12	10	$ 1,635	No	No	2
Biking in France	9/23/2013	7	12	7	$ 2,110	No	No	5
Biking in Scotland	6/11/2013	10	15	10	$ 2,600	Yes	No	5
Biking in Scotland	7/11/2013	10	15	9	$ 2,600	Yes	No	6
Biking in Scotland	8/11/2013	10	15	6	$ 2,600	Yes	No	9
Catalonia Adventure	5/9/2013	14	51	30	$ 2,587	Yes	No	21
Catalonia Adventure	6/9/2013	14	51	15	$ 2,100	Yes	No	36
Catalonia Adventure	10/9/2013	14	51	11	$ 2,100	Yes	No	40
Corfu Sailing Voyage	6/10/2013	21	12	10	$ 2,190	Yes	No	2
Corfu Sailing Voyage	7/9/2013	21	12	1	$ 2,190	Yes	No	11
Costa Rica	1/19/2013	10	31	28	$ 1,833	Yes	Yes	3
Costa Rica	1/30/2013	7	20	0	$ 1,927	Yes	Yes	20
Costa Rica	4/18/2013	10	30	20	$ 2,800	Yes	Yes	10
Exotic Morocco	6/12/2013	7	38	25	$ 1,900	Yes	No	13
Exotic Morocco	10/31/2013	7	38	15	$ 1,900	Yes	No	23

1. Which element do you click to set a range in a table that will print using Quick Print?
2. Which element do you click to print field names at the top of every page?
3. Which element do you click to sort field data on a worksheet?
4. Which element points to a second-level sort field?
5. Which element points to a top-level sort field?

Match each term with the statement that best describes it.

6. Sort
7. Field
8. Table
9. Record
10. Header row

a. Organized collection of related information in Excel
b. Arrange records in a particular sequence
c. Column in an Excel table
d. First row of a table containing field names
e. Row in an Excel table

Select the best answer from the list of choices.

11. **Which of the following Excel sorting options do you use to sort a table of employee names in order from Z to A?**
    a. Ascending
    b. Absolute
    c. Descending
    d. Alphabetic

12. **Which of the following series appears in descending order?**
    a. 8, 6, 4, C, B, A
    b. 4, 5, 6, A, B, C
    c. C, B, A, 6, 5, 4
    d. 8, 7, 6, 5, 6, 7

13. **You can easily add formatting to a table by using:**
    a. Print titles.
    b. Table styles.
    c. Print areas.
    d. Calculated columns.

14. **When printing a table on multiple pages, you can define a print title to:**
    a. Include the sheet name in table reports.
    b. Include appropriate fields in the printout.
    c. Exclude from the printout all rows under the first row.
    d. Include field names at the top of each printed page.

Skills Review

1. **Create and format a table.**
    a. Start Excel, open the file EX G-2.xlsx from the drive and folder where you store your data files, then save it as **EX G-Employees**.
    b. Using the Practice sheet, enter the field names in the first row and the first two records in rows two and three, as shown in Table G-3. Create a table using the data you entered.

TABLE G-3

Last Name	First Name	Years Employed	Department	Full/Part Time	Training Completed
Lane	Sarah	4	Print Books	F	Y
Magnum	Darrin	3	E-Books	P	N

   c. On the Staff sheet, create a table with a header row. Adjust the column widths, if necessary, to display the field names.
   d. Apply a table style of Light 12 to the table, and adjust the column widths if necessary.
   e. Enter your name in the center section of the worksheet footer, then save the workbook.

2. **Add table data.**
    a. Add a new record in row seven for **Hank Worthen**, a 5-year employee in print book sales. Hank works full time and has completed training. Adjust the height of the new row to match the other table rows.
    b. Insert a table row above Jill Krosby's record, and add a new record for **Stacy Atkins**. Stacy works full time, has worked at the company for 2 years in E-Books, and has not completed training.
    c. Insert a new data field in cell G1 with a label **Weeks Vacation**. Adjust the column width, and wrap the label in the cell to display the field name with **Weeks** above **Vacation**. (*Hint*: Use the Wrap Text button in the Alignment group on the Home tab.)
    d. Add a new column to the table by dragging the table's sizing handle, and give the new field a label of **Employee #**. Widen the column to fit the label.
    e. Save the file.

3. **Find and replace table data.**
    a. Return to cell A1.
    b. Open the Find and Replace dialog box and if necessary uncheck the Match Case option. Find the first record that contains the text **Print Books**.
    c. Find the second and third records that contain the text **Print Books**.
    d. Replace all **Print Books** text in the table with **Books**, then save the file.

Skills Review (continued)

4. Delete table data.

   a. Go to cell A1.

   b. Delete the record for Sarah Lane.

   c. Use the Remove Duplicates button to confirm that the table does not have any duplicate records.

   d. Delete the Employee # table column, then delete its column header, if necessary.

   e. Save the file.

5. Sort table data.

   a. Sort the table by years employed in largest to smallest order.

   b. Sort the table by last name in A to Z order.

   c. Perform a multilevel sort: Sort the table first by Full/Part Time in A to Z order and then by last name in A to Z order.

   d. Check the table to make sure the records appear in the correct order.

   e. Save the file.

6. Use formulas in a table.

   a. In cell G2, enter the formula that calculates an employee's vacation time; base the formula on the company policy that employees working at the company less than 3 years have 2 weeks of vacation. At 3 years of employment and longer, an employee has 3 weeks of vacation time. Use the table's field names where appropriate. (*Hint*: The formula is: =IF([Years Employed]<3,2,3.)

   b. Check the table to make sure the formula filled into the cells in column G and that the correct vacation time is calculated for all cells in the column.

   c. Add a Total Row to display the total number of vacation weeks.

   d. Change the function in the Total Row to display the average number of vacation weeks.

   e. Compare your table to Figure G-23, then save the workbook.

FIGURE G-23

	A	B	C	D	E	F	G
1	Last Name	First Name	Years Employed	Department	Full/Part Time	Training Complete	Weeks Vacation
2	Atkins	Stacy	2	E-Books	F	N	2
3	Gray	Jen	1	Books	F	N	2
4	Krosby	Jill	2	E-Books	F	Y	2
5	Worthen	Hank	5	Books	F	Y	3
6	Magnum	Darrin	3	E-Books	P	N	3
7	Rogers	Mary	1	E-Books	P	Y	2
8	Total						2.333333333
9							

7. Print a table.

   a. Add a header that reads **Employees** in the center section, then format the header in bold with a font size of 16.

   b. Add column A as a print title that repeats at the left of each printed page.

   c. Preview your table to check that the last names appear on both pages.

   d. Change the page orientation to landscape, save the workbook.

   e. Submit your worksheet to your instructor. Close the workbook, then exit Excel.

Independent Challenge 1

You are the marketing director for a national pharmaceutical firm. Your administrative assistant created an Excel worksheet with customer data including the results of an advertising survey. You will create a table using the customer data, and analyze the survey results to help focus the company's advertising expenses in the most successful areas.

a. Start Excel, open the file EX G-3.xlsx from the drive and folder where you store your Data Files, then save it as **EX G-Customers**.

b. Create a table from the worksheet data, and apply Table Style Light 16. Widen the columns as necessary to display the table data.

c. Add the two records shown in Table G-4 to the table:

TABLE G-4

Last Name	First Name	Street Address	City	State	Zip	Area Code	Ad Source
Ross	Cathy	92 Arrow St.	Seattle	WA	98101	206	TV
Jones	Sarah	402 9th St.	Seattle	WA	98001	206	Newspaper

d. Find the record for Mary Riley, then delete it.

e. Click cell A1 and replace all instances of **TV** with **Cable TV**. Compare your table to Figure G-24.

FIGURE G-24

	A	B	C	D	E	F	G	H
1	Last Name	First Name	Street Address	City	State	Zip	Area Code	Ad Source
2	Kelly	Karen	19 North St.	San Francisco	CA	94177	415	Newspaper
3	Johnson	Mel	Hamilton Park St.	San Francisco	CA	94107	415	Newspaper
4	Markette	Kathy	1 Spring St.	San Luis	CA	94018	510	Radio
5	Worthen	Sally	2120 Central St.	San Francisco	CA	93772	415	Retail Website
6	Herbert	Greg	1192 Dome St.	San Diego	CA	93303	619	Newspaper
7	Chavez	Jane	11 Northern St.	San Diego	CA	92206	619	Cable TV
8	Chelly	Yvonne	900 Sola St.	San Diego	CA	92106	619	Retail Website
9	Smith	Carolyn	921 Lopez St.	San Diego	CA	92104	619	Newspaper
10	Oren	Scott	72 Yankee St.	Brookfield	CT	06830	203	Health Website
11	Warner	Salvatore	100 Westside St.	Chicago	IL	60620	312	Newspaper
12	Roberts	Bob	56 Water St.	Chicago	IL	60618	771	Retail Website
13	Miller	Hope	111 Stratton St.	Chicago	IL	60614	773	Newspaper
14	Duran	Maria	Galvin St.	Chicago	IL	60614	773	Health Website
15	Roberts	Bob	56 Water St.	Chicago	IL	60614	312	Newspaper
16	Graham	Shelley	989 26th St.	Chicago	IL	60611	773	Education Website
17	Kelly	Janie	9 First St.	San Francisco	CA	94177	415	Newspaper
18	Kim	Janie	9 First St.	San Francisco	CA	94177	415	Health Website
19	Williams	Tasha	1 Spring St.	Reading	MA	03882	413	Newspaper
20	Juarez	Manuel	544 Cameo St.	Belmont	MA	02483	617	Newspaper
21	Masters	Latrice	88 Las Puntas Rd.	Boston	MA	02205	617	Education Website
22	Kooper	Peter	671 Main St.	Cambridge	MA	02138	617	Cable TV
23	Kelly	Shawn	22 Kendall St.	Cambridge	MA	02138	617	Education Website
24	Rodriguez	Virginia	123 Main St.	Boston	MA	02007	617	Radio
25	Frei	Carol	123 Elm St.	Salem	MA	01970	978	Newspaper
26	Stevens	Crystal	14 Waterford St.	Salem	MA	01970	508	Radio
27	Ichikawa	Pam	232 Shore Rd.	Boston	MA	01801	617	Newspaper
28	Paxton	Gail	100 Main St.	Woburn	MA	01801	508	Newspaper
29	Spencer	Robin	293 Serenity Dr.	Concord	MA	01742	508	Radio
30	Lopez	Luis	1212 City St.	Kansas City	MO	64105	816	Cable TV

f. Remove duplicate records where all fields are identical.

g. Sort the list by Last Name in A to Z order.

h. Sort the list again by Area Code in Smallest to Largest order.

i. Sort the table first by State in A to Z order, then within the state, by Zip in Smallest to Largest order.

j. Enter your name in the center section of the worksheet footer.

k. Add a centered header that reads **Customer Survey Data** in bold with a font size of 16.

l. Add print titles to repeat the first row at the top of printed pages.

m. Save the workbook, then preview it.

Advanced Challenge Exercise

■ Create a print area that prints only the first six columns of the table.
■ Print the print area.
■ Clear the print area.

n. Save the workbook, close the workbook, submit the workbook to your instructor, then exit Excel.

Independent Challenge 2

You own Green Place, a paint store that sells environmentally friendly paint by the gallon. Your customers are primarily contractors who purchase items in quantities of 10 or more for their customers. You decide to plan and build a table of sales information with eight records using the items sold.

a. Prepare a plan for a table that states your goal, outlines the data you need, and identifies the table elements.

b. Sketch a sample table on a piece of paper, indicating how the table should be built. Create a table documenting the table design including the field names, type of data, and description of the data. Some examples of items are clay paint, lime wash, low VOC paint, milk paint, and zero VOC paint.

c. Start Excel, create a new workbook, then save it as **EX G-Store Items** in the drive and folder where you store your Data Files. Enter the field names from Table G-6 in the designated cells.

d. Enter eight data records using your own data.

e. Create a table using the data in the range A1:E9. Adjust the column widths as necessary.

f. Apply the Table Style Light 18 to the table.

g. Add a field named **Total** in cell F1.

h. Enter a formula to calculate the total (Quantity*Cost) in cell F2. Check that the formula was filled down in the column.

i. Format the Cost and Total columns using the Accounting number format with two decimal places and the dollar symbol ($). Adjust the column widths as necessary.

j. Add a new record to your table in row 10. Add another record above row 4.

k. Sort the table in ascending order by Item.

l. Enter your name in the worksheet footer, then save the workbook.

m. Preview the worksheet, then submit your worksheet to your instructor.

n. Close the workbook, then exit Excel.

TABLE G-6

cell	field name
A1	Customer Last
B1	Customer First
C1	Item
D1	Quantity
E1	Cost

Independent Challenge 3   *Do this*

You are the project manager at a construction firm. You are managing your accounts using an Excel worksheet and have decided that a table will provide additional features to help you keep track of the accounts. You will use the table sorting features and table formulas to analyze your account data.

a. Start Excel, open the file EX G-4.xlsx from the drive and folder where you store your Data Files, then save it as **EX G-Accounts**.

b. Create a table with the worksheet data, and apply Table Style Light 10. Adjust the column widths as necessary.

c. Sort the table on the Budget field using the Smallest to Largest order.

d. Sort the table using two fields, by Contact in A to Z order, then by Budget in Smallest to Largest order. Compare your table to Figure G-25.

FIGURE G-25

	A	B	C	D	E	F
1	Project	Deadline	Code	Budget	Expenses	Contact
2	Town of Northfield Dam	6/1/2013	AA1	$ 200,000	$ 30,000	Cathy Brown
3	South Apartments	4/30/2013	C43	$ 200,000	$ 170,000	Cathy Brown
4	Warren Condominium	10/10/2013	C21	$ 450,000	$ 400,000	Cathy Brown
5	Langley Parking Lot	7/10/2013	V13	$ 690,000	$ 700,000	Cathy Brown
6	Route 100	1/15/2013	C43	$ 100,000	$ 150,000	Jill Saunders
7	1st Street Bridge	11/15/2013	V53	$ 200,000	$ 210,000	Jill Saunders
8	Green Ridge Condominium	5/1/2013	AA5	$ 400,000	$ 230,210	Jill Saunders
9	Rangely Industrial Park	9/30/2013	V51	$ 400,000	$ 320,000	Jill Saunders
10	Northridge School	3/15/2013	A3A	$ 600,000	$ 610,000	Kim Jess
11	West Mall	11/15/2013	B12	$ 710,000	$ 600,000	Kim Jess
12						

Independent Challenge 3 (continued)

e. Add the new field label **Balance** in cell G1, and adjust the column width as necessary. Format the Budget, Expenses, and Balance columns using the Accounting format with no decimal places and the dollar symbol ($).

f. Enter a formula in cell G2 that uses structured references to table fields to calculate the balance on an account as the Budget minus the Expenses.

g. Add a new record for a project named **North Mall** with a deadline of **2/15/2013**, a code of **AB2**, a budget of **$300,000**, expenses of **$150,000**, and a contact of **Cathy Brown**.

h. Verify that the formula accurately calculated the balance for the new record.

i. Replace all of the Jill Saunders data with **Jill Jones**.

j. Enter your name in the center section of the worksheet footer, add a center section header of **Accounts** using formatting of your choice, change the page orientation to landscape, then save the workbook.

Advanced Challenge Exercise

- Sort the table on the Balance field using the Smallest to Largest order.
- Use conditional formatting to format the cells of the table containing negative balances with a light red fill with dark red text.
- Sort the table using the Balance field with the order of no cell color on top.
- Format the table to emphasize the Balance column, and turn off the banded rows. (*Hint*: Use the Table Style Options on the Table Tools Design tab.)
- Compare your table with Figure G-26. Save the workbook.

FIGURE G-26

	A	B	C	D	E	F	G
1	Project	Deadline	Code	Budget	Expenses	Contact	Balance
2	South Apartments	4/30/2013	C43	$ 200,000	$ 170,000	Cathy Brown	$ 30,000
3	Warren Condominium	10/10/2013	C21	$ 450,000	$ 400,000	Cathy Brown	$ 50,000
4	Rangely Industrial Park	9/30/2013	V51	$ 400,000	$ 320,000	Jill Jones	$ 80,000
5	West Mall	11/15/2013	B12	$ 710,000	$ 600,000	Kim Jess	$ 110,000
6	North Mall	2/15/2013	AB2	$ 300,000	$ 150,000	Cathy Brown	$ 150,000
7	Green Ridge Condominium	5/1/2013	AA5	$ 400,000	$ 230,210	Jill Jones	$ 169,790
8	Town of Northfield Dam	6/1/2013	AA1	$ 200,000	$ 30,000	Cathy Brown	$ 170,000
9	Route 100	1/15/2013	C43	$ 100,000	$ 150,000	Jill Jones	$ (50,000)
10	Langley Parking Lot	7/10/2013	V13	$ 690,000	$ 700,000	Cathy Brown	$ (10,000)
11	1st Street Bridge	11/15/2013	V53	$ 200,000	$ 210,000	Jill Jones	$ (10,000)
12	Northridge School	3/15/2013	A3A	$ 600,000	$ 610,000	Kim Jess	$ (10,000)
13							
14							

k. Submit the worksheet to your instructor, close the workbook, then exit Excel.

Real Life Independent Challenge

You have decided to organize your recording collection using a table in Excel. This will enable you to easily find songs in your music library. You will add records as you purchase new music and delete records if you discard a recording.

a. Using the fields Title, Artist, Genre, and Format, prepare a diagram of your table structure.

b. Document the table design by detailing the type of data that will be in each field and a description of the data. For example, in the Format field you may have .mp3, .aac, .wma, or other formats.

c. Start Excel, create a new workbook, then save it as **EX G-Music** in the drive and folder where you store your Data Files.

d. Enter the field names into the worksheet, enter the records for seven of your music recordings, then save the workbook.

e. Create a table that contains your music information. Resize the columns as necessary.

f. Choose a Table Style, and apply it to your table.

g. Add a new field with a label of **Media/Player**. Enter information in the new table column describing the media or player where your music is stored, such as iPod, iPhone, CD, or Computer.

h. Add a record to the table for the next recording you will purchase.

i. Sort the records by the Format field using A to Z order.

j. Add a Total row to your table, and verify that the Count function accurately calculated the number of your recordings.

k. Enter your name in the worksheet footer, then save the workbook.

l. Submit the worksheet to your instructor, close the workbook, then exit Excel.

Visual Workshop

Start Excel, open the file EX G-5.xlsx from the drive and folder where you store your Data Files, then save it as **EX G-Products**. Create the table and sort the data as shown in Figure G-27. (*Hint*: The table is formatted using Table Style Medium 7.) Add a worksheet header with the sheet name in the center section that is formatted in bold with a size of 14. Enter your name in the center section of the worksheet footer. Save the workbook, preview the table, close the workbook, submit the worksheet to your instructor, then exit Excel.

FIGURE G-27

Order Number	Order date	Amount	Shipping	Sales Rep
1533	10/14/2013	$ 10,057	Air	Ellie Cranson
7897	3/15/2013	$ 22,587	Ground	Ellie Cranson
1123	5/30/2013	$ 125,879	Air	Ellie Cranson
2199	2/15/2013	$ 236,014	Air	Ellie Cranson
1154	10/15/2013	$ 312,845	Air	Ellie Cranson
5423	2/1/2013	$ 1,369	Air	Gene Coburn
2186	6/1/2013	$ 132,558	Ground	Gene Coburn
9021	1/15/2013	$ 198,257	Ground	Gene Coburn
1115	8/30/2013	$ 200,521	Ground	Gene Coburn
2100	2/10/2013	$ 32,987	Ground	Neil Boxer
2130	11/15/2013	$ 82,496	Air	Neil Boxer

Managing Data Using Tables

Analyzing Table Data

Excel tables let you manipulate and analyze data in many ways. One way is to filter a table so that it displays only the rows that meet certain criteria. In this unit, you will display selected records using the AutoFilter feature, create a custom filter, and filter a table using an Advanced Filter. In addition, you will learn to insert automatic subtotals, use lookup functions to locate table entries, and apply database functions to summarize table data that meet specific criteria. You'll also learn how to restrict entries in a column by using data validation. The vice president of sales, Kate Morgan, asks you to display information from a table of the 2013 scheduled tours to help the sales representatives with customer inquiries. She also asks you to prepare summaries of the tour sales for a presentation at the international sales meeting.

OBJECTIVES

Filter a table

Create a custom filter

Filter a table with the Advanced Filter

Extract table data

Look up values in a table

Summarize table data

Validate table data

Create subtotals

Filtering a Table

An Excel table lets you easily manipulate large amounts of data to view only the data you want, using a feature called **AutoFilter**. When you create a table, arrows automatically appear next to each column header. These arrows are called **filter list arrows**, **AutoFilter list arrows**, or **list arrows**, and you can use them to **filter** a table to display only the records that meet criteria you specify, temporarily hiding records that do not meet those criteria. For example, you can use the filter list arrow next to the Tour field header to display only records that contain Nepal Trekking in the Tour field. Once you filter data, you can copy, chart, and print the displayed records. You can easily clear a filter to redisplay all the records. Kate asks you to display only the records for the Yellowstone tours. She also asks for information about the tours that sell the most seats and the tours that depart in March.

STEPS

1. **Start Excel, open the file** EX H-1.xlsx **from the drive and folder where you save your Data Files, then save it as** EX H-Tours

2. **Click the** Tour list arrow

   Sort options appear at the top of the menu, advanced filtering options appear in the middle, and at the bottom is a list of the tour data from column A, as shown in Figure H-1. Because you want to display data for only the Yellowstone tours, your **search criterion** (the text you are searching for) is Yellowstone. You can select one of the Tour data options in the menu, which acts as your search criterion.

   > **QUICK TIP**
   > You can also filter the table to display only the Yellowstone tour information by clicking the Tour list arrow, entering "Yellowstone" in the Search text box on the menu options below Text Filters, then clicking OK.

3. **In the list of tours for the Tour field, click** Select All **to clear the checks from the tours, scroll down the list of tours, click** Yellowstone, **then click** OK

   Only those records containing "Yellowstone" in the Tour field appear, as shown in Figure H-2. The row numbers for the matching records change to blue, and the list arrow for the filtered field has a filter icon. Both indicate that there is a filter in effect and that some of the records are temporarily hidden.

4. **Move the pointer over the** Tour list arrow

   The ScreenTip Tour: Equals "Yellowstone" describes the filter for the field, meaning that only the Yellowstone records appear. You decide to remove the filter to redisplay all of the table data.

5. **Click the** Tour list arrow, **then click** Clear Filter From "Tour"

   You have cleared the Yellowstone filter, and all the records reappear. You want to display the most popular tours, those that are in the top five percent of seats reserved.

   > **QUICK TIP**
   > You can also filter or sort a table by the color of the cells if conditional formatting has been applied.

6. **Click the** Seats Reserved list arrow, **point to** Number Filters, **click** Top 10, **select** 10 **in the middle box, type** 5, **click the** Items list arrow, **click** Percent, **then click** OK

   Excel displays the records for the top five percent in the number of Seats Reserved field, as shown in Figure H-3. You decide to clear the filter to redisplay all the records.

7. **On the Home tab, click the** Sort & Filter button **in the Editing group, then click** Clear

   You can clear a filter using either the AutoFilter menu command or the Sort and Filter menu on the Home tab. You have cleared the filter and all the records reappear. The Sort and Filter button is convenient for clearing multiple filters at once. You want to find all of the tours that depart in March.

8. **Click the** Depart Date list arrow, **point to** Date Filters, **point to** All Dates in the Period, **then click** March

   Excel displays the records for only the tours that leave in March. You decide to clear the filter and display all of the records.

   > **QUICK TIP**
   > You can also clear a filter by clicking the Clear button in the Sort & Filter group on the Data tab.

9. **Click the** Sort & Filter button **in the Editing group, click** Clear, **then save the workbook**

FIGURE H-1: **Worksheet showing filter options**

Tour Filter list arrow •

Sort Options •

Advanced filtering options •

List of tours •

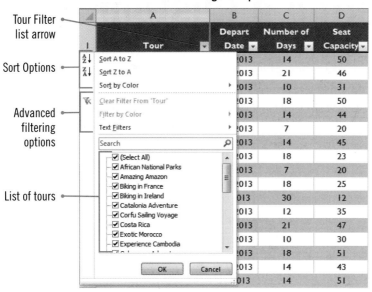

	A	B	C	D
	Tour	Depart Date	Number of Days	Seat Capacity
		2013	14	50
		2013	21	46
		2013	10	31
		2013	18	50
		2013	14	44
		2013	7	20
		2013	14	45
		2013	18	23
		2013	7	20
		2013	18	25
		2013	30	12
		2013	12	35
		2013	21	47
		2013	10	30
		2013	18	51
		2013	14	43
		2013	14	51

Filter menu contents:
- Sort A to Z
- Sort Z to A
- Sort by Color ▸
- Clear Filter From "Tour"
- Filter by Color ▸
- Text Filters ▸
- Search
- ☑ (Select All)
- ☑ African National Parks
- ☑ Amazing Amazon
- ☑ Biking in France
- ☑ Biking in Ireland
- ☑ Catalonia Adventure
- ☑ Corfu Sailing Voyage
- ☑ Costa Rica
- ☑ Exotic Morocco
- ☑ Experience Cambodia
- OK   Cancel

Excel 2010

FIGURE H-2: **Table filtered to show Yellowstone tours**

List arrow changed to filter icon •

Matching row numbers are blue and sequence indicates that not all rows appear •

	A	B	C	D	E	F	G	H
	Tour	Depart Date	Number of Days	Seat Capacity	Seats Reserved	Price	Air Included	Insurance Included
5	Yellowstone	1/21/2013	18	50	40	$ 1,700	Yes	Yes
16	Yellowstone	4/20/2013	18	51	31	$ 1,652	Yes	Yes
41	Yellowstone	8/20/2013	18	51	20	$ 2,922	Yes	Yes
45	Yellowstone	9/11/2013	18	51	20	$ 2,922	Yes	Yes
63	Yellowstone	12/30/2013	18	51	15	$ 2,922	Yes	Yes

Filter displays only Yellowstone tours

FIGURE H-3: **Table filtered with top 5% of Seats Reserved**

Table filtered with top 5% in this field •

	A	B	C	D	E	F	G	H
	Tour	Depart Date	Number of Days	Seat Capacity	Seats Reserved	Price	Air Included	Insurance Included
2	Pacific Odyssey	1/12/2013	14	50	50	$ 2,105	Yes	No
3	Old Japan	1/13/2013	21	46	41	$ 1,964	Yes	No
5	Yellowstone	1/21/2013	18	50	40	$ 1,700	Yes	Yes

Creating a Custom Filter

While AutoFilter lists can display records that are equal to certain amounts, you will often need more detailed filters. You can use more complex filters with the help of options in the Custom AutoFilter dialog box. For example, your criteria can contain comparison operators such as "greater than" or "less than" that let you display values above or below a certain amount. You can also use **logical conditions** like And and Or to narrow a search even further. You can have Excel display records that meet a criterion in a field *and* another criterion in that same field. This is often used to find records between two values. For example, by specifying an And logical condition, you can display records for customers with incomes between $40,000 *and* $70,000. You can also have Excel display records that meet either criterion in a field by specifying an Or condition. The Or condition is used to find records that satisfy either of two values. For example, in a table of book data you can use the Or condition to find records that contain either Beginning *or* Introduction in the title name. Kate wants to locate tours for customers who like active vacations. She also wants to find tours that depart between February 15, 2013, and April 15, 2013. She asks you to create custom filters to find the tours satisfying these criteria.

1. **Click the** Tour list arrow, **point to** Text Filters, **then click** Contains

   The Custom AutoFilter dialog box opens. You enter your criteria in the text boxes. The left text box on the first line currently displays "contains." You want to display tours that contain the word "sailing" in their names.

2. **Type** sailing **in the right text box on the first line**

   You want to see entries that contain either sailing or biking.

QUICK TIP

When specifying criteria in the Custom Filter dialog box, you can use the (?) wildcard to represent any single character and the (*) wildcard to represent any series of characters.

3. **Click the** Or option button **to select it, click the** left text box list arrow **on the second line, scroll to and select** contains, **then type** biking **in the right text box on the second line**

   Your completed Custom AutoFilter dialog box should match Figure H-4.

4. **Click** OK

   The dialog box closes, and only those records having "sailing" or "biking" in the Tour field appear in the worksheet. You want to find all tours that depart between February 15, 2013 and April 15, 2013.

5. **Click the** Tour list arrow, **click** Clear Filter From "Tour", **click the** Depart Date list arrow, **point to** Date Filters, **then click** Custom Filter

   The Custom AutoFilter dialog box opens. The word "equals" appears in the left text box on the first line. You want to find the departure dates that are between February 15, 2013 and April 15, 2013 (that is, after February 15 *and* before April 15).

6. **Click the** left text box list arrow **on the first line, click** is after, **then type** 2/15/2013 **in the right text box on the first line**

   The And condition is selected, which is correct.

7. **Click the** left text box list arrow **on the second line, select** is before, **type** 4/15/2013 **in the right text box on the second line, then click** OK

   The records displayed have departing dates between February 15, 2013, and April 15, 2013. Compare your records to those shown in Figure H-5.

8. **Click the** Depart Date list arrow, **click** Clear Filter From "Depart Date", **then add your name to the center section of the footer**

   You have cleared the filter, and all the tour records reappear.

Analyzing Table Data

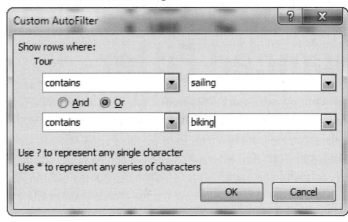

	A	B	C	D	E	F	G	H
1	Tour	Depart Date	Number of Days	Seat Capacity	Seats Reserved	Price	Air Included	Insurance Included
6	Amazing Amazon	2/22/2013	14	44	38	$ 2,154	No	No
7	Hiking Patagonia	2/28/2013	7	20	15	$ 2,822	Yes	No
8	Pearls of the Orient	3/13/2013	14	45	15	$ 2,400	Yes	No
9	Silk Road Travels	3/19/2013	18	23	19	$ 2,031	Yes	Yes
10	Photographing France	3/20/2013	7	20	20	$ 1,541	Yes	Yes
11	Green Adventures in Ecuador	3/23/2013	18	25	22	$ 2,450	No	No
12	African National Parks	4/8/2013	30	12	10	$ 3,115	Yes	Yes
13	Experience Cambodia	4/11/2013	12	35	21	$ 2,441	Yes	No

Departing dates are between 2/15 and 4/15

Using more than one rule when conditionally formatting data

You can apply conditional formatting to table cells in the same way that you can format a range of worksheet data. You can add multiple rules by clicking the Home tab, clicking the Conditional Formatting button in the Styles group, then clicking New Rule for each additional rule that you want to apply. You can also add rules using the Conditional Formatting Rules Manager, which displays all of the rules for a data range. To use the Rules Manager, click the Home tab, click the Conditional Formatting button in the Styles group, click Manage Rules, then click New Rule for each rule that you want to apply to the data range. After you have applied conditional formatting such as color fills, icon sets, or color scales to a numeric table range, you can use AutoFilter to sort or filter based on the colors or symbols.

Filtering a Table with the Advanced Filter

If you would like to see more specific information in a table, such as view date and insurance information for a specific tour or tours, then the Advanced Filter command is very helpful. Using the Advanced Filter, you can specify data that you want to display from the table using And and Or conditions. Rather than entering the criteria in a dialog box, you enter the criteria in a criteria range on your worksheet. A **criteria range** is a cell range containing one row of labels (usually a copy of the column labels) and at least one additional row underneath the row of labels that contains the criteria you want to match. Placing the criteria in the same row indicates that the records you are searching for must match both criteria; that is, it specifies an **And condition**. Placing the criteria in the different rows indicates that the records you are searching for must match only one of the criterion; that is, it specifies an **Or condition**. With the criteria range on the worksheet, you can easily see the criteria by which your table is sorted. You can also use the criteria range to create a macro using the Advanced Filter feature to automate the filtering process for data that you filter frequently. Another advantage of the Advanced Filter is that you can move filtered table data to a different area of the worksheet or to a new worksheet, as you will see in the next lesson. Kate wants to identify tours that depart after 6/1/2013 and that cost less than $2,000. She asks you to use the Advanced Filter to retrieve these records. You begin by defining the criteria range.

STEPS

1. **Select** table rows 1 through 6, **click the** Insert list arrow **in the Cells group, click** Insert Sheet Rows; **click cell** A1, **type** Criteria Range, **then click the** Enter button ✔ **on the Formula bar**

   Six blank rows are added above the table. Excel does not require the label "Criteria Range", but it is useful to see the column labels as you organize the worksheet and use filters.

2. **Select the range** A7:H7, **click the** Copy button 🖹 **in the Clipboard group, click cell** A2, **click the** Paste button **in the Clipboard group, then press** [Esc]

   Next, you want to insert criteria that will display records for only those tours that depart after June 1, 2013 and that cost under $2,000.

QUICK TIP

You can apply multiple criteria by using AutoFilter a second time on the results of the previously filtered data. Each additional filter builds on the results of the filtered data and filters the data further.

3. **Click cell** B3, **type** >6/1/2013, **click cell** F3, **type** <2000, **then click** ✔

   You have entered the criteria in the cells directly beneath the Criteria Range labels, as shown in Figure H-6.

4. **Click any cell in the table, click the** Data tab, **then click the** Advanced button **in the Sort & Filter group**

   The Advanced Filter dialog box opens, with the table (list) range already entered. The default setting under Action is to filter the table in its current location ("in-place") rather than copy it to another location.

TROUBLE

If your filtered records don't match Figure H-7, make sure there are no spaces between the > symbol and the 6 in cell B3 and the < symbol and the 2 in cell F3.

5. **Click the** Criteria range text box, **select the range** A2:H3 **in the worksheet, then click** OK

   You have specified the criteria range and used the filter. The filtered table contains eight records that match both criteria—the departure date is after 6/1/2013 and the price is less than $2,000, as shown in Figure H-7. You'll filter this table even further in the next lesson.

FIGURE H-6: **Criteria in the same row**

	A	B	C	D	E	F	G	H
1	Criteria Range							
2	Tour	Depart Date	Number of Days	Seat Capacity	Seats Reserved	Price	Air Included	Insurance Included
3		>6/1/2013				<2000		
4								
5								
6								
7	Tour	Depart Date	Number of Days	Seat Capacity	Seats Reserved	Price	Air Included	Insurance Included
8	Pacific Odyssey	1/12/2013	14	50	50	$ 2,105	Yes	No

Filtered records will
match these criteria

FIGURE H-7: **Filtered table**

	A	B	C	D	E	F	G	H
1	Criteria Range							
2	Tour	Depart Date	Number of Days	Seat Capacity	Seats Reserved	Price	Air Included	Insurance Included
3		>6/1/2013				<2000		
4								
5								
6								
7	Tour	Depart Date	Number of Days	Seat Capacity	Seats Reserved	Price	Air Included	Insurance Included
33	Exotic Morocco	6/12/2013	7	38	25	$ 1,900	Yes	No
34	Kayak Newfoundland	6/12/2013	7	20	15	$ 1,970	Yes	Yes
37	Wild River Escape	6/27/2013	10	21	21	$ 1,944	No	No
42	Kayak Newfoundland	7/12/2013	7	20	15	$ 1,970	Yes	Yes
44	Magnificent Montenegro	7/27/2013	10	48	0	$ 1,890	No	No
46	Kayak Newfoundland	8/12/2013	7	20	12	$ 1,970	Yes	Yes
49	Wild River Escape	8/27/2013	10	21	11	$ 1,944	No	No
61	Exotic Morocco	10/31/2013	7	38	15	$ 1,900	Yes	No

Depart dates are after 6/1/2013   Prices are less than $2,000

Using advanced conditional formatting options

You can emphasize top- or bottom-ranked values in a field using conditional formatting. To highlight the top or bottom values in a field, select the field data, click the Conditional Formatting button in the Styles group on the Home tab, point to Top/Bottom Rules, select a Top or Bottom rule, if necessary enter the percentage or number of cells in the selected range that you want to format, select the format for the cells that meet the top or bottom criteria, then click OK. You can also format your worksheet or table data using icon sets and color scales based on the cell values. A **color scale** uses a set of two, three, or four fill colors to convey relative values. For example, red could fill cells to indicate they have higher values and green could signify lower values. To add a color scale, select a data range, click the Home tab, click the Conditional Formatting button in the Styles group, then point to Color Scales. On the submenu, you can select preformatted color sets or click More Rules to create your own color sets. **Icon sets** let you visually communicate relative cell values by adding icons to cells based on the values they contain. An upward-pointing green arrow might represent the highest values, and downward-pointing red arrows could represent lower values. To add an icon set to a data range, select a data range, click the Conditional Formatting button in the Styles group, then point to Icon Sets. You can customize the values that are used as thresholds for color scales and icon sets by clicking the Conditional Formatting button in the Styles group, clicking Manage Rules, clicking the rule in the Conditional Formatting Rules Manager dialog box, then clicking Edit Rule.

Extracting Table Data

Whenever you take the time to specify a complicated set of search criteria, it's a good idea to extract the matching records, rather than filtering it in place. When you **extract** data, you place a copy of a filtered table in a range that you specify in the Advanced Filter dialog box. This way, you won't accidentally clear the filter or lose track of the records you spent time compiling. To extract data, you use an Advanced Filter and enter the criteria beneath the copied field names, as you did in the previous lesson. You then specify the location where you want the extracted data to appear. Kate needs to filter the table one step further to reflect only the Wild River Escape or Kayak Newfoundland tours in the current filtered table. She asks you to complete this filter by specifying an Or condition, which you will do by entering two sets of criteria in two separate rows. You decide to save the filtered records by extracting them to a different location in the worksheet.

STEPS

1. **In cell A3, enter** Wild River Escape, **then in cell A4, enter** Kayak Newfoundland

   The new sets of criteria need to appear in two separate rows, so you need to copy the previous filter criteria to the second row.

2. **Copy the criteria in B3:F3 to** B4:F4

   The criteria are shown in Figure H-8. When you use the Advanced Filter this time, you indicate that you want to copy the filtered table to a range beginning in cell A75, so that Kate can easily refer to the data, even if you use more filters later.

3. **If necessary, click the** Data tab, **then click** Advanced **in the Sort & Filter group**

4. **Under Action, click the** Copy to another location option button **to select it, click the** Copy to **text box, then type** A75

   The last time you filtered the table, the criteria range included only rows 2 and 3, and now you have criteria in row 4.

> **QUICK TIP**
> Make sure the criteria range in the Advanced Filter dialog box includes the field names and the number of rows underneath the names that contain criteria. If you leave a blank row in the criteria range, Excel filters nothing and shows all records.

5. **Edit the contents of the** Criteria range text box **to show the range** $A$2:$H$4, **click** OK, **then if necessary scroll down until row 75 is visible**

   The matching records appear in the range beginning in cell A75, as shown in Figure H-9. The original table, starting in cell A7, contains the records filtered in the previous lesson.

6. **Press [Ctrl][Home], then click the** Clear button **in the Sort & Filter group**

   The original table is displayed starting in cell A7, and the extracted table remains in A75:H80.

7. **Save the workbook**

Analyzing Table Data

FIGURE H-8: **Criteria in separate rows**

	A	B	C	D	E	F	G	H
1	Criteria Range							
2	Tour	Depart Date	Number of Days	Seat Capacity	Seats Reserved	Price	Air Included	Insurance Included
3	Wild River Escape	>6/1/2013				<2000		
4	Kayak Newfoundland	>6/1/2013				<2000		
5								

Criteria on two lines indicates an OR condition

FIGURE H-9: **Extracted data records**

	Tour	Depart Date	Number of Days	Seat Capacity	Seats Reserved	Price	Air Included	Insurance Included
75	Tour	Depart Date	Number of Days	Seat Capacity	Seats Reserved	Price	Air Included	Insurance Included
76	Kayak Newfoundland	6/12/2013	7	20	15	$ 1,970	Yes	Yes
77	Wild River Escape	6/27/2013	10	21	21	$ 1,944	No	No
78	Kayak Newfoundland	7/12/2013	7	20	15	$ 1,970	Yes	Yes
79	Kayak Newfoundland	8/12/2013	7	20	12	$ 1,970	Yes	Yes
80	Wild River Escape	8/27/2013	10	21	11	$ 1,944	No	No
81								

Only Wild River Escape and Kayak Newfoundland tours   Depart date after 6/1/2013   Price is less than $2,000

Understanding the criteria range and the copy-to location

When you define the criteria range and the copy-to location in the Advanced Filter dialog box, Excel automatically creates the range names Criteria and Extract for these ranges in the worksheet. The Criteria range includes the field names and any criteria rows underneath them. The Extract range includes just the field names above the extracted table. You can select these ranges by clicking the Name box list arrow, then clicking the range name. If you click the Name Manager button in the Defined Names group on the Formulas tab, you will see these new names and the ranges associated with each one.

Looking Up Values in a Table

The Excel VLOOKUP function helps you locate specific values in a table. VLOOKUP searches vertically (V) down the far left column of a table, then reads across the row to find the value in the column you specify, much as you might look up a number in a phone book: You locate a person's name, then read across the row to find the phone number you want. ▓▓▓▓ Kate wants to be able to find a tour destination by entering the tour code. You will use the VLOOKUP function to accomplish this task. You begin by viewing the table name so you can refer to it in a lookup function.

STEPS

QUICK TIP

You can change table names to better represent their content so they are easier to use in formulas. Click the table in the list of names in the Name Manager text box, click Edit, type the new table name in the Name text box, then click OK.

1. **Click the** Lookup sheet tab, **click the** Formulas tab **in the Ribbon, then click the** Name Manager button **in the Defined Names group**

    The named ranges for the workbook appear in the Name Manager dialog box, as shown in Figure H-10. The Criteria and Extract ranges appear at the top of the range name list. At the bottom of the list is information about the three tables in the workbook. Table1 refers to the table on the Tours sheet, Table2 refers to the table on the Lookup sheet, and Table3 refers to the table on the Subtotals worksheet. The Excel structured reference feature automatically created these table names when the tables were created.

2. **Click** Close

    You want to find the tour represented by the code 653S. The VLOOKUP function lets you find the tour name for any trip code. You will enter a trip code in cell L2 and a VLOOKUP function in cell M2.

3. **Click cell L2, enter** 653S, **click cell M2, click the** Lookup & Reference button **in the Function Library group, then click** VLOOKUP

    The Function Arguments dialog box opens, with boxes for each of the VLOOKUP arguments. Because the value you want to find is in cell L2, L2 is the Lookup_value. The table you want to search is the table on the Lookup sheet, so its assigned name, Table2, is the Table_array.

QUICK TIP

If you want to find only the closest match for a value, enter TRUE in the Range_lookup text box. However, this can give misleading results if you are looking for an exact match. If you use FALSE and Excel can't find the value, you see an error message.

4. **With the insertion point in the Lookup_value text box, click cell L2, click the** Table_array text box, **then type** Table2

    The column containing the information that you want to find and display in cell M2 is the second column from the left in the table range, so the Col_index_num is 2. Because you want to find an exact match for the value in cell L1, the Range_lookup argument is FALSE.

5. **Click the** Col_index_num text box, **type** 2, **click the** Range_lookup text box, **then enter** FALSE

    Your completed Function Arguments dialog box should match Figure H-11.

6. **Click** OK

    Excel searches down the far-left column of the table until it finds a trip code that matches the one in cell L2. It then looks in column 2 of the table range and finds the tour for that record, Green Adventures in Ecuador, and displays it in cell M2. You use this function to determine the tour for one other trip code.

7. **Click cell L2, type** 325B, **then click the** Enter button ✔ **on the formula bar**

    The VLOOKUP function returns the value of Costa Rica in cell M2.

8. **Press [Ctrl][Home], then save the workbook**

Finding records using the DGET function

You can also use the DGET function to find a record in a table that matches specified criteria. For example, you could use the criteria of L1:L2 in the DGET function. When using DGET, you need to include [#All] after your table name in the formula to include the column labels that are used for the criteria range.

FIGURE H-10: Named ranges in the workbook

Created by Advanced Filter •

Tables in the workbook •

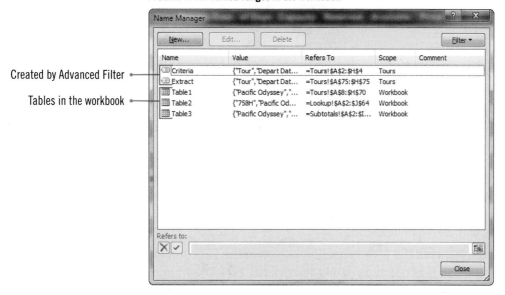

FIGURE H-11: Completed Function Arguments dialog box for VLOOKUP

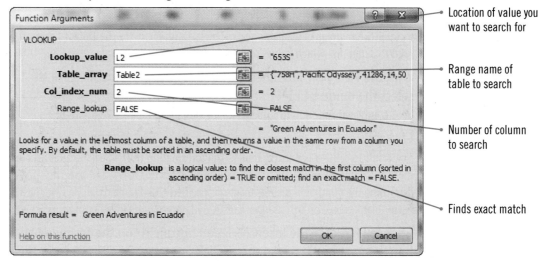

Location of value you want to search for

Range name of table to search

Number of column to search

Finds exact match

Using the HLOOKUP and MATCH functions

The VLOOKUP (Vertical Lookup) function is useful when your data is arranged vertically, in columns. When your data is arranged horizontally in rows, use the HLOOKUP (Horizontal Lookup) function. HLOOKUP searches horizontally across the upper row of a table until it finds the matching value, then looks down the number of rows you specify. The arguments for this function are identical to those for the VLOOKUP function, with one exception. Instead of a Col_index_number, HLOOKUP uses a Row_index_number, which indicates the location of the row you want to search. For example, if you want to search the fourth row from the top of the table range, the Row_index_number should be 4. You can use the MATCH function when you want the position of an item in a range. The MATCH function uses the syntax: MATCH (lookup_value,lookup_array,match_ type) where the lookup_value is the value you want to match in the lookup_array range. The match_type can be 0 for an exact match, 1 for matching the largest value that is less than or equal to lookup_ value, or –1 for matching the smallest value that is greater than or equal to the lookup_value.

Summarizing Table Data

Because a table acts much like a database, database functions allow you to summarize table data in a variety of ways. When working with a sales activity table, for example, you can use Excel to count the number of client contacts by sales representative or to total the amount sold to specific accounts by month. Table H-1 lists database functions commonly used to summarize table data. Kate is considering adding tours for the 2013 schedule. She needs your help in evaluating the number of seats available for scheduled tours.

1. **Review the criteria range for the Yellowstone tour in the range** L4:L5

   The criteria range in L4:L5 tells Excel to summarize records with the entry "Yellowstone" in the Tour column. The functions will be in cells N6 and N7. You use this criteria range in a DSUM function to sum the seats available for only the Yellowstone tours.

2. **Click cell** N6, **click the** Insert Function button **in the Function Library group, in the Search for a function text box type** database, **click** Go, **click** DSUM **under Select a function, then click** OK

   The first argument of the DSUM function is the table, or database.

   QUICK TIP

   Because the DSUM formula uses the column headings to locate and sum the table data, the header row needs to be included in the database range.

3. **In the Function Arguments dialog box, with the insertion point in the Database text box, move the pointer over the upper-left corner of cell A1 until the pointer becomes** ↘, **click once, then click again**

   The first click selects the table's data range, and the second click selects the entire table, including the header row. The second argument of the DSUM function is the label for the column that you want to sum. You want to total the number of available seats. The last argument for the DSUM function is the criteria that will be used to determine which values to total.

   QUICK TIP

   You can move the Function Arguments dialog box if it overlaps a cell or range that you need to click. You can also click the Collapse Dialog Box button ▦, select the cell or range, then click the Expand Dialog box button ▦ to return to the Function Arguments dialog box.

4. **Click the** Field text box, **then click cell** G1, **Seats Available; click the** Criteria text box **and select the range** L4:L5

   Your completed Function Arguments dialog box should match Figure H-12.

5. **Click** OK

   The result in cell N6 is 8. Excel totaled the information in the Seats Available column for those records that meet the criterion of Tour equals Yellowstone. The DCOUNT and the DCOUNTA functions can help you determine the number of records meeting specified criteria in a database field. DCOUNTA counts the number of nonblank cells. You will use DCOUNTA to determine the number of tours scheduled.

6. **Click cell** N7, **click the** Insert Function button *fx* **on the formula bar, in the Search for a function text box type** database, **click** Go, **select** DCOUNTA **from the Select a function list, then click** OK

7. **With the insertion point in the Database text box, move the pointer over the upper-left corner of cell A1 until the pointer becomes** ↘, **click once, click again to include the header row, click the Field text box and click cell** B1, **click the** Criteria text box **and select the range** L4:L5, **then click** OK

   The result in cell N7 is 5, and it indicates that there are five Yellowstone tours scheduled for the year. You also want to display the number of seats available for the Hiking Patagonia tours.

8. **Click cell** L5, **type** Hiking Patagonia, **then click the** Enter button ✓ **on the formula bar**

   Figure H-13 shows that 18 seats are available in the two Hiking Patagonia tours.

FIGURE H-12: Completed Function Arguments dialog box for DSUM

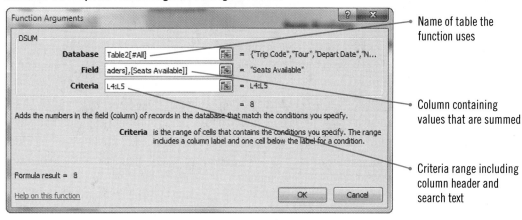

Name of table the function uses

Column containing values that are summed

Criteria range including column header and search text

FIGURE H-13: Result generated by database functions

	Seats Reserved	Seats Available	Price	Air Included	Insurance Included		Trip Code	Tour		
2	50	0	$2,105	Yes	No		325B	Costa Rica		
3	41	5	$1,964	Yes	No					
4	28	3	$1,833	Yes	Yes		Tour			
5	48	2	$1,700	Yes	Yes		Hiking Patagonia			
6	38	6	$2,154	No	No			Seats Available		18
7	15	5	$2,822	Yes	No			Number of tours scheduled		2
8	15	30	$2,400	Yes	No					
9	19	4	$2,031	Yes	Yes					

Information for Hiking Patagonia tours

TABLE H-1: Common database functions

function	result
DGET	Extracts a single record from a table that matches criteria you specify
DSUM	Totals numbers in a given table column that match criteria you specify
DAVERAGE	Averages numbers in a given table column that match criteria you specify
DCOUNT	Counts the cells that contain numbers in a given table column that match criteria you specify
DCOUNTA	Counts the cells that contain nonblank data in a given table column that match criteria you specify

Validating Table Data

When setting up tables, you want to help ensure accuracy when you or others enter data. The Excel data validation feature allows you to do this by specifying what data users can enter in a range of cells. You can restrict data to whole numbers, decimal numbers, or text. You can also specify a list of acceptable entries. Once you've specified what data the program should consider valid for that cell, Excel displays an error message when invalid data is entered and can prevent users from entering any other data that it considers to be invalid. Kate wants to make sure that information in the Air Included column is entered consistently in the future. She asks you to restrict the entries in that column to two options: Yes and No. First, you select the table column you want to restrict.

STEPS

1. **Click the top edge of the Air Included column header**
   The column data is selected.

2. **Click the Data tab, click the Data Validation button in the Data Tools group, click the Settings tab if necessary, click the Allow list arrow, then click List**
   Selecting the List option lets you type a list of specific options.

3. **Click the Source text box, then type Yes, No**
   You have entered the list of acceptable entries, separated by commas, as shown in Figure H-14. You want the data entry person to be able to select a valid entry from a drop-down list.

4. **Click the In-cell dropdown check box to select it if necessary, then click OK**
   The dialog box closes, and you return to the worksheet.

5. **Click the Home tab, click any cell in the last table row, click the Insert list arrow in the Cells group, click Insert Table Row Below, click the last cell in the Air Included column, then click its list arrow to display the list of valid entries**
   The drop-down list is shown in Figure H-15. You could click an item in the list to have it entered in the cell, but you want to test the data restriction by entering an invalid entry.

6. **Click the list arrow to close the list, type Maybe, then press [Enter]**
   A warning dialog box appears and prevents you from entering the invalid data, as shown in Figure H-16.

7. **Click Cancel, click the list arrow, then click Yes**
   The cell accepts the valid entry. The data restriction ensures that records contain only one of the two correct entries in the Air Included column. The table is ready for future data entry.

8. **Delete the last table row, add your name to the center section of the footer, then save the workbook**

Restricting cell values and data length

In addition to providing an in-cell drop-down list for data entry, you can use data validation to restrict the values that are entered into cells. For example, if you want to restrict cells to values less than a certain number, date, or time, click the Data tab, click the Data Validation button in the Data Tools group, and on the Settings tab, click the Allow list arrow, select Whole number, Decimal, Date, or Time, click the Data list arrow, select less than, then in the bottom text box, enter the maximum value. You can also limit the length of data entered into cells by choosing Text length in the Allow list, clicking the Data list arrow and selecting less than, then entering the maximum length in the Maximum text box.

FIGURE H-14: **Creating data restrictions**

Restricts entries to a
list of valid options

List of valid options

Displays a list of valid
options during data entry

FIGURE H-15: **Entering data in restricted cells**

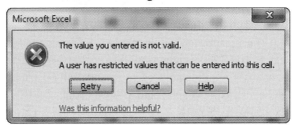

60	592D	Galapagos Adventure	12/20/2013	14	15	1	14	$2,100	Yes	Yes
61	793T	Galapagos Adventure	12/20/2013	14	15	1	14	$2,100	Yes	Yes
62	307R	Pacific Odyssey	12/21/2013	14	50	10	40	$2,105	Yes	No
63	927F	Yellowstone	12/30/2013	18	51	51	0	$2,922	Yes	Yes
64	448G	Old Japan	12/31/2013	21	47	4	43	$2,100	Yes	No
65							0			
66									Yes	
67									No	

Dropdown
list

FIGURE H-16: **Invalid data warning**

> Microsoft Excel
>
> The value you entered is not valid.
>
> A user has restricted values that can be entered into this cell.
>
> [Retry] [Cancel] [Help]
>
> Was this information helpful?

Adding input messages and error alerts

You can customize the way data validation works by using the two other tabs in the Data Validation dialog box: Input Message and Error Alert. The Input Message tab lets you set a message that appears when the user selects that cell. For example, the message might contain instructions about what type of data to enter. On the Input Message tab, enter a message title and message, then click OK. The Error Alert tab lets you set one of three alert levels if a user enters invalid data. The Information level displays your message with the information icon but allows the user to proceed with data entry. The Warning level displays your information with the warning icon and gives the user the option to proceed with data entry or not. The Stop level, which you used in this lesson, displays your message and only lets the user retry or cancel data entry for that cell.

Creating Subtotals

In a large range of data, you will often need ways to perform calculations that summarize groups within the data. For example, you might need to subtotal the sales for several sales reps listed in a table. The Excel Subtotals feature provides a quick, easy way to group and summarize a range of data. It lets you create not only subtotals using the SUM function, but other statistics as well, including COUNT, AVERAGE, MAX, and MIN. However, subtotals cannot be used in an Excel table, nor can it rearrange data. Before you can add subtotals to table data, you must first convert the data to a range and sort it. ⬛⬛⬛⬛ Kate wants you to group data by tours, with subtotals for the number of seats available and the number of seats reserved. You begin by converting the table to a range.

STEPS

1. **Click the Subtotals sheet tab, click any cell inside the table, click the Table Tools Design tab, click the Convert to Range button in the Tools group, then click Yes**

   Before you can add the subtotals, you must first sort the data. You decide to sort it in ascending order, first by tour and then by departure date.

2. **Click the Data tab, click the Sort button in the Sort & Filter group, in the Sort dialog box click the Sort by list arrow, click Tour, then click the Add Level button, click the Then by list arrow, click Depart Date, verify that the order is Oldest to Newest, then click OK**

   You have sorted the range in ascending order, first by tour, then by departure date.

3. **Click any cell in the data range, then click the Subtotal button in the Outline group**

   The Subtotal dialog box opens. Here you specify the items you want subtotaled, the function you want to apply to the values, and the fields you want to summarize.

4. **Click the At each change in list arrow, click Tour, click the Use function list arrow, click Sum; in the "Add subtotal to" list, click the Seats Reserved and Seats Available check boxes to select them, if necessary, then click the Insurance Included check box to deselect it**

5. **If necessary, click the Replace current subtotals and Summary below data check boxes to select them**

   Your completed Subtotal dialog box should match Figure H-17.

QUICK TIP

You can click the ⊟ button to hide or the ⊞ button to show a group of records in the subtotaled structure.

6. **Click OK, then scroll down so you can see row 90**

   The subtotaled data appears, showing the calculated subtotals and grand total in columns E and F, as shown in Figure H-18. Excel displays an outline to the left of the worksheet, with outline buttons to control the level of detail that appears. The button number corresponds to the detail level that is displayed. You want to show the second level of detail, the subtotals and the grand total.

7. **Click the outline symbol ②**

   Only the subtotals and the grand total appear.

QUICK TIP

You can remove subtotals in a worksheet by clicking the Subtotal button and clicking Remove All. The subtotals no longer appear, and the Outline feature is turned off automatically.

8. **Add your name to the center section of the footer, preview the worksheet, click the No Scaling list arrow, click Fit Sheet on One Page to scale the worksheet to print on one page, then save the workbook**

9. **Close the workbook, exit Excel, then submit the workbook to your instructor**

FIGURE H-17: **Completed Subtotal dialog box**

Field to use in grouping data

Function to apply to groups

Subtotal these fields

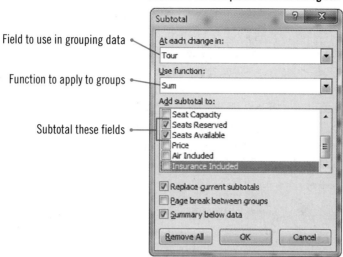

FIGURE H-18: **Portion of subtotaled table**

Outline symbols

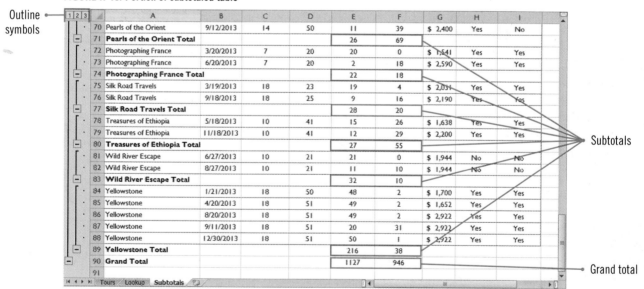

Subtotals

Grand total

Practice

Concepts Review

For current SAM information, including versions and content details, visit SAM Central (http://www.cengage.com/samcentral). If you have a SAM user profile, you may have access to hands-on instruction, practice, and assessment of the skills covered in this unit. Since various versions of SAM are supported throughout the life of this text, check with your instructor for the correct instructions and URL/Web site for accessing assignments.

FIGURE H-19

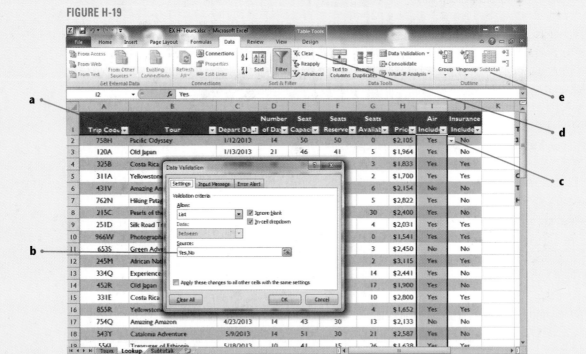

1. Which element would you click to remove a filter?
2. Which element points to an in-cell drop-down list arrow?
3. Which element do you click to group and summarize data?
4. Which element points to a field's list arrow?
5. Where do you specify acceptable data entries for a table?

Match each term with the statement that best describes it.

6. Extracted table
7. Table_array
8. Criteria range
9. Data validation
10. DSUM

a. Cell range when Advanced Filter results are copied to another location
b. Range in which search conditions are set
c. Restricts table entries to specified options
d. Name of the table searched in a VLOOKUP function
e. Function used to total table values that meet specified criteria

Select the best answer from the list of choices.

11. The _____ logical condition finds records matching both listed criteria.
    a. And
    b. Or
    c. True
    d. False

12. What does it mean when you select the Or option when creating a custom filter?
    a. Either criterion can be true to find a match.
    b. Neither criterion has to be 100% true.
    c. Both criteria must be true to find a match.
    d. A custom filter requires a criteria range.

Skills Review

1. Filter a table.

a. Start Excel, open the file EX H-2.xlsx from the drive and folder where you store your Data Files, then save it as **EX H-NE Compensation**.

b. With the Compensation sheet active, filter the table to list only records for employees in the Boston branch.

c. Clear the filter, then add a filter that displays the records for employees in the Boston and Philadelphia branches.

d. Redisplay all employees, then use a filter to show the three employees with the highest annual salary.

e. Redisplay all the records.

2. Create a custom filter.

a. Create a custom filter showing employees hired before 1/1/2010 or after 12/31/2010.

b. Create a custom filter showing employees hired between 1/1/2010 and 12/31/2010.

c. Enter your name in the worksheet footer, then preview the filtered worksheet.

d. Redisplay all records.

e. Save the workbook.

3. Filter and extract a table with the Advanced Filter.

a. You want to retrieve a list of employees who were hired before 1/1/2011 and who have an annual salary of more than $70,000 a year. Define a criteria range by inserting six new rows above the table on the worksheet and copying the field names into the first row.

b. In cell D2, enter the criterion **<1/1/2011**, then in cell G2 enter **>70000**.

c. Click any cell in the table.

d. Open the Advanced Filter dialog box.

e. Indicate that you want to copy to another location, enter the criteria range **A1:J2**, verify that the List range is $A$7:$J$17, then indicate that you want to place the extracted list in the range starting at cell **A20**.

f. Confirm that the retrieved list meets the criteria as shown in Figure H-20.

g. Save the workbook, then preview the worksheet.

FIGURE H-20

4. Look up values in a table.

a. Click the Summary sheet tab. Use the Name Manager to view the table names in the workbook, then close the dialog box.

b. You will use a lookup function to locate an employee's annual compensation; enter the Employee Number **2214** in cell A17.

c. In cell B17, use the VLOOKUP function and enter **A17** as the Lookup_value, **Table2** as the Table_array, **10** as the Col_index_num, and **FALSE** as the Range_lookup; observe the compensation displayed for that employee number, then check it against the table to make sure it is correct.

d. Enter another Employee Number, **4177**, in cell A17, and view the annual compensation for that employee.

e. Format cell B17 with the Accounting format with the $ symbol and no decimal places.

f. Save the workbook.

5. Summarize table data.

a. You want to enter a database function to average the annual salaries by branch, using the New York branch as the initial criterion. In cell E17, use the DAVERAGE function, and click the upper-left corner of cell A1 twice to select the table and its header row as the Database, select cell G1 for the Field, and select the range D16:D17 for the Criteria. Verify that the average New York salary is 45460.

b. Test the function further by entering the text **Philadelphia** in cell D17. When the criterion is entered, cell E17 should display 91480.

Skills Review (continued)

   c. Format cell E17 in Accounting format with the $ symbol and no decimal places.

   d. Save the workbook.

6. **Validate table data.**

   a. Select the data in column E of the table, and set a validation criterion specifying that you want to allow a list of valid options.

   b. Enter a list of valid options that restricts the entries to **New York**, **Boston**, and **Philadelphia**. Remember to use a comma between each item in the list.

   c. Indicate that you want the options to appear in an in-cell drop-down list, then close the dialog box.

   d. Add a row to the table. Go to cell E12, then select Boston in the drop-down list.

   e. Select the data in column F in the table, and indicate that you want to restrict the data entered to only whole numbers. In the Minimum text box, enter **1000**; in the Maximum text box, enter **10000**. Close the dialog box.

   f. Click cell F12, enter **15000**, then press [Enter]. You should get an error message.

   g. Click Cancel, then enter **7000**.

   h. Complete the new record by adding an Employee Number of **1112**, a First Name of **Caroline**, a Last Name of **Schissel**, a Hire Date of **2/1/2013**, and an Annual Bonus of **$1000**. Format the range F12:J12 as Accounting with no decimal places and using the $ symbol. Compare your screen to Figure H-21.

FIGURE H-21

	A	B	C	D	E	F	G	H	I	J
1	Employee Number	First Name	Last Name	Hire Date	Branch	Monthly Salary	Annual Salary	Annual Bonus	Benefits Dollars	Annual Compensation
2	1210	Maria	Lawson	2/12/2010	New York	$ 4,600	$ 55,200	$ 1,350	$ 12,696	$ 69,246
3	4510	Laurie	Warton	4/1/2011	Boston	$ 5,900	$ 70,800	$ 5,700	$ 16,284	$ 92,784
4	4177	Donna	Donnolly	5/6/2009	Philadelphia	$ 7,500	$ 90,000	$ 15,000	$ 20,700	$ 125,700
5	2571	Maria	Marlin	12/10/2010	Boston	$ 8,500	$ 102,000	$ 18,000	$ 23,460	$ 143,460
6	2214	John	Greeley	2/15/2012	Boston	$ 2,900	$ 34,800	$ 570	$ 8,004	$ 43,374
7	6587	Peter	Erickson	3/25/2010	New York	$ 2,775	$ 33,300	$ 770	$ 7,659	$ 41,729
8	2123	Erin	Mallo	6/23/2009	New York	$ 3,990	$ 47,880	$ 2,500	$ 11,012	$ 61,392
9	4439	Martin	Meng	8/3/2012	Philadelphia	$ 6,770	$ 81,240	$ 5,000	$ 18,685	$ 104,925
10	9807	Harry	Rumeriz	9/29/2011	Philadelphia	$ 8,600	$ 103,200	$ 14,000	$ 23,736	$ 140,936
11	3944	Joyce	Roberts	5/12/2010	Boston	$ 3,500	$ 42,000	$ 900	$ 9,660	$ 52,560
12	1112	Caroline	Schissel	2/1/2013	Boston	$ 7,000	$ 84,000	$ 1,000	$ 19,320	$ 104,320
13										
14										
15										
16	Employee Number	Annual Compensation			Branch	Average Annual Salary				
17	4177	$ 125,700			Philadelphia	$ 91,480				

   i. Add your name to the center section of the footer, save the worksheet, then preview the worksheet.

7. **Create subtotals.**

   a. Click the Subtotals sheet tab.

   b. Use the Branch field list arrow to sort the table in ascending order by branch.

   c. Convert the table to a range.

   d. Group and create subtotals of the Annual Compensation data by branch, using the SUM function.

   e. Click the 2 outline button on the outline to display only the subtotals and the grand total. Compare your screen to Figure H-22.

FIGURE H-22

	A	B	C	D	E	F	G	H	I	J
1	Employee Number	First Name	Last Name	Hire Date	Branch	Monthly Salary	Annual Salary	Annual Bonus	Benefits Dollars	Annual Compensation
6					Boston Total					$ 332,178
10					New York Total					$ 172,367
14					Philadelphia Total					$ 371,561
15					Grand Total					$ 876,107
16										

   f. Enter your name in the worksheet footer, save the workbook, then preview the worksheet.

   g. Save the workbook, close the workbook, exit Excel, then submit your workbook to your instructor.

Independent Challenge 1

As the manager of Miami Dental, a dental supply company, you spend a lot of time managing your inventory. To help with this task, you have created an Excel table that you can extract information from using filters. You also need to add data validation and summary information to the table.

   a. Start Excel, open the file EX H-3.xlsx from the drive and folder where you store your Data Files, then save it as **EX H-Dental**.

   b. Using the table data on the Inventory sheet, create a filter to display information about only the product bond refill. Clear the filter.

Independent Challenge 1 (continued)

c. Use a Custom Filter to generate a list of products with a quantity greater than 20. Clear the filter.

d. Copy the labels in cells A1:F1 into A16:F16. Type **Bond Refill** in cell A17, and type **Small** in cell C17. Use the Advanced Filter with a criteria range of A16:F17 to extract a table of small bond refills to the range of cells beginning in cell A20. Enter your name in the worksheet footer, save the workbook, then preview the worksheet.

e. Click the Summary sheet tab, select the table data in column B. Open the Data Validation dialog box, then indicate you want to use a validation list with the acceptable entries of **Berkley**, **Bromen**, **Lincoln**, **Mallory**. Make sure the In-cell dropdown check box is selected.

f. Test the data validation by trying to change a cell in column B of the table to **Loring**.

g. Using Figure H-23 as a guide, enter a function in cell E18 that calculates the total quantity of bond refill available in your inventory. Enter your name in the worksheet footer, preview the worksheet, then save the workbook.

FIGURE H-23

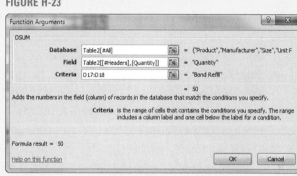

h. On the Subtotals sheet, sort the table in ascending order by product. Convert the table to a range. Insert subtotals by product using the Subtotal function, then select Quantity in the "Add Subtotal to" box. Remove the check box for the Total field, if necessary. Use the appropriate button on the outline to display only the subtotals and grand total. Save the workbook, then preview the worksheet.

Advanced Challenge Exercise

- Clear the subtotals from the worksheet.
- Use conditional formatting to add icons to the quantity field using the following criteria: quantities greater than or equal to 20 are formatted with a green check mark, quantities greater than or equal to 10 but less than 20 are formatted with a yellow exclamation point, and quantities less than 10 are formatted with a red x. Use Figure H-24 as a guide to adding the formatting rule, then compare your Quantity values to Figure H-25. (*Hint*: You may need to click in the top Value text box for the correct value to display for the red x.)
- Save the workbook then preview the worksheet.

i. Submit the workbook to your instructor. Close the workbook, then exit Excel.

FIGURE H-24

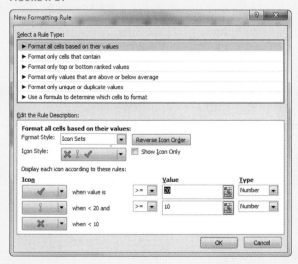

FIGURE H-25

	A	B	C	D	E	F
1	Product	Manufacturer	Size	Unit Price	Quantity	Total
2	Bond Refill	Berkley	Small	$6.55	12	$78.60
3	Bond Refill	Bromen	Medium	$10.25	11	$112.75
4	Bond Refill	Lincoln	Small	$6.25	21	$131.25
5	Bond Refill	Mallory	Small	$6.75	6	$40.50
6	Composite Kit	Berkley	Medium	$33.99	11	$373.89
7	Composite Kit	Mallory	Medium	$34.19	24	$820.56
8	Composite Syringe	Berkley	Small	$21.97	5	$109.85
9	Composite Syringe	Lincoln	Small	$21.88	31	$678.28
10	Masking Agent	Bromen	Small	$30.39	12	$364.68
11	Masking Agent	Lincoln	Medium	$42.99	18	$773.82
12	Mixing Well	Lincoln	Medium	$25.19	15	$377.85
13	Mixing Well	Mallory	Small	$19.99	8	$159.92

Independent Challenge 2

You are an accountant for an electrical supply company where you track the accounts receivables. The business supplies both residential and commercial electricians. You have put together an invoice table to track sales for the month of October. Now that you have this table, you would like to manipulate it in several ways. First, you want to filter the table to show only invoices over a certain amount with certain order dates. You also want to subtotal the total column by residential and commercial supplies. To prevent data entry errors you will restrict entries in the Order Date column. Finally, you would like to add database and lookup functions to your worksheet to efficiently retrieve data from the table.

a. Start Excel, open the file EX H-4.xlsx from the drive and folder where you store your Data Files, then save it as **EX H-Invoices**.

b. Use the Advanced Filter to show invoices with amounts more than $100.00 ordered before 10/15/2013, using cells A27:B28 to enter your criteria and extracting the results to cell A33. (*Hint*: You don't need to specify an entire row as the criteria range.) Enter your name in the worksheet footer.

c. Use the Data Validation dialog box to restrict entries to those with order dates between 10/1/2013 and 10/31/2013. Test the data restrictions by attempting to enter an invalid date in cell B25.

d. Enter **23721** in cell G28. Enter a VLOOKUP function in cell H28 to retrieve the total based on the invoice number entered in cell G28. Make sure you have an exact match with the invoice number. Test the function with the invoice number 23718.

e. Enter the date **10/1/2013** in cell J28. Use the database function, DCOUNT, in cell K28 to count the number of invoices for the date in cell J28. Save the workbook, then preview the worksheet.

f. On the Subtotals worksheet, sort the table in ascending order by Type, then convert the table to a range. Create subtotals showing the totals for commercial and residential invoices. (*Hint*: Sum the Total field.) Display only the subtotals for the commercial and residential accounts along with the grand total.

g. Save the workbook, preview the worksheet, close the workbook, then exit Excel. Submit the workbook to your instructor.

Independent Challenge 3

You are the manager of Home Design, a paint and decorating store. You have created an Excel table that contains your order data, along with the amounts for each item ordered and the date the order was placed. You would like to manipulate this table to display product categories and ordered items meeting specific criteria. You would also like to add subtotals to the table and add database functions to total orders. Finally, you want to restrict entries in the Category column.

a. Start Excel, open the file EX H-5.xlsx from the drive and folder where you store your Data Files, then save it as **EX H-Home**.

b. Create an advanced filter that extracts records with the following criteria to cell A42: orders greater than $1000 having dates either before 9/10/2013 or after 9/24/2013. (*Hint*: Recall that when you want records to meet one criterion or another, you need to place the criteria on separate lines.) Enter your name in the worksheet footer.

c. Use the DSUM function in cell H2 to let worksheet users find the total order amounts for the category entered in cell G2. Format the cell containing the total order using the Accounting format with the $ symbol and no decimals. Test the DSUM function using the Paint category name. (The sum for the Paint category should be $10,668.) Preview the worksheet.

d. Use data validation to create an in-cell drop-down list that restricts category entries to "Paint", "Wallpaper", "Hardware", and "Tile". Use the Error Alert tab of the Data Validation dialog box to set the alert level to the Warning style with the message "Data is not valid." Test the validation in the table with valid and invalid entries. Save the workbook, then preview the worksheet.

e. Using the Subtotals sheet, sort the table by category in ascending order. Convert the table to a range, and add Subtotals to the order amounts by category.

f. Use the outline to display only category names with subtotals and the grand total.

Independent Challenge 3 (continued)

Advanced Challenge Exercise

- Clear the subtotals from the worksheet.
- Conditionally format the Order data using Top/Bottom Rules to emphasize the cells containing the top 10 percent with yellow fill and dark yellow text.
- Add another rule to format the bottom 10 percent in the Order column with a light red fill.

g. Save the workbook, then preview the worksheet.

h. Close the workbook, exit Excel, then submit the workbook to your instructor.

A8-K........   due 10/27/13

Real Life Independent Challenge

You decide to organize your business and personal contacts using the Excel table format to allow you to easily look up contact information. You want to include addresses and a field documenting whether the contact relationship is personal or business. You enter your contact information in an Excel worksheet that you will convert to a table so you can easily filter the data. You also use lookup functions to locate phone numbers when you provide a last name in your table. Finally, you restrict the entries in the Relationship field to values in drop-down lists to simplify future data entry and reduce errors.

a. Start Excel, open a new workbook, then save it as **EX H-Contacts** in the drive and folder where you store your Data Files.

b. Use the structure of Table H-2 to enter at least six of your personal and business contacts into a worksheet. (*Hint*: You will need to format the Zip column using the Zip Code type of the Special category.) In the Relationship field, enter either Business or Personal. If you don't have phone numbers for all the phone fields, leave them blank.

TABLE H-2

Last name	First name	Cell phone	Home phone	Work phone	Street address	City	State	Zip	Relationship

c. Use the worksheet information to create a table. Use the Name Manager dialog box to edit the table name to **Contacts**.

d. Create a filter that retrieves records of personal contacts. Clear the filter.

e. Create a filter that retrieves records of business contacts. Clear the filter.

f. Restrict the Relationship field entries to Business or Personal. Provide an in-cell drop-down list allowing the selection of these two options. Add an input message of **Select from the dropdown list**. Add an Information-level error message of **Choose Business or Personal**. Test the validation by adding a new record to your table.

g. Below your table, create a phone lookup area with the following labels in adjacent cells: **Last name**, **Cell phone**, **Home phone**, **Work phone**.

h. Enter one of the last names from your table under the label Last Name in your phone lookup area.

i. In the phone lookup area, enter lookup functions to locate the cell phone, home phone, and work phone numbers for the contact last name that you entered in the previous step. Make sure you match the last name exactly.

j. Enter your name in the center section of the worksheet footer, save the workbook, then preview the worksheet.

k. Close the workbook, exit Excel, then submit the workbook to your instructor.

Visual Workshop

Open the file EX H-6.xlsx from the drive and folder where you save your Data Files, then save it as **EX H-Schedule**. Complete the worksheet as shown in Figure H-26. An in-cell drop-down list has been added to the data entered in the Room field. The range A18:G21 is extracted from the table using the criteria in cells A15:A16. Add your name to the worksheet footer, save the workbook, preview the worksheet, then submit the workbook to your instructor.

FIGURE H-26

	A	B	C	D	E	F	G	H
1	Spring 2013 Schedule of Yoga Classes							
2								
3	Class Code	Class	Time	Day	Room	Fee	Instructor	
4	Y100	Basics	8:00	Monday	Mat Room	$10	Martin	
5	Y101	Power	9:00	Tuesday	Equipment Room	$15	Grey	
6	Y102	Hatha	10:00	Wednesday	Mat Room	$10	Marshall	
7	Y103	Kripalu	11:00	Monday	Mat Room	$10	Bradley	
8	Y104	Basics	1:00	Friday	Mat Room	$10	Pauley	
9	Y105	Power	2:00	Saturday	Equipment Room	$15	Dash	
10	Y106	Hatha	3:00	Tuesday	Mat Room	$10	Robinson	
11	Y107	Power	4:00	Monday	Equipment Room	$15	Walsh	
12	Y108	Basics	5:00	Tuesday	Mat Room	10	Matthews	
13					Please select Mat Room or Equipment Room			
14								
15	Class							
16	Power							
17								
18	Class Code	Class	Time	Day	Room	Fee	Instructor	
19	Y101	Power	9:00	Tuesday	Equipment Room	$15	Grey	
20	Y105	Power	2:00	Saturday	Equipment Room	$15	Dash	
21	Y107	Power	4:00	Monday	Equipment Room	$15	Walsh	
22								
23								

A9 Due Wed. Nov 6th

5 Powerpoint slides on Me

20 excredpoints for Voice over

Automating Worksheet Tasks

Files You Will Need:

EX I-1.xlsx
EX I-2.xlsx

A **macro** is a named set of instructions you can create that performs tasks automatically, in an order you specify. You create macros to automate Excel tasks that you perform frequently. Because they perform tasks rapidly, macros can save you a great deal of time. For example, if you usually enter your name and date in a worksheet footer, you can record the keystrokes in an Excel macro that enters the text and inserts the current date automatically when you run the macro. In this unit, you will plan and design a simple macro, then record and run it. You will then edit the macro and explore ways to make it more easily available as you work. Kate Morgan, the North America regional vice president of sales at Quest, wants you to create a macro for the sales division. The macro needs to automatically insert text that identifies the worksheet as a sales division document.

OBJECTIVES

Plan a macro

Enable a macro

Record a macro

Run a macro

Edit a macro

Assign keyboard shortcuts to macros

Use the Personal Macro Workbook

Assign a macro to a button

Planning a Macro

You create macros for Excel tasks that you perform frequently. For example, you can create a macro to enter and format text or to save and print a worksheet. To create a macro, you record the series of actions using the macro recorder built into Excel, or you write the instructions in a special programming language. Because the sequence of actions in a macro is important, you need to plan the macro carefully before you record it. ▰▰▰ Kate wants you to create a macro for the sales division that inserts the text "Quest Sales" in the upper-left corner of any worksheet. You work with her to plan the macro.

DETAILS

To plan a macro, use the following guidelines:

- **Assign the macro a descriptive name**

  The first character of a macro name must be a letter; the remaining characters can be letters, numbers, or underscores. Letters can be uppercase or lowercase. Spaces are not allowed in macro names; use underscores in place of spaces. Press [Shift][-] to enter an underscore character. Kate wants you to name the macro "DivStamp". See Table I-1 for a list of macros that could be created to automate other tasks at Quest.

- **Write out the steps the macro will perform**

  This planning helps eliminate careless errors. Kate writes a description of the macro she wants, as shown in Figure I-1.

- **Decide how you will perform the actions you want to record**

  You can use the mouse, the keyboard, or a combination of the two. Kate wants you to use both the mouse and the keyboard.

- **Practice the steps you want Excel to record, and write them down**

  Kate has written down the sequence of actions she wants you to include in the macro.

- **Decide where to store the description of the macro and the macro itself**

  Macros can be stored in an active workbook, in a new workbook, or in the **Personal Macro Workbook**, a special workbook used only for macro storage. Kate asks you to store the macro in a new workbook.

Automating Worksheet Tasks

FIGURE I-1: **Paper description of planned macro**

Macro to create stamp with the division name	
Name:	DivStamp
Description:	Adds a stamp to the top left of the worksheet, identifying it as a Quest sales worksheet
Steps:	1. Position the cell pointer in cell A1.
	2. Type Sales Division, then click the Enter button.
	3. Click the Format button, then click Format Cells.
	4. Click the Font tab, under Font style click Bold; under Underline click Single; under Color click Red; then click OK.

TABLE I-1: **Possible macros and their descriptive names**

description of macro	descriptive name for macro
Enter a frequently used proper name, such as "Kate Morgan"	KateMorgan
Enter a frequently used company name, such as Quest	Company_Name
Print the active worksheet on a single page, in landscape orientation	FitToLand
Add a footer to a worksheet	FooterStamp
Add totals to a worksheet	AddTotals

Enabling a Macro

Because a macro may contain a **virus**—destructive software that can damage your computer files—the default security setting in Excel disables macros from running. Although a workbook containing a macro will open, if macros are disabled, they will not function. You can manually change the Excel security setting to allow macros to run if you know a macro came from a trusted source. When saving a workbook with a macro, you need to save it as a macro-enabled workbook with the extension .xlsm. 🔳🔳🔳 Kate asks you to change the security level to enable all macros. You will change the security level back to the default setting after you create and run your macros.

STEPS

1. **Start Excel, click the** Save button 🔲 **on the Quick Access toolbar, in the Save As dialog box click the** Save as type list arrow, **click** Excel Macro-Enabled Workbook (*.xlsm), **then in the File name text box type** EX I-Macro Workbook

2. **Navigate to the drive and folder where you store your Data Files, then click** Save

   The security settings that enable macros are available on the Developer tab. The Developer tab does not appear by default, but you can display it by customizing the Ribbon.

QUICK TIP

If the Developer tab is displayed on your Ribbon, skip steps three and four.

3. **Click the** File tab, **click** Options, **then click** Customize Ribbon **in the category list**

   The Customize the Ribbon options open in the Excel Options dialog box, as shown in Figure I-2.

4. **Click the** Developer check box **in the Main Tabs area on the right side of the screen to select it, then click** OK

   The Developer tab appears on the Ribbon. You are ready to change the security settings.

5. **Click the** Developer tab, **then click the** Macro Security button **in the Code group**

   The Trust Center dialog box opens, as shown in Figure I-3.

6. **Click** Macro Settings **if necessary, click the** Enable all macros (not recommended; potentially dangerous code can run) option button **to select it, then click** OK

   The dialog box closes. Macros remain enabled until you disable them by deselecting the Enable all macros option. As you work with Excel, you should disable macros when you are not working with them.

FIGURE I-2: Excel Options dialog box

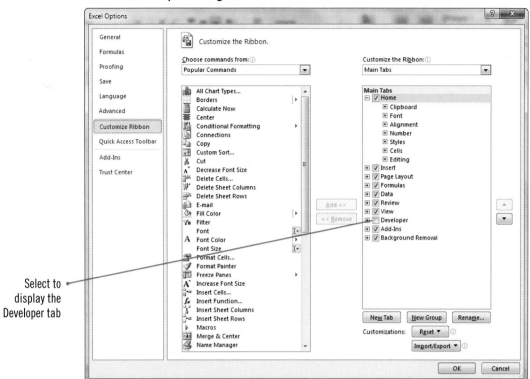

Select to
display the
Developer tab

FIGURE I-3: Trust Center dialog box

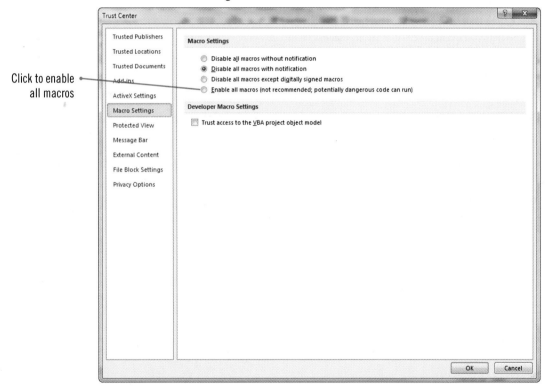

Click to enable
all macros

Disabling macros

To prevent viruses from running on your computer, you should disable all macros when you are not working with them. To disable macros, click the Developer tab, then click the Macro Security button in the Code group. Clicking any of the first three options disables macros. The first option disables all macros without notifying you. The second option notifies you when macros are disabled, and the third option allows only digitally signed macros to run.

Recording a Macro

The easiest way to create a macro is to record it using the Excel Macro Recorder. You turn the Macro Recorder on, name the macro, enter the keystrokes and select the commands you want the macro to perform, then stop the recorder. As you record the macro, Excel automatically translates each action into program code that you can later view and modify. You can take as long as you want to record the macro; a recorded macro contains only your actions, not the amount of time you took to record it. ▰▰▰▰ Kate wants you to create a macro that enters a division "stamp" in cell A1 of the active worksheet. You create this macro by recording your actions.

STEPS

QUICK TIP

You can also click the Record Macro button in the Code group on the Developer tab, or the Macros button in the Macros group of the View tab to record a new macro.

1. **Click the Record Macro button 🔲 on the left side of the status bar**

   The Record Macro dialog box opens, as shown in Figure I-4. The default name Macro1 is selected. You can either assign this name or enter a new name. This dialog box also lets you assign a shortcut key for running the macro and assign a storage location for the macro.

2. **Type DivStamp in the Macro name text box**

3. **If the Store macro in list box does not display "This Workbook", click the list arrow and select This Workbook**

4. **Type your name in the Description text box, then click OK**

   The dialog box closes, and the Record Macro button on the status bar is replaced with a Stop Recording button. Take your time performing the steps below. Excel records every keystroke, menu selection, and mouse action that you make.

5. **Press [Ctrl][Home]**

   When you begin an Excel session, macros record absolute cell references. By beginning the recording with a command to move to cell A1, you ensure that the macro includes the instruction to select cell A1 as the first step, in cases where A1 is not already selected.

QUICK TIP

You can press [Ctrl] [Enter] instead of clicking the Enter button.

6. **Type Quest Sales in cell A1, then click the Enter button ✔ on the Formula Bar**

7. **Click the Home tab, click the Format button in the Cells group, then click Format Cells**

8. **Click the Font tab, in the Font style list box click Bold, click the Underline list arrow and click Single, click the Color list arrow and click the Red, Accent 2 Theme color (first row, sixth color from the left), then compare your dialog box to Figure I-5**

QUICK TIP

You can also click the Stop Recording button in the Code group on the Developer tab to stop recording a macro.

9. **Click OK, click the Stop Recording button 🔳 on the left side of the status bar, click cell D1 to deselect cell A1, then save the workbook**

   Figure I-6 shows the result of recording the macro.

FIGURE I-4: **Record Macro dialog box**

Type macro name here

Type your name and description of macro here

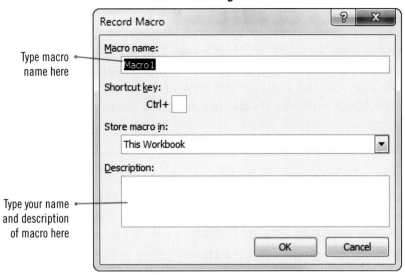

FIGURE I-5: **Font tab of the Format Cells dialog box**

Macro will apply these formatting attributes to the text

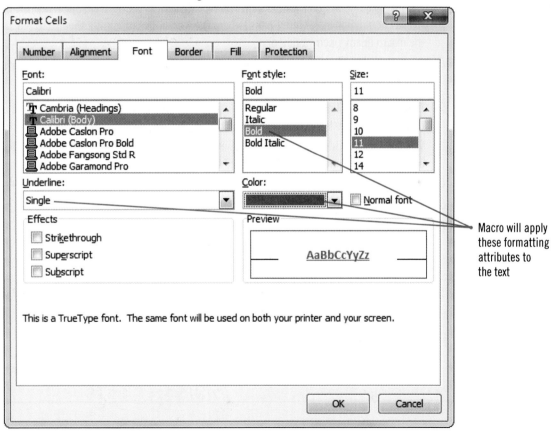

FIGURE I-6: **Sales Division stamp**

	A	B	C
1	Quest Sales		
2			
3			

Running a Macro

Once you record a macro, you should test it to make sure that the actions it performs are correct. To test a macro, you **run** (play) it. You can run a macro using the Macros button in the Code group of the Developer tab. Kate asks you to clear the contents of cell A1, and then test the DivStamp macro. After you run the macro in the Macro workbook, she asks you to test the macro once more from a newly opened workbook.

STEPS

1. **Click cell A1, click the Home tab if necessary, click the Clear button in the Editing group, click Clear All, then click any other cell to deselect cell A1**

   When you delete only the contents of a cell, any formatting still remains in the cell. By using the Clear All option you can be sure that the cell is free of contents and formatting.

2. **Click the Developer tab, then click the Macros button in the Code group**

   The Macro dialog box, shown in Figure I-7, lists all the macros contained in the open workbooks. If other people have used your computer, other macros may be listed.

3. **Make sure DivStamp is selected, as you watch cell A1 click Run, then deselect cell A1**

   The macro quickly plays back the steps you recorded in the previous lesson. When the macro is finished, your screen should look like Figure I-8. As long as the workbook containing the macro remains open, you can run the macro in any open workbook.

4. **Click the File tab, click New, then in the Blank Workbook area click Create**

   Because the EX I-Macro Workbook.xlsm is still open, you can use its macros.

5. **Deselect cell A1, click the Macros button in the Code group, make sure 'EX I-Macro Workbook.xlsm'!DivStamp is selected, click Run, then deselect cell A1**

   When multiple workbooks are open, the macro name in the Macro dialog box includes the workbook name between single quotation marks, followed by an exclamation point, indicating that the macro is outside the active workbook. Because you only used this workbook to test the macro, you don't need to save it.

6. **Close Book2.xlsx without saving changes**

   The EX I-Macro Workbook.xlsm workbook remains open.

FIGURE I-7: **Macro dialog box**

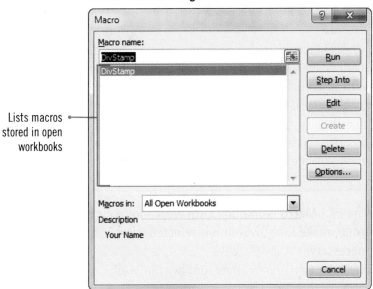

Lists macros stored in open workbooks

FIGURE I-8: **Result of running DivStamp macro**

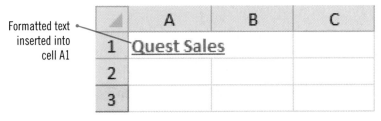

Formatted text inserted into cell A1

Running a macro automatically

You can create a macro that automatically performs certain tasks when the workbook in which it is saved is opened. This is useful for actions you want to do every time you open a workbook. For example, you may import data from an external data source into the workbook or format the worksheet data in a certain way. To create a macro that will automatically run when the workbook is opened, you need to name the macro Auto_Open and save it in the workbook.

Editing a Macro

When you use the Macro Recorder to create a macro, the program instructions, called **program code**, are recorded automatically in the **Visual Basic for Applications (VBA)** programming language. Each macro is stored as a **module**, or program code container, attached to the workbook. After you record a macro, you might need to change it. If you have a lot of changes to make, it might be best to record the macro again. But if you need to make only minor adjustments, you can edit the macro code directly using the **Visual Basic Editor**, a program that lets you display and edit your macro code. Kate wants you to modify the DivStamp macro to change the point size of the department stamp to 14.

STEPS

1. **Make sure the EX I-Macro Workbook.xlsm workbook is open, click the Macros button in the Code group, make sure DivStamp is selected, click Edit, then maximize the Code window, if necessary**

   The Visual Basic Editor starts, showing three windows: the Project Explorer window, the Properties window, and the Code window, as shown in Figure I-9.

TROUBLE

If the Properties window does not appear in the lower-left portion of your screen, click the Properties Window button 🖼 in the Visual Basic Standard toolbar, then resize it as shown in the figure if necessary.

2. **Click Module 1 in the Project Explorer window if it's not already selected, then examine the steps in the macro, comparing your screen to Figure I-9**

   The name of the macro and your name appear at the top of the module window. Below this area, Excel has translated your keystrokes and commands into macro code. When you open and make selections in a dialog box during macro recording, Excel automatically stores all the dialog box settings in the macro code. For example, the line .FontStyle = "Bold" was generated when you clicked Bold in the Format Cells dialog box. You also see lines of code that you didn't generate directly while recording the DivStamp macro, for example, .Name = "Calibri".

3. **In the line .Size = 11, double-click 11 to select it, then type 14**

   Because Module1 is attached to the workbook and not stored as a separate file, any changes to the module are saved automatically when you save the workbook.

4. **Review the code in the Code window**

QUICK TIP

You can return to Excel without closing the module by clicking the View Microsoft Excel button 🗷 on the Visual Basic Editor toolbar.

5. **Click File on the menu bar, then click Close and Return to Microsoft Excel**

   You want to rerun the DivStamp macro to make sure the macro reflects the change you made using the Visual Basic Editor. You begin by clearing the division name from cell A1.

6. **Click cell A1, click the Home tab, click the Clear button 🔲 in the Editing group, then click Clear All**

QUICK TIP

Another way to start the Visual Basic Editor is to click the Developer tab, then click the Visual Basic button in the Code group.

7. **Click any other cell to deselect cell A1, click the Developer tab, click the Macros button in the Code group, make sure DivStamp is selected, click Run, then deselect cell A1**

   The department stamp is now in 14-point type, as shown in Figure I-10.

8. **Save the workbook**

FIGURE I-9: Visual Basic Editor showing Module1

Properties window button

Project Explorer window with Module1 selected

Properties window showing properties for Module1

Comments appear in green

Code window

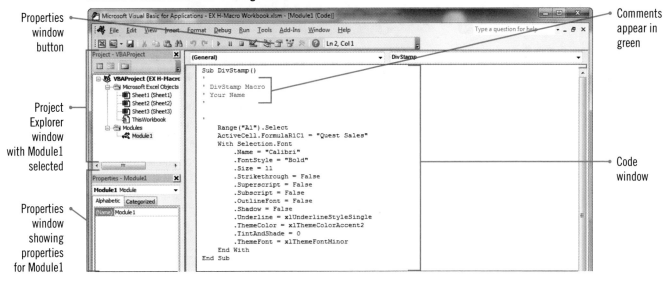

```
Sub DivStamp()
'
' DivStamp Macro
' Your Name
'
'
    Range("A1").Select
    ActiveCell.FormulaR1C1 = "Quest Sales"
    With Selection.Font
        .Name = "Calibri"
        .FontStyle = "Bold"
        .Size = 11
        .Strikethrough = False
        .Superscript = False
        .Subscript = False
        .OutlineFont = False
        .Shadow = False
        .Underline = xlUnderlineStyleSingle
        .ThemeColor = xlThemeColorAccent2
        .TintAndShade = 0
        .ThemeFont = xlThemeFontMinor
    End With
End Sub
```

FIGURE I-10: Result of running edited DivStamp macro

Font size is enlarged to 14 point

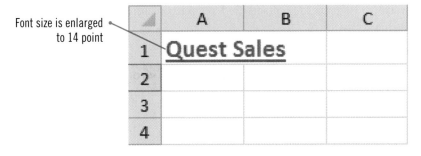

Adding comments to Visual Basic code

With practice, you will be able to interpret the lines of macro code. Others who use your macro, however, might want to review the code to, for example, learn the function of a particular line. You can explain the code by adding comments to the macro. **Comments** are explanatory text added to the lines of code. When you enter a comment, you must type an apostrophe (') before the comment text. Otherwise, the program tries to interpret it as a command. On the screen, comments appear in green after you press [Enter], as shown in Figure I-9. You can also insert blank lines as comments in the macro code to make the code more readable. To do this, type an apostrophe, then press [Enter].

Assigning Keyboard Shortcuts to Macros

For macros that you run frequently, you can run them by using shortcut key combinations instead of the Macro dialog box. You can assign a shortcut key combination to any macro. Using shortcut keys saves you time by reducing the number of actions you need to take to run a macro. You assign shortcut key combinations in the Record Macro dialog box. ░░░░░ Kate also wants you to create a macro called Region to enter the company region into a worksheet. You assign a shortcut key combination to run the macro.

STEPS

1. **Click cell B2**

   You want to record the macro in cell B2, but you want the macro to enter the region of North America anywhere in a worksheet. Therefore, you do not begin the macro with an instruction to position the cell pointer, as you did in the DivStamp macro.

2. **Click the Record Macro button 🔲 on the status bar**

   The Record Macro dialog box opens. Notice the option Shortcut key: Ctrl+ followed by a blank box. You can type a letter (A–Z) in the Shortcut key text box to assign the key combination of [Ctrl] plus that letter to run the macro. Because some common Excel shortcuts use the [Ctrl][letter] combination, such as [Ctrl][C] for Copy, you decide to use the key combination [Ctrl][Shift] plus a letter to avoid overriding any of these shortcut key combinations.

3. **With the default macro name selected, type Region, click the Shortcut key text box, press and hold [Shift], type C, then in the Description box type your name**

   You have assigned the shortcut key combination [Ctrl][Shift][C] to the Region macro. After you create the macro, you will use this shortcut key combination to run it. Compare your screen with Figure I-11. You are ready to record the Region macro.

4. **Click OK to close the dialog box**

5. **Type North America in cell B2, click the Enter button ✔ on the formula bar, press [Ctrl][I] to italicize the text, click the Stop Recording button 🔲 on the status bar, then deselect cell B2**

   North America appears in italics in cell B2. You are ready to run the macro in cell A5 using the shortcut key combination.

6. **Click cell A5, press and hold [Ctrl][Shift], type C, then deselect the cell**

   The region appears in cell A5, as shown in Figure I-12. The macro played back in the selected cell (A5) instead of the cell where it was recorded (B2) because you did not begin recording the macro by clicking cell B2.

FIGURE I-11: **Record Macro dialog box with shortcut key assigned**

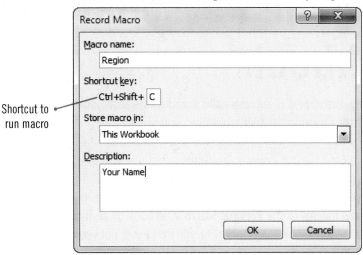

Shortcut to run macro

Record Macro

Macro name:
Region

Shortcut key:
Ctrl+Shift+ C

Store macro in:
This Workbook

Description:
Your Name

OK   Cancel

FIGURE I-12: **Result of running the CompanyName macro**

	A	B	C
1	**Quest Sales**		
2		*North America*	
3			
4			
5	*North America*		
6			
7			
8			

Result of recording macro in cell B2

Result of running macro in cell A5

Using relative referencing when creating a macro

By default, Excel records absolute cell references in macros. You can record a macro's actions based on the relative position of the active cell by clicking the Use Relative References button in the Code group prior to recording the action. For example, when you create a macro using the default setting of absolute referencing, bolding the range A1:D1 will always bold that range when the macro is run. However, if you click the Use Relative References button when recording the macro before bolding the range, then running the macro will not necessarily result in bolding the range A1:D1. The range that will be bolded will depend on the location of the active cell when the macro is run. If the active cell is A4, then the range A4:D4 will be bolded. Selecting the Use Relative References button highlights the button name, indicating it is active, as shown in Figure I-13. The button remains active until you click it again to deselect it. This is called a **toggle**, meaning that it acts like an off/on switch: it retains the relative reference setting until you click it again to turn it off or you exit Excel.

FIGURE I-13: **Relative Reference button selected**

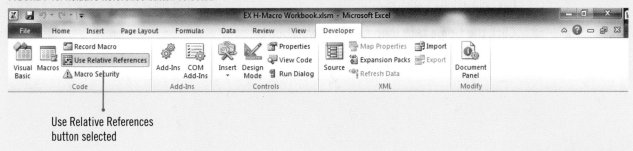

Use Relative References button selected

Excel 2010

Using the Personal Macro Workbook

When you create a macro, it is automatically stored in the workbook in which you created it. But if you wanted to use that macro in another workbook, you would have to copy the macro to that workbook. Instead, it's easier to store commonly used macros in the Personal Macro Workbook. The **Personal Macro Workbook** is an Excel file that is always available, unless you specify otherwise, and gives you access to all the macros it contains, regardless of which workbooks are open. The Personal Macro Workbook file is automatically created the first time you choose to store a macro in it, and is named PERSONAL.XLSB. You can add additional macros to the Personal Macro Workbook by saving them in the workbook. By default, the PERSONAL.XLSB workbook opens each time you start Excel, but you don't see it because Excel designates it as a hidden file. **▓▓▓▓** Kate often likes to print her worksheets in landscape orientation with 1" left, right, top, and bottom margins. She wants you to create a macro that automatically formats a worksheet for printing this way. Because she wants to use this macro in future workbooks, she asks you to store the macro in the Personal Macro Workbook.

STEPS

1. **Click the Record Macro button ▤ on the status bar**

   The Record Macro dialog box opens.

2. **Type FormatPrint in the Macro name text box, click the Shortcut key text box, press and hold [Shift], type F, then click the Store macro in list arrow**

   You have named the macro FormatPrint and assigned it the shortcut combination [Ctrl][Shift][F]. This Workbook storage option is selected by default, indicating that Excel automatically stores macros in the active workbook, as shown in Figure I-14. You can also choose to store the macro in a new workbook or in the Personal Macro Workbook.

   > **TROUBLE**
   >
   > If a dialog box appears saying that a macro is already assigned to this shortcut combination, choose another letter for a keyboard shortcut. If a dialog box appears with the message that a macro named FormatPrint already exists, click Yes to replace it.

3. **Click Personal Macro Workbook, in the Description text box enter your name, then click OK**

   The recorder is on, and you are ready to record the macro keystrokes.

4. **Click the Page Layout tab, click the Orientation button in the Page Setup group, click Landscape, click the Margins button in the Page Setup group, click Custom Margins, then enter 1 in the Top, Left, Bottom, and Right text boxes**

   Compare your margin settings to Figure I-15.

5. **Click OK, then click the Stop Recording button ▤ on the status bar**

   You want to test the macro.

   > **TROUBLE**
   >
   > You may have to wait a few moments for the macro to finish. If you are using a different letter for the shortcut key combination, type that letter instead of the letter F.

6. **Activate Sheet2, in cell A1 type Macro Test, press [Enter], press and hold [Ctrl][Shift], then type F**

   The FormatPrint macro plays back the sequence of commands.

7. **Preview Sheet2 and verify that the orientation is landscape and the margins are 1" on the left, right, top, and bottom**

8. **Click the Home tab, then save the workbook**

FIGURE I-14: **Record Macro dialog box showing macro storage options**

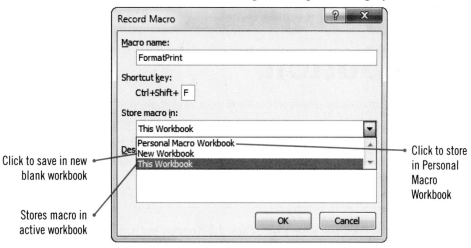

Click to save in new blank workbook

Stores macro in active workbook

Click to store in Personal Macro Workbook

FIGURE I-15: **Margin settings for the FormatPrint macro**

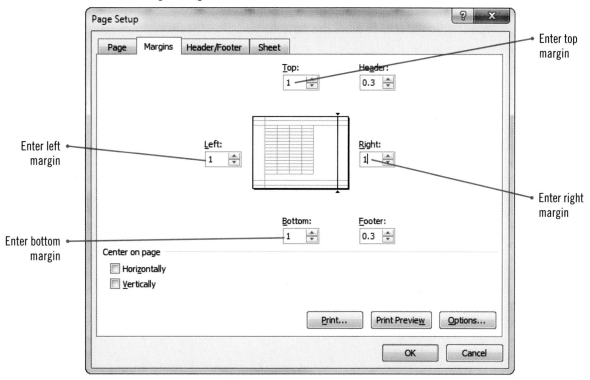

Enter top margin

Enter left margin

Enter right margin

Enter bottom margin

Working with the Personal Macro Workbook

Once you use the Personal Macro Workbook, it opens automatically each time you start Excel so you can add macros to it. By default, the Personal Macro Workbook is hidden in Excel as a precautionary measure so you don't accidentally delete anything from it. If you need to delete a macro from the Personal Macro Workbook, click the View tab, click Unhide in the Window group, click PERSONAL.XLSB, then click OK. To hide the Personal Macro Workbook, make it the active workbook, click the View tab, then click Hide in the Window group. If you should see a message that Excel is unable to record to your Personal Macro Workbook, check to make sure it is enabled: Click the File tab, click Options, click Add-ins, click Disabled Items, then click Go. If your Personal Macro Workbook is listed in the Disabled items dialog box, click its name, then click Enable.

Assigning a Macro to a Button

When you create macros for others who will use your workbook, you might want to make the macros more visible so they're easier to use. In addition to using shortcut keys, you can run a macro by assigning it to a button on your worksheet. Then when you click the button the macro will run.  To make it easier for people in the sales division to run the DivStamp macro, Kate asks you to assign it to a button on the workbook. You begin by creating the button.

STEPS

1. **Click** Sheet3, **click the** Insert tab, **click the** Shapes button **in the Illustrations group, then click the** first rectangle **in the Rectangles group**

   The mouse pointer changes to a + symbol.

2. **Click at the top-left corner of cell** A8, **and drag the pointer to the lower-right corner of cell B9**

   Compare your screen to Figure I-16.

3. **Type** Division Macro **to label the button**

   Now that you have created the button, you are ready to assign the macro to it.

4. **Right-click the** new button, **then on the shortcut menu click** Assign Macro

   The Assign Macro dialog box opens.

5. **Click** DivStamp **under "Macro name", then click** OK

   You have assigned the DivStamp macro to the button.

6. **Click any cell to deselect the button, then click the button**

   The DivStamp macro plays, and the text Quest Sales appears in cell A1, as shown in Figure I-17.

7. **Save the workbook, preview Sheet3, close the workbook, then exit Excel, clicking** No **when asked to save changes to the Personal Macro Workbook**

8. **Submit the workbook to your instructor**

FIGURE I-16: **Button shape**

Rectangle shape will become button

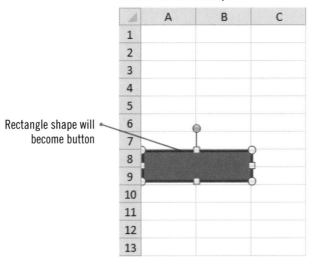

FIGURE I-17: **Sheet3 with the Sales Division text**

Result of running macro using the button

	A	B	C
1	Quest Sales		
2			
3			
4			
5			
6			
7			
8	Division Macro		
9			
10			
11			

Formatting a macro button

You can format macro buttons using 3-D effects, clip art, photographs, fills, and shadows. To format a button, right-click it and select Format Shape from the shortcut menu. In the Format Shape dialog box you can select from many features such as Fill, Line Color, Line Style, Shadow, Reflection, Glow and Soft Edges, 3-D Format, 3-D Rotation, Picture Color, and Text Box. To add an image to the button, click Fill, then click the Picture or texture fill option button. To insert a picture from a file, click File, select a picture, then click Insert. To insert a clip art picture, click Clip Art, select a picture, then

click OK. You may need to resize your button to fully display a picture. You may also want to move the text on the button if it overlaps the image. Figure I-18 shows a button formatted with clip art.

FIGURE I-18: **Button formatted with clip art**

Practice

 SAM

For current SAM information, including versions and content details, visit SAM Central (http://www.cengage.com/samcentral). If you have a SAM user profile, you may have access to hands-on instruction, practice, and assessment of the skills covered in this unit. Since various versions of SAM are supported throughout the life of this text, check with your instructor for the correct instructions and URL/Web site for accessing assignments.

Concepts Review

FIGURE I-19

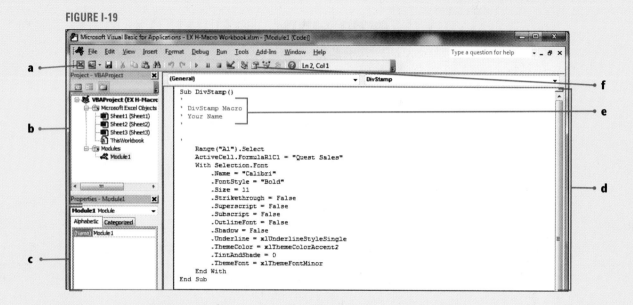

1. **Which element do you click to return to Excel without closing the module?**
2. **Which element points to comments?**
3. **Which element points to the Properties Window button?**
4. **Which element points to the Code window?**
5. **Which element points to the Properties window?**
6. **Which element points to the Project Explorer window?**

Match each term or button with the statement that best describes it.

7. **Virus**
8. **Macro**
9. **Personal Macro Workbook**
10. **Comments**
11. **Visual Basic Editor**

a. Set of instructions that performs a task in a specified order
b. Statements that appear in green explaining the macro
c. Destructive software that can damage computer files
d. Used to make changes to macro code
e. Used to store frequently used macros

Select the best answer from the list of choices.

12. **Which of the following is the best candidate for a macro?**
    a. Nonsequential tasks
    b. Often-used sequences of commands or actions
    c. Seldom-used commands or tasks
    d. One-button or one-keystroke commands
13. **You can open the Visual Basic Editor by clicking the _____ button in the Macro dialog box.**
    a. Programs
    b. Edit
    c. Modules
    d. Visual Basic Editor
14. **A Macro named _____ will automatically run when the workbook it is saved in opens.**
    a. Auto_Open
    b. Default
    c. Macro1
    d. Open_Macro

15. **Which of the following is *not* true about editing a macro?**
    a. You edit macros using the Visual Basic Editor.
    b. You can type changes directly in the existing program code.
    c. A macro cannot be edited and must be recorded again.
    d. You can make more than one editing change in a macro.

16. **Why is it important to plan a macro?**
    a. Planning helps prevent careless errors from being introduced into the macro.
    b. Macros can't be deleted.
    c. It is impossible to edit a macro.
    d. Macros won't be stored if they contain errors.

17. **Macros are recorded with relative references:**
    a. In all cases.
    b. Only if the Use Relative References button is selected.
    c. By default.
    d. Only if the Use Absolute References button is not selected.

18. **You can run macros:**
    a. From the Macro dialog box.
    b. From shortcut key combinations.
    c. From a button on the worksheet.
    d. Using all of the above.

19. **Macro security settings can be changed using the _____ tab.**
    a. Developer
    b. Home
    c. Security
    d. Review

Skills Review

1. **Plan and enable a macro.**
   a. You need to plan a macro that enters and formats your name and e-mail address in a worksheet.
   b. Write out the steps the macro will perform.
   c. Write out how the macro could be used in a workbook.
   d. Start Excel, open a new workbook, then save it as a Macro-Enabled workbook named **EX I-Macros** in the drive and folder where you store your Data Files. (*Hint*: The file will have the file extension .xlsm.)
   e. Use the Excel Options feature to display the Developer tab if it is not showing in the Ribbon.
   f. Using the Trust Center dialog box, enable all macros.

2. **Record a macro.**
   a. You want to record a macro that enters and formats your name and e-mail address in the range A1:A2 in a worksheet using the steps below.
   b. Name the macro **MyEmail**, store it in the current workbook, and make sure your name appears as the person who recorded the macro.
   c. Record the macro, entering your name in cell A1 and your e-mail address in cell A2. (*Hint*: You need to press [Ctrl][Home] first to ensure cell A1 will be selected when the macro runs.)
   d. Resize column A to fit the information entirely in that column.
   e. Add an outside border around the range A1:A2 and format the font using red from the Standard Colors.
   f. Add bold formatting to the text in the range A1:A2.
   g. Stop the recorder and save the workbook.

3. **Run a macro.**
   a. Clear cell entries and formats in the range affected by the macro, then resize the width of column A to 8.43.
   b. Run the MyEmail macro to place your name and e-mail information in the range A1:A2.
   c. On the worksheet, clear all the cell entries and formats generated by running the MyEmail macro. Resize the width of column A to 8.43.
   d. Save the workbook.

Skills Review (continued)

4. **Edit a macro.**
   a. Open the MyEmail macro in the Visual Basic Editor.
   b. Change the line of code above the last line from Selection.Font.
      Bold = True to Selection.Font.Bold = False.
   c. Use the Close and Return to Microsoft Excel option on the File
      menu to return to Excel.
   d. Test the macro on Sheet1, and compare your worksheet to Figure I-20
      verifying that the text is not bold.
   e. Save the workbook.

FIGURE I-20

◢	A	B
1	Your Name	
2	yourname@yourschool.edu	
3		
4		
5		

5. **Assign keyboard shortcuts to macros.**
   a. You want to record a macro that enters your e-mail address in italics with a font color of green, without underlining, in
      the selected cell of a worksheet, using the steps below.
   b. Record the macro called **EmailStamp** in the current workbook, assigning your macro the shortcut key combination
      [Ctrl][Shift][E], storing it in the current workbook, with your name in the description.
   c. After you record the macro, clear the contents and formats from the cell
      containing your e-mail address that you used to record the macro.
   d. Use the shortcut key combination to run the EmailStamp macro in a cell other
      than the one in which it was recorded. Compare your macro result to
      Figure I-21. Your e-mail address may appear in a different cell.
   e. Save the workbook.

FIGURE I-21

	E	F	G
	yourname@yourschool.edu		

6. **Use the Personal Macro Workbook.**
   a. Using Sheet1, record a new macro called **FitToLand** and store it in the
      Personal Macro Workbook with your name in the Description text box. If you already have a macro named FitToLand
      replace that macro. The macro should set the print orientation to landscape.
   b. After you record the macro, display Sheet2, and enter **Test data for FitToLand macro** in cell A1.
   c. Preview Sheet2 to verify that the orientation is set to portrait.
   d. Run the FitToLand macro. (You may have to wait a few moments.)
   e. Add your name to the Sheet2 footer, then preview Sheet2 and verify that it is now in Landscape orientation.
   f. Save the workbook.

7. **Assign a macro to a button.**
   a. Enter **Button Test** in cell A1 of Sheet3.
   b. Using the rectangle shape, draw a rectangle in the range A7:B8. Compare your
      worksheet to Figure I-22.
   c. Label the button with the text **Landscape**.
   d. Assign the macro PERSONAL.XLSB!FitToLand to the button.
   e. Verify that the orientation of Sheet3 is set to portrait.
   f. Run the FitToLand macro using the button.
   g. Preview the worksheet, and verify that it is in landscape view.
   h. Add your name to the Sheet3 footer, then save the workbook.
   i. Close the workbook, exit Excel without saving the FitToLand macro in the
      Personal Macro Workbook, then submit your workbook to your instructor.

FIGURE I-22

◢	A	B	C
1	Button Test		
2			
3			
4			
5			
6			
7		Landscape	
8			
9			

Independent Challenge 1

As a computer-support employee of Smith and Jones Consulting Group, you need to develop ways to help your fellow
employees work more efficiently. Employees have asked for Excel macros that can do the following:
- Adjust the column widths to display all column data in a worksheet.
- Place the company name of Smith and Jones Consulting Group in the header of a worksheet.

Independent Challenge 1 (continued)

a. Plan and write the steps necessary for each macro.

b. Start Excel, open the Data File EX I-1.xlsx from the drive and folder where you store your Data Files, then save it as a macro-enabled workbook called **EX I-Consulting**.

c. Check your macro security on the Developer tab to be sure that macros are enabled.

d. Create a macro named **ColumnFit**, save it in the EX I-Consulting.xlsm workbook, assign the ColumnFit macro a shortcut key combination of [Ctrl][Shift][C], and add your name in the description area for the macro. Record the macro using the following instructions:

   • Record the ColumnFit macro to adjust a worksheet's column widths to display all data. (*Hint*: Select the entire sheet, click the Home tab, click the Format button in the Cells group, select AutoFit Column Width, then click cell A1 to deselect the worksheet.)

   • End the macro recording.

e. Format the widths of columns A through G to 8.43, then test the ColumnFit macro with the shortcut key combination [Ctrl][Shift][C].

f. Create a macro named **CompanyName**, and save it in the EX I-Consulting.xlsm workbook. Assign the macro a shortcut key combination of [Ctrl][Shift][D], and add your name in the description area for the macro.

g. Record the CompanyName macro. The macro should place the company name of Smith and Jones Consulting Group in the center section of the worksheet header.

FIGURE I-23

h. Enter **CompanyName test data** in cell A1 of Sheet2, and test the CompanyName macro using the shortcut key combination [Ctrl][Shift][D]. Preview Sheet2 to view the header.

i. Edit the CompanyName macro in the Visual Basic Editor to change the company name from Smith and Jones Consulting Group to **Smith Consulting Group**. Close the Visual Basic Editor and return to Excel.

j. Add a rectangle button to the Sheet3 in the range A6:B7. Label the button with the text **Company Name**.

k. Assign the CompanyName macro to the button.

l. Enter **New CompanyName Test** in cell A1. Use the button to run the CompanyName macro. Preview the worksheet checking the header to be sure it is displaying the new company name. Compare your screen to Figure I-23.

Advanced Challenge Exercise

   ■ Format the button using the fill color of your choice. (*Hint*: Right-click the button and select Format Shape from the shortcut menu.)

   ■ Format the button to add the 3-D effect of your choice.

   ■ Add a shadow in the color of your choice to the button.

m. Enter your name in the footers of all three worksheets. Save the workbook, close the workbook, then submit the workbook to your instructor and exit Excel.

Independent Challenge 2

You are an assistant to the VP of Sales at American Beverage Company, a distributor of juices, water, and soda to supermarkets. As part of your work, you create spreadsheets with sales projections for different regions of the company. You frequently have to change the print settings so that workbooks print in landscape orientation with custom margins of 1" on the top and bottom. You also add a header with the company name on every worksheet. You have decided that it's time to create a macro to streamline this process.

a. Plan and write the steps necessary to create the macro.

b. Check your macro security settings to confirm that macros are enabled.

Independent Challenge 2 (continued)

c. Start Excel, create a new workbook, then save it as a macro-enabled file named **EX I-Sales Macro** in the drive and folder where you store your Data Files.

d. Create a macro that changes the page orientation to landscape, adds custom margins of 1" on the top and bottom of the page, adds a header of **American Beverage Company** in the center section formatted as Bold with a font size of 14 points. Name the macro **Format**, add your name in the description, assign it the shortcut key combination [Ctrl][Shift][W], and store it in the current workbook.

e. Go to Sheet2 and enter the text **Format Test** in cell A1. Test the macro using the shortcut key combination of [Ctrl][Shift][W]. Preview Sheet2 to check the page orientation, margins, and the header.

f. Enter the text **Format Test** in cell A1 of Sheet3, add a rectangular button with the text Format Worksheet to run the Format macro, then test the macro using the button.

g. Preview the Visual Basic code for the macro.

h. Save the workbook, close the workbook, exit Excel, then submit the workbook to your instructor.

Independent Challenge 3

You are the eastern region sales manager of Bio Pharma, a biotech consulting firm. You manage the California operations and frequently create workbooks with data from the office locations. It's tedious to change the tab names and colors every time you open a new workbook, so you decide to create a macro that will add the office locations and colors to your three default worksheet tabs, as shown in Figure I-24.

FIGURE I-24

a. Plan and write the steps to create the macro described above.

b. Start Excel and open a new workbook.

c. Create the macro using the plan you created in Step a, name it **SheetFormat**, assign it the shortcut key combination [Ctrl][Shift][Z], store it in the Personal Macro Workbook, and add your name in the description area.

d. After recording the macro, close the workbook without saving it.

e. Open a new workbook, then save it as a macro-enabled workbook named **EX I-Office Test** in the drive and folder where you store your Data Files. Use the shortcut key combination of [Ctrl][Shift][Z] to test the macro in the new workbook.

f. Unhide the PERSONAL.XLSB workbook. (*Hint*: Click the View tab, click the Unhide button in the Window group, then click PERSONAL.XLSB.)

g. Edit the SheetFormat macro using Figure I-25 as a guide, changing the San Diego sheet name to Berkeley. (*Hint*: There are three instances of San Diego that need to be changed.)

FIGURE I-25

```
Sub SheetFormat()
'
' SheetFormat Macro
' Your Name
'
' Keyboard Shortcut: Ctrl+Shift+Z
'
    Sheets("Sheet1").Select
    Sheets("Sheet1").Name = "San Francisco"
    Sheets("San Francisco").Select
    With ActiveWorkbook.Sheets("San Francisco").Tab
        .Color = 12611584
        .TintAndShade = 0
    End With
    Sheets("Sheet2").Select
    Sheets("Sheet2").Name = "Los Angeles"
    Sheets("Los Angeles").Select
    With ActiveWorkbook.Sheets("Los Angeles").Tab
        .Color = 65535
        .TintAndShade = 0
    End With
    Sheets("Sheet3").Select
    Sheets("Sheet3").Name = "Berkeley"
    Sheets("Berkeley").Select
    With ActiveWorkbook.Sheets("Berkeley").Tab
        .Color = 10498160
        .TintAndShade = 0
    End With
End Sub
```

Independent Challenge 3 (continued)

h. Open a new workbook, then save it as a macro-enabled workbook named **EX I-Office Test New** in the drive and folder where you store your Data Files. Test the edited macro using the shortcut key combination of [Ctrl][Shift][Z].

i. Add a new sheet in the workbook, and name it **Code**. Copy the SheetFormat macro code from the Personal Macro Workbook, and paste it in the Code sheet beginning in cell A1. Save the workbook, close the workbook, then submit the EX I-Office Test New workbook to your instructor.

j. Hide the PERSONAL.XLSB workbook. (*Hint*: With the PERSONAL.XLSB workbook active, click the View tab, then click the Hide button in the Window group.)

k. Close the workbook, click No to save the PERSONAL.XLSB changes, then exit Excel.

Real Life Independent Challenge

Excel can be a helpful tool in keeping track of hours worked at a job or on a project. A macro can speed up the repetitive process of entering a formula to total your hours each week.

a. Start Excel, create a new workbook, then save it as **EX I-Hours** in the drive and folder where you store your Data Files. Be sure to save it as a macro-enabled file.

b. If necessary, change your security settings to enable macros.

c. Use Table I-2 as a guide in entering labels and hours into a worksheet tracking your work or project effort.

d. Create a macro named **TotalHours** in the cell adjacent to the Total label that can be activated by the [Ctrl][Shift][T] key combination. Save the macro in the EX I-Hours workbook, and add your name in the description area.

e. The TotalHours macro should do the following:
- Total the hours for the week.
- Boldface the Total amount and the Total label to its left.

f. Test the macro using the key combination [Ctrl][Shift][T].

g. Add a button to the range A11:B12 with the label **Total**.

h. Assign the TotalHours macro to the Total button.

i. Test the macro using the button.

j. Enter your name in the footer, then save your workbook.

k. Open the macro in the Visual Basic Editor, and preview the macro code.

TABLE I-2

Monday	5
Tuesday	8
Wednesday	5
Thursday	8
Friday	9
Saturday	5
Sunday	0
Total	

Advanced Challenge Exercise

- Edit the macro code to add a comment with a description of your work or project.
- Add another comment with your e-mail address.
- Above the keyboard comment enter the comment **Macro can be run using the Total button**.

l. Return to Excel, save and close the workbook, exit Excel, then submit the workbook to your instructor.

Visual Workshop

Start Excel, open the Data File EX I-2.xlsx from the drive and folder where you store your Data Files, then save it as a macro-enabled workbook called **EX I-Payroll**. Create a macro with the name **TotalHours** in the EX I-Payroll workbook that does the following:

- Totals the weekly hours for each employee by totaling the hours for the first employee and copying that formula for the other employees
- Adds a row at the top of the worksheet and inserts a label of **Hours** in a font size of 14 point, centered across all columns
- Adds your name in the worksheet footer

Compare your macro results to Figure I-26. Test the macro, edit the macro code as necessary, then save the workbook. Submit the workbook to your instructor.

FIGURE I-26

	A	B	C	D	E	F	G	H	I	J
1				Hours						
2		Monday	Tuesday	Wednesday	Thursday	Friday	Saturday	Sunday	Total	
3	Mary Jones	8	2	8	8	2	2	0	30	
4	Jack McKay	4	8	7	8	8	5	1	41	
5	Keith Drudge	5	4	6	5	4	4	0	28	
6	Sean Lavin	7	6	5	6	6	2	2	34	
7	Kerry Baker	9	6	8	7	6	6	0	42	
8	Justin Regan	6	3	6	3	3	7	0	28	
9	Carol Hodge	7	5	2	6	8	5	3	36	
10	Rick Thomas	2	7	8	6	7	2	0	32	
11	Kris Young	0	4	4	4	4	4	1	21	
12	Lisa Russell	7	8	2	8	8	1	0	34	
13										

UNIT
J
Excel 2010

Enhancing Charts

Files You Will Need:

EX J-1.xlsx
EX J-2.xlsx
EX J-3.xlsx
EX J-4.xlsx
EX J-5.xlsx
EX J-6.xlsx
chartlogo.gif
cookie.gif
golfball.gif

Although Excel offers a variety of eye-catching chart types, you can customize your charts for even greater impact. In this unit, you learn to enhance your charts by manipulating chart data, formatting axes, and rotating the chart. You clarify your data display by adding a data table, special text effects, and a picture. You also show trends in data using sparklines and trendlines. As you enhance your charts, keep in mind that too much customization can be distracting. Your goal in enhancing charts should be to communicate your data more clearly and accurately. Quest's vice president of sales, Kate Morgan, has requested charts comparing sales in the Quest regions over the first two quarters. You will produce these charts and enhance them to improve their appearance and make the worksheet data more accessible.

OBJECTIVES

Customize a data series

Change a data source and add data labels

Format the axes of a chart

Add a data table to a chart

Rotate a chart

Enhance a chart with WordArt and pictures

Add sparklines to a worksheet

Identify data trends

Customizing a Data Series

A **data series** is the sequence of values that Excel uses to **plot**, or create, a chart. You can format the data series in a chart to make the chart more attractive and easier to read. As with other Excel elements, you can change the data series borders, patterns, or colors. ░░░░░ Kate wants you to create a chart showing the sales for each region in January and February. You begin by creating a column chart, which you will customize to make it easier to compare the sales for each region.

STEPS

1. **Start Excel, open the file EX J-1.xlsx from the drive and folder where you store your Data Files, then save it as EX J-Region Sales**

   To begin, Kate wants to see how each region performed over January and February. The first step is to select the data you want to appear in the chart. In this case, you want the row labels in cells A3:A6 and the data for January and February in cells B2:C6, including the column labels.

2. **Select the range A2:C6**

TROUBLE

If your chart over-laps the worksheet data, you can drag its edge to move it below row 6.

3. **Click the Insert tab, click the Column button in the Charts group, then click the 3-D Clustered Column chart (the first chart in the 3-D Column group)**

   The column chart compares the January and February sales for each branch, as shown in Figure J-1. You decide to display the data so that it is easier to compare the monthly sales for each branch.

4. **Click the Switch Row/Column button in the Data group**

   The legend now contains the region data, and the horizontal axis groups the bars by month. Kate can now easily compare the branch sales for each month. The graph will be easier to read if the U.S. data series is plotted in a color that is easier to distinguish.

QUICK TIP

You can also format a data series by click-ing the data series on the chart, clicking the Chart Tools Layout tab, then clicking the Format Selection button in the Current Selec-tion group.

5. **Right-click the Jan U.S. data series bar (the far-left bar on the graph), click Format Data Series from the shortcut menu, click Fill in the left pane of the Format Data Series dialog box, click the Solid fill option button, click the Color list arrow, select Purple, Accent 6 in the Theme Colors group, then click Close**

6. **Point to the edge of the chart, then drag the chart to place its upper-left corner in cell A8**

   You can resize a chart by dragging its corner sizing handles. When a chart is resized this way, all of the elements are resized to maintain its appearance.

7. **Drag the chart's lower-right sizing handle to fit the chart in the range A8:H23, then compare your chart to Figure J-2**

8. **Save the workbook**

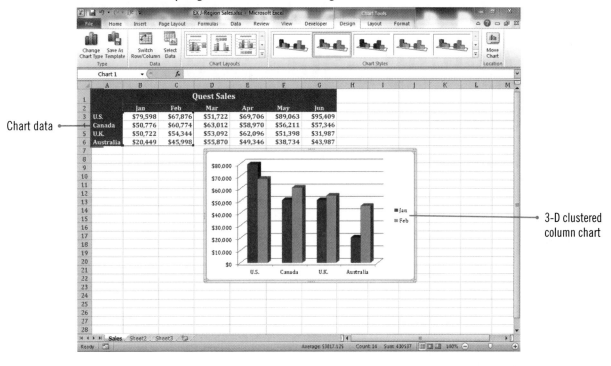

Chart data

3-D clustered column chart

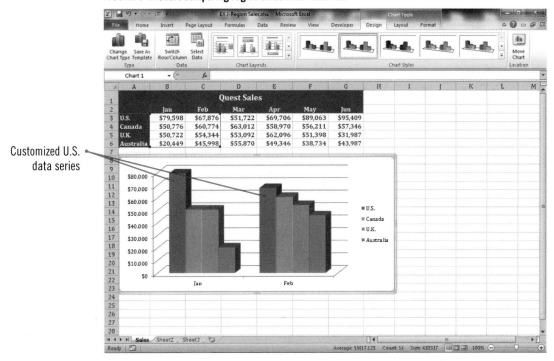

Customized U.S. data series

Adding width and depth to data series

You can change the gap depth and the gap width in 3-D bar or column charts by right-clicking one of the data series of the chart then clicking Format Data Series from the shortcut menu. With Series Options selected in the left pane of the Format Data Series dialog box, you can move the Gap Depth and Gap Width sliders from No Gap (or 0%) to Large Gap (or 500%). Increasing the gap width adds space between each set of data on the chart by increasing the width of the chart's data series. Increasing the gap depth adds depth to all categories of data.

Excel 2010

Changing a Data Source and Adding Data Labels

As you update your workbooks with new data, you may also need to add data series to (or delete them from) a chart. Excel makes it easy to revise a chart's data source and to rearrange chart data. To communicate chart data more clearly, you can add descriptive text, called a **data label**, which appears above a data marker in a chart. Kate wants you to create a chart showing the branch sales for the first quarter. You need to add the March data to your chart so that it reflects the first-quarter sales. Kate asks you to add data labels to clarify the charted data and to make the chart more attractive. It will be easier to compare the branch sales in a 3-D column chart that is not clustered.

STEPS

1. **Click the Chart Tools Design tab if necessary, click the Change Chart Type button in the Type group, in the Change Chart Type dialog box click 3-D Column (the last chart in the first row), then click OK**

   The chart bars are no longer clustered. You want to change the data view to compare branch sales for each month in the new chart type.

2. **Click the Switch Row/Column button in the Data group**

   The labels that were in the legend are now on the horizontal axis. You want to add the March data to the chart.

> **QUICK TIP**
> You can also add data to a chart by clicking the Select Data button in the Data group of the Chart Tools Design tab, selecting the new range of cells in the Select Data Source dialog box, then click OK.

3. **Click the edge of the chart to select it if necessary, then drag the lower-right corner of the data border in worksheet cell C6 to the right to include the data in column D**

   The March data series appears on the chart, as shown in Figure J-3. You want to make the columns more attractive and decide to use one of the preformatted chart styles.

4. **Click the More button ⊽ in the Chart Styles group, then click Style 26**

   The January data bars are now a maroon color, and all of the data bars have shadows. You want to add data labels to your chart indicating the exact amount of sales each bar represents.

> **QUICK TIP**
> You can also add data labels by clicking the Chart Tools Design tab, clicking the More button in the Chart Layouts group, and selecting a chart layout with data labels.

5. **Click the Chart Tools Layout tab, click the Data Labels button in the Labels group, click More Data Label Options, then drag the dialog box to the right of the chart**

   Data labels on the chart show the exact value of each data point above each bar. The data labels are hard to read against the dark shadows of the columns. You decide to add a white background fill to the labels.

6. **With the Jan data labels selected, click Fill in the Format Data Labels dialog box, click the Solid fill option button to select it, click the Color list arrow, then click White, Background1 (the first theme color)**

   The January data labels now have a white background.

7. **Click one of the Feb data labels on the chart, click Fill in the Format Data labels dialog box, click the Solid fill option button, click one of the Mar data labels on the chart, click Fill in the Format Data labels dialog box, click the Solid fill option button, then click Close**

   The data labels are still difficult to read because they are crowded together. You decide to resize the chart to add space between the columns.

8. **Drag the chart's lower-right sizing handle to fit the chart in the range A8:L30, then compare your chart to Figure J-4**

FIGURE J-3: Chart with March data series added

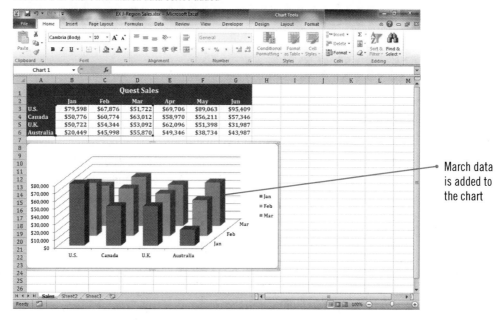

March data
is added to
the chart

FIGURE J-4: Chart with data labels

U.S. data
labels

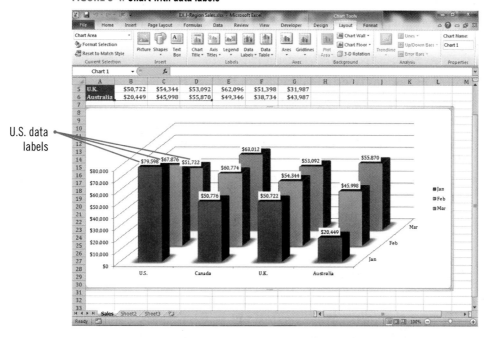

Moving, removing, and formatting legends

To change the position of a legend or to remove it, click the Chart Tools Layout tab, click the Legend button in the Labels group, then select the desired legend position or select None to remove the legend. To format a legend's position, fill, border color and style, or shadows, click More Legend Options at the bottom of the Legend menu. You can add textured fills or pictures and customize the border and shadow characteristics. If you position the Format Legend dialog box next to the legend, you can use the Excel Live Preview feature to try out different effects, such as those shown in Figure J-5. To change a legend's font size, right-click the legend text, click Font on the shortcut menu, then adjust the font size in the Font dialog box. You can also drag a legend to any location.

FIGURE J-5: Formatted legend

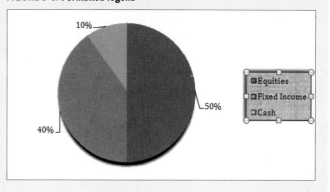

Formatting the Axes of a Chart

Excel plots and formats chart data and places the chart axes within the chart's **plot area**. Data values in two-dimensional charts are plotted on the vertical y-axis (often called the **value axis** because it usually shows value levels). Categories are plotted on the horizontal x-axis (often called the **category axis** because it usually shows data categories). Excel creates a scale for the value (*y*) axis based on the highest and lowest values in the series and places intervals along the scale. A three-dimensional (3-D) chart, like the one in Figure J-6, has a third axis displaying the chart's depth. You can override the Excel default formats for chart axes at any time by using the Format Axis dialog box. ▰▰▰▰ Kate asks you to increase the maximum number on the value axis and change the axis number format. She would also like you to add axes titles to explain the plotted data.

STEPS

1. **Click the chart to select it if necessary, click the** Chart Tools Layout tab, **click the** Axes **button in the Axes group, point to** Primary Vertical Axis, **then click** More Primary Vertical Axis Options

    The Format Axis dialog box opens. The minimum, maximum, and unit Axis Options are set to Auto, and the default scale settings appear in the text boxes on the right. You can override any of these settings by clicking the Fixed option buttons and entering new values.

2. **With Axis Options selected in the list on the left, click the** Fixed option button **in the Maximum line, press [Tab], in the Fixed text box type** 90000, **then click** Close

    Now 90,000 appears as the maximum value on the value axis, and the chart bar heights adjust to reflect the new value. Next, you want the vertical axis values to appear without additional zeroes to make the chart data easier to read.

3. **Click the** Axes button **in the Axes group, point to** Primary Vertical Axis, **then click** Show Axis in Thousands

    The values are reduced to two digits and the word "Thousands" appears in a text box to the left of the values. You decide that vertical and horizontal axis titles would improve the clarity of the chart information.

4. **Click the** Axis Titles button **in the Labels group, point to** Primary Vertical Axis Title, **then click** Rotated Title

    A text box containing the text "Axis Title" appears on the vertical axis, next to "Thousands".

5. **Type** Sales, **then click outside the text box to deselect it**

    The word "Sales" appears in the Vertical axis label. You decide to label the horizontal axis.

6. **Click the** Axis Titles button **in the Labels group, point to** Primary Horizontal Axis Title, **click** Title Below Axis, **type** Regions, **then click outside the text box to deselect it**

7. **Drag the** Thousands text box **on the vertical axis lower in the Chart Area to match Figure J-7, then deselect it**

FIGURE J-6: Chart elements in a 3-D chart

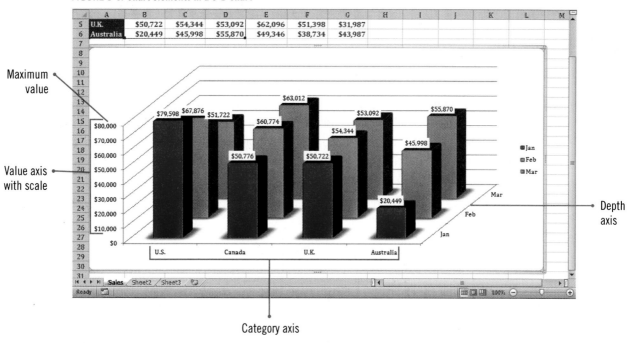

Maximum value

Value axis with scale

Depth axis

Category axis

FIGURE J-7: Chart with formatted axes

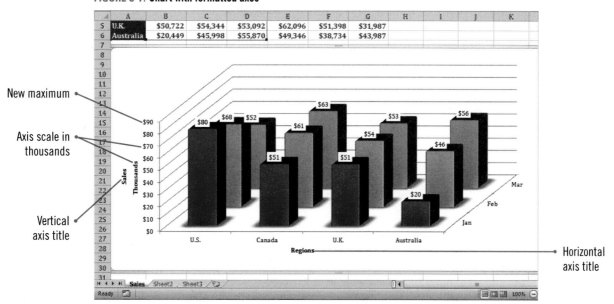

New maximum

Axis scale in thousands

Vertical axis title

Horizontal axis title

Adding a Data Table to a Chart

A **data table** is a grid containing the chart data, attached to the bottom of a chart. Data tables are useful because they display—directly on the chart itself—the data you used to generate a chart. It's good practice to add data tables to charts that are stored separately from worksheet data. You can display data tables in line, area, column, and bar charts, and print them automatically along with a chart. Kate wants you to move the chart to its own worksheet and add a data table to emphasize the chart's first-quarter data.

STEPS

1. **Click the chart object to select it if necessary, click the Chart Tools Design tab, then click the Move Chart button in the Location group**
   The Move Chart dialog box opens. You want to place the chart on a new sheet named First Quarter.

2. **Click the New sheet option button, type First Quarter in the New sheet text box, then click OK**

QUICK TIP
You can also add a data table by clicking the Chart Tools Design tab, and selecting a chart with a data table from the Chart Layouts gallery.

3. **Click the Chart Tools Layout tab, click the Data Table button in the Labels group, then click Show Data Table with Legend Keys**
   A data table with the first-quarter data and a key to the legend appears at the bottom of the chart, as shown in Figure J-8. The data table would stand out more if it were formatted.

4. **Click the Data Table button in the Labels group, then click More Data Table Options**
   The Format Data Table dialog box opens.

QUICK TIP
To hide a data table, click the Data Table button in the Labels group, then click None.

5. **Click Border Color in the left pane, click the Solid line option button to select it, click the Color list arrow, click the Orange, Accent2 color in the Theme Colors section, click Close, then click the chart area to deselect the data table**
   The data table now has orange borders. The left side of the data table contains legend keys, showing which series each color represents, so you don't need the legend that appears on the right of the chart.

QUICK TIP
You can also remove a legend by clicking the Legend button in the Labels group of the Chart Tools Layout tab and clicking None.

6. **Click the legend to select it, then press [Delete]**
   Now the only legend for the chart is part of the data table, as shown in Figure J-9.

7. **Save the workbook**

FIGURE J-8: **Chart with data table**

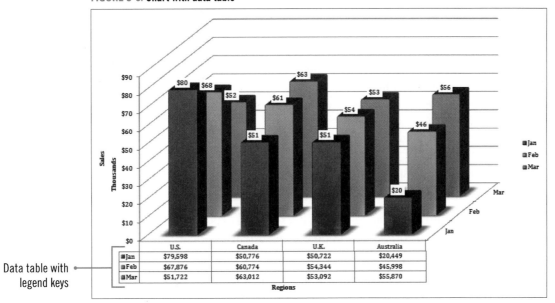

Data table with legend keys

	U.S.	Canada	U.K.	Australia
▣ Jan	$79,598	$50,776	$50,722	$20,449
▣ Feb	$67,876	$60,774	$54,344	$45,998
▣ Mar	$51,722	$63,012	$53,092	$55,870

Regions

FIGURE J-9: **Chart with formatted data table**

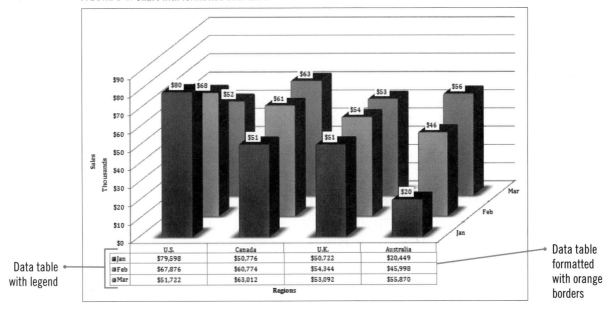

Data table with legend

Data table formatted with orange borders

	U.S.	Canada	U.K.	Australia
▣ Jan	$79,598	$50,776	$50,722	$20,449
▣ Feb	$67,876	$60,774	$54,344	$45,998
▣ Mar	$51,722	$63,012	$53,092	$55,870

Regions

Using the Modeless Format dialog box

Many of the buttons on the Chart Tools Layout tab have a More ...Options command at the bottom of the menu that appears when you click them. For example, clicking the Data Table button allows you to click More Data Table Options. The Format dialog box that opens when you click it allows you to format the selected data table. But while the dialog box is open, you can also click and format other elements. The Format dialog boxes are **modeless,** which means that when they are open, you can click on other chart elements and then change their formatting in the same dialog box, whose options adjust to reflect the selected element. You are not restricted to changing only one object—you are not in a single **mode** or limited set of possible choices. For example if the Format Data Table dialog box is open and you click a data label, the dialog box changes to Format Data Labels. If you click the legend, the dialog box becomes the Format Legend dialog box, allowing you to modify the legend characteristics.

Rotating a Chart

Three-dimensional (3-D) charts do not always display data in the most effective way. In many cases, one or more of a chart's data points can obscure the view of other data points, making the chart difficult to read. By rotating and/or changing the chart's depth, you can make the data easier to understand. Kate wants you to rotate the chart and increase the depth. You will begin by hiding the data table so it doesn't overlap the view of the data.

STEPS

1. **Click the chart to select it if necessary, click the** Chart Tools Layout tab**, click the** Data Table **button in the Labels group, then click** None

2. **Click the** 3-D Rotation button **in the Background group, then if necessary click** 3-D Rotation **in the list on the left pane of the Format Chart Area dialog box**

   The 3-D rotation options are shown in Figure J-10.

3. **In the Chart Scale section, click the** Right Angle Axes **check box to deselect it, double-click the** X: text box **in the Rotation section, then enter** 50

   The X: Rotation setting rotates the chart to the left and right. You can also click the Left and Right buttons or the up and down arrows to rotate the chart.

QUICK TIP
You can also click the Up and Down buttons in the Rotation area of the dialog box to rotate the chart up and down.

4. **Double-click the** Y: text box**, then enter** 30

   The Y: Rotation setting rotates the chart up and down. You decide to change the depth of the columns.

5. **Double-click the** Depth (% of base) text box **in the Chart Scale section, then enter** 200**, then click** Close

   Deleting the data table removed the legend so you decide to add a legend to the chart. Also, the axes titles need to be adjusted for the new chart layout.

6. **Click the** Legend button **in the Labels group, click** Show Legend at Bottom**, right-click the text** Sales **in the vertical axis title, click the** Font Size list arrow **in the Mini toolbar, then click** 18

   The vertical axis label is now easier to read. You will format the horizontal axis similarly.

7. **Right-click the text** Regions **in the horizontal axis title, click the** Font Size list arrow **in the Mini toolbar, click** 18**, then drag the Regions title closer to the horizontal axis**

8. **Right-click the text** Thousands **in the vertical axis display units label, click the** Font Size list arrow **in the Mini toolbar, click** 14**, drag the Thousands title closer to the vertical axis, drag the Sales title to the left of the Thousands title, then compare your chart to Figure J-11.**

   The chart columns now appear deeper and less crowded, with labels positioned in the correct place, making the chart easier to read.

9. **Save the workbook**

Making 3-D charts easier to read

In addition to rotating a chart, there are other ways to view smaller data points that may be obscured by larger data markers in the front of a 3-D chart. To reverse the order in which the data series are charted, you can click the Axes button in the Axes group of the Chart Tools Layout tab, point to Depth Axis, click More Depth Axis Options, click the Series in reverse order check box in the Format Axis dialog box to select it, then click Close. Another way to see smaller data series in the back of a 3-D chart is to add transparency to the large data markers in the front of the chart. To do this, right-click the data series that you want to make transparent, click Format Data Series on the shortcut menu, click Fill in the Format Data Series dialog box, click either the Solid fill or Gradient fill option buttons, move the slider on the Transparency bar to a percentage that allows you to see the other data series on the chart, then click Close. If you have a picture on the chart's back wall, adding transparency to the series in front of it makes more of the picture visible.

FIGURE J-10: **3-D Rotation options**

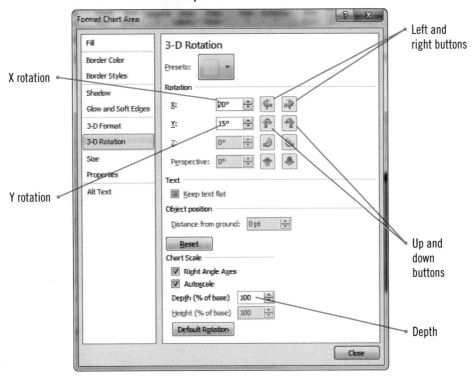

X rotation

Y rotation

Left and right buttons

Up and down buttons

Depth

FIGURE J-11: **Chart with increased depth and rotation**

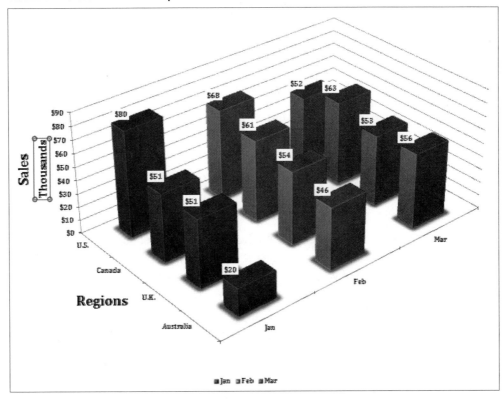

Charting data accurately

The purpose of a chart is to help viewers to interpret the worksheet data. When creating charts, you need to make sure that your chart accurately portrays your data. Charts can sometimes misrepresent data and thus mislead people. For example, you can change the y-axis units or its starting value to make charted sales values appear larger than they are. Even though you may have correctly labeled the sales values on the chart, the height of the data points will lead people viewing the chart to think the sales are higher than the labeled values. So use caution when you modify charts to make sure you accurately represent your data.

Enhancing a Chart with WordArt and Pictures

You can enhance your chart or worksheet titles using **WordArt**, which is preformatted text. Once you've added WordArt text, you can edit or format it by adding 3-D effects and shadows. WordArt text is a shape rather than text. This means that you cannot treat WordArt objects as if they were labels entered in a cell; that is, you cannot sort, use the spell checker, or use their cell references in formulas. You can further enhance your chart by adding a picture to one of the chart elements. Kate wants you to add a WordArt title to the first-quarter chart. She also wants you to add the Quest logo to the chart. You will begin by adding a title to the chart.

STEPS

QUICK TIP

To delete a chart title, right-click it, then select Delete from the shortcut menu. You can also select the chart title and press [Delete].

1. **Click the chart to select it if necessary, click the Chart Tools Layout tab, click the Chart Title button in the Labels group, then click Above Chart**

   A chart title text box appears above the chart.

2. **With the Chart Title text box selected, type First Quarter Sales, then click the Enter button ✓ on the Formula Bar**

3. **Click the Chart Tools Format tab, then click the More button ⊽ in the WordArt Styles group**

   The WordArt Gallery opens, as shown in Figure J-12. This is where you select the style for your text.

4. **Click Fill – White, Outline – Accent 1 (the fourth style in the first row), then click outside the chart title to deselect it**

   The title text becomes formatted with outlined letters. You decide the chart would look better if the gridlines were not visible.

5. **Click the Chart Tools Layout tab, click the Gridlines button in the Axes group, click Primary Horizontal Gridlines, then click None**

   Kate wants you to add the Quest logo to the back wall of the chart to identify the company data.

QUICK TIP

You can also enhance a chart by adding a picture to the data markers, chart area, plot area, legend, or chart floor.

6. **Click the chart to select it if necessary, click the Chart Tools Format tab, click the Chart Elements list arrow in the Current Selection group, then click Back Wall**

   The back wall of the chart is selected, as shown by the four small circles on its corners.

7. **Click the Format Selection button in the Current Selection group, click the Picture or texture fill option button to select it in the Format Wall dialog box, click File, navigate to the location where you store your Data Files, click the chartlogo.gif file, click Insert, then click Close**

8. **Click the Insert tab, click the Header & Footer button in the Text group, click the Custom Footer button, enter your name in the Center section, click OK, then click OK again**

   The Quest logo appears on the back wall of the chart. Compare your chart to Figure J-13.

Adding WordArt to a worksheet

You can use WordArt to add interest to the text on a worksheet. To insert WordArt, click the Insert tab, click the WordArt button in the Text group, choose a WordArt Style from the gallery, then replace the WordArt text "Your Text Here" with your text. You can use the Text Fill list arrow in the WordArt Styles group to add a solid, picture, gradient, or texture fill to your text. The Text Outline list arrow in the WordArt Styles group allows you to add color, weight, and dashes to the text outline. You can use the Text Effects button in the WordArt Styles group to add shadows, reflections, glows, bevels, 3-D rotations, and transformations to the WordArt text.

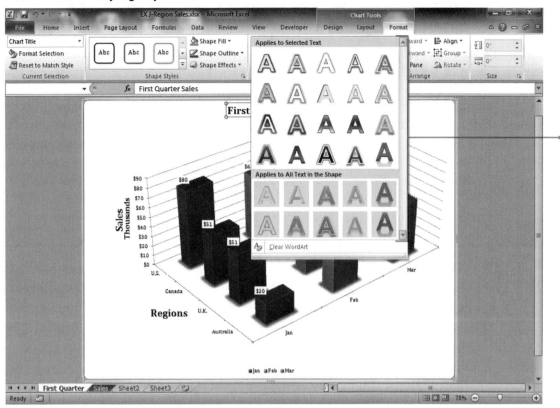

Select
style
from the
gallery

FIGURE J-13: **Chart with WordArt title**

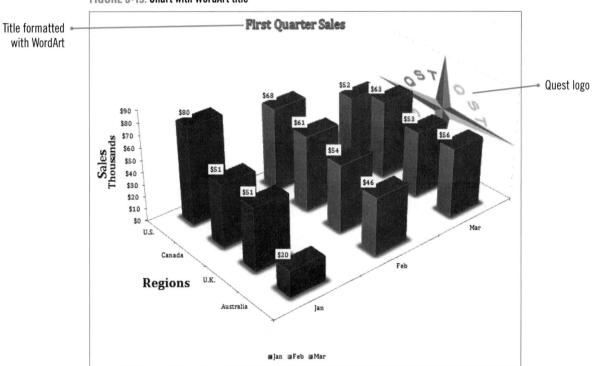

Title formatted
with WordArt

First Quarter Sales

Quest logo

Rotating chart labels

You can rotate the category labels on a chart so that longer labels won't appear crowded. Select the Category Axis on the chart, click the Chart Tools Format tab, click the Format Selection button in the Current Selection group, click Alignment in the left pane of the dialog box, click the Text direction list arrow, then select the rotation option for the labels. Rotating labels works best in two-dimensional charts because labels on three-dimensional charts often overlap as they are moved. You can also select a custom angle for horizontally aligned axis labels on two-dimensional charts.

Adding Sparklines to a Worksheet

You can enhance your worksheets by adding sparklines to the worksheet cells. **Sparklines** are miniature charts that show data trends in a worksheet range such as sales increases or decreases. Sparklines are also used to highlight maximum and minimum values in a range of data. Sparklines usually appear close to the data they represent. Any changes that you make to a worksheet are reflected in the sparklines that represent the data. After you add sparklines to a worksheet, you can change the sparkline and color. You can also format high and low data points in special colors. Kate wants you to add sparklines to the Sales worksheet to illustrate the sales trends for the first half of the year.

STEPS

1. **Click the Sales sheet, click cell H3 to select it, click the Insert tab if necessary, click Line in the Sparklines group, verify that the insertion point is in the Data Range text box, select the range B3:G3 on the worksheet, then click OK**

    A sparkline showing the sales trend for the U.S. appears in cell H3. You can copy the sparkline to cells representing other regions.

2. **With cell H3 selected, drag the fill handle to fill the range H4:H6**

    The sparklines for all four regions are shown in Figure J-14. You decide to change the sparklines to columns.

3. **Click cell H3, then click the Column button in the Type group of the Sparkline Tools Design tab**

    All of the sparklines in column H appear as columns. The column heights represent the values of the data in the adjacent rows. You want the sparklines to appear in a theme color.

    QUICK TIP
    You can also change the color scheme of your sparklines by choosing a format from the Style gallery on the Sparkline Tools Design tab.

4. **Click the Sparkline Color list arrow in the Style group, then click Indigo Accent 5 from the Theme colors**

    The sparklines match the worksheet format. You want to highlight the high and low months using theme colors.

5. **Click the Marker Color list arrow in the Style group, point to High Point, then select Orange Accent 2 from the Theme Colors**

6. **Click the Marker Color list arrow in the Style group, point to Low Point, select Olive Green Accent 3 from the Theme Colors, then compare your worksheet to Figure J-15**

Creating a chart template

After you create a custom chart with specific formatting, you can save it as a chart template. You can create future charts based on your saved chart templates, and they will reflect your custom formatting. Chart templates have .crtx as their file extension. If you use a custom chart frequently, you can save the template as the default chart type. To save a chart as a chart template, click the Chart Tools Design tab, click Save As Template in the Type group, enter a file-name in the Save Chart Template dialog box, then click Save. Your chart template will be saved in the Microsoft\Templates\Charts folder. When you want to format a chart like your chart template, you need to apply the template. Select your chart, click the Insert tab, click a chart type in the Charts group, click All Chart Types, click the Templates folder in the Change Chart Type dialog box, select a template in the My Templates area, then click OK.

FIGURE J-14: Sales trend sparklines

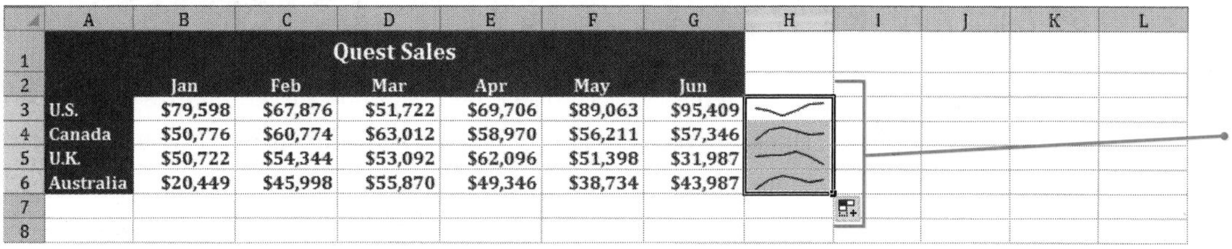

◢	A	B	C	D	E	F	G	H	I	J	K	L
1				Quest Sales								
2		Jan	Feb	Mar	Apr	May	Jun					
3	U.S.	$79,598	$67,876	$51,722	$69,706	$89,063	$95,409					
4	Canada	$50,776	$60,774	$63,012	$58,970	$56,211	$57,346					
5	U.K.	$50,722	$54,344	$53,092	$62,096	$51,398	$31,987					
6	Australia	$20,449	$45,998	$55,870	$49,346	$38,734	$43,987					
7												
8												

Sparklines for all regions

FIGURE J-15: Formatted sparklines

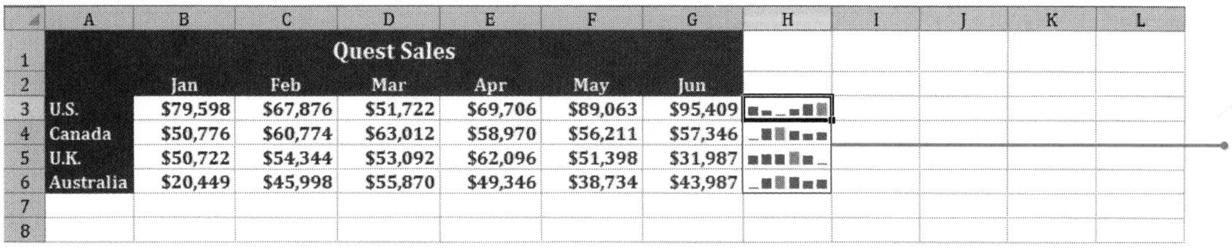

◢	A	B	C	D	E	F	G	H	I	J	K	L
1				Quest Sales								
2		Jan	Feb	Mar	Apr	May	Jun					
3	U.S.	$79,598	$67,876	$51,722	$69,706	$89,063	$95,409					
4	Canada	$50,776	$60,774	$63,012	$58,970	$56,211	$57,346					
5	U.K.	$50,722	$54,344	$53,092	$62,096	$51,398	$31,987					
6	Australia	$20,449	$45,998	$55,870	$49,346	$38,734	$43,987					
7												
8												

Formatted Sparklines

Identifying Data Trends

You often use charts to visually represent data over a period of time. To emphasize patterns in data, you can add trendlines to your charts. A **trendline** is a series of data points on a line that shows data values representing the general direction in a data series. In some business situations, you can use trendlines to predict future data based on past trends. Kate wants you to compare the U.S. and U.K. sales performance over the first two quarters and to project sales for each region in the following 3 months, assuming past trends. You begin by charting the 6-months sales data in a 2-D Column chart.

STEPS

1. **On the Sales sheet select the range A2:G6, click the Insert tab, click the Column button in the Charts group, then click the Clustered Column button (the first chart in the 2-D Column group)**

2. **Drag the chart left until its upper-left corner is at the upper-left corner of cell A8, then drag the middle-right sizing handle right to the border between column G and column H**
   You are ready to add a trendline for the U.S. data series.

3. **Click the U.S. January data point (the far-left column in the chart) to select the U.S. data series, click the Chart Tools Layout tab, click the Trendline button in the Analysis group, then click Linear Trendline**
   A linear trendline identifying U.S. sales trends in the first 6 months is added to the chart, along with an entry in the legend identifying the line. You need to compare the U.S. sales trend with the U.K. sales trend.

4. **Click the U.K. January data point (the third column in the chart) to select the U.K. data series, click the Trendline button, then click Linear Trendline**
   The chart now has two trendlines, making it easy to compare the sales trends of the U.S. and the U.K. branches. Now you want to project the next 3-months sales for the U.S. and U.K. sales branches based on the past 6-month trends.

TROUBLE
If you have trouble selecting the trend-line, you can click the Chart Tools Layout tab, click the Chart Elements list arrow in the Current Selection group, then select Series "U.S." Trendline 1.

5. **Click the U.S. data series trendline, click the Trendline button, then click More Trendline Options**
   The Format Trendline dialog box opens, as shown in Figure J-16.

6. **In the Forecast section, enter 3 in the Forward text box, click Close, click the U.K. data series trendline, click the Trendline button, click More Trendline Options, enter 3 in the Forward text box, then click Close**
   The trendlines project an additional 3 months, predicting the future sales trends for the U.S. and U.K. regions, assuming that past trends continue. The two trendlines look identical, so you decide to format them.

7. **Click the U.S. data series trendline, click the Trendline button, click More Trendline Options, click the Custom option button in the Trendline Name section, then type U.S. Trends in the Custom text box**

8. **Click Line Color in the left pane of the dialog box, click the Solid line option button, click the Color list arrow, select Red in the Standard colors section, click Line Style in the left pane, click the Dash type list arrow, select the Dash option, then click Close**
   The U.S. data series trendline is now a red dashed line and is clearly identified in the legend.

9. **Select the U.K. data series trendline, repeat Steps 7 and 8 but use the name U.K. Trends and a Purple dashed line, then click outside the chart and go to cell A1**

10. **Enter your name in the center section of the Sales sheet footer, save the workbook, preview the Sales sheet, close the workbook, submit the workbook to your instructor, then exit Excel**
    The completed worksheet is shown in Figure J-17

FIGURE J-16: **Format Trendline dialog box**

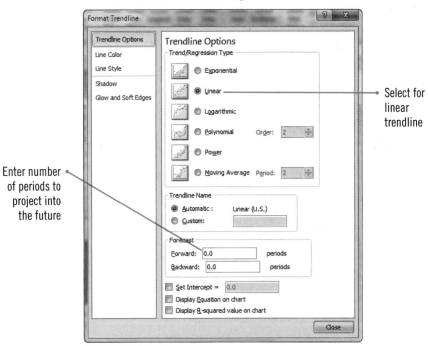

Enter number of periods to project into the future

Select for linear trendline

FIGURE J-17: **Sales chart with trendlines for U.S. and U.K. data**

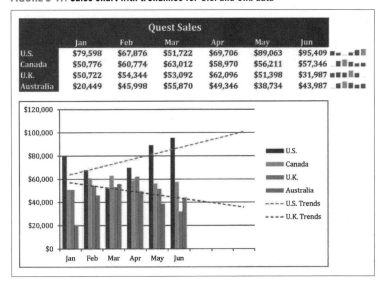

Choosing the right trendline for your chart

Trendlines can help you forecast where your data is headed and understand its past values. This type of data analysis is called **regression analysis** in mathematics. You can choose from four types of trendlines: Linear, Exponential, Linear Forecast, and Two-Period Moving Average. A **linear trendline** is used for data series with data points that have the pattern of a line. An exponential trendline is a curved line that is used when data values increase or decrease quickly. You cannot use an exponential trendline if your data contains negative values. A linear forecast trendline is a linear trendline with a two-period forecast. A two-period moving average smooths out fluctuations in data by averaging the data points.

Practice

For current SAM information, including versions and content details, visit SAM Central (http://www.cengage.com/samcentral). If you have a SAM user profile, you may have access to hands-on instruction, practice, and assessment of the skills covered in this unit. Since various versions of SAM are supported throughout the life of this text, check with your instructor for the correct instructions and URL/Web site for accessing assignments.

Concepts Review

1. Which element points to the vertical axis title?
2. Which element points to the vertical axis?
3. Which element points to the chart title?
4. Which element points to the chart legend?
5. Which element points to a data label?
6. Which element points to the horizontal category axis?

FIGURE J-18

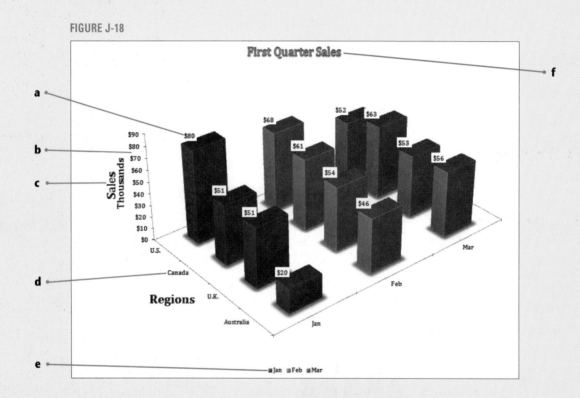

Match each term with the statement that best describes it.

7. Plot area
8. Data series
9. X-axis
10. Sparklines
11. Trendlines

a. Category axis
b. Miniature charts that show data trends
c. Line charts that can be used to predict future data
d. Sequence of values plotted on a chart
e. Location holding data charted on the axes

Select the best answer from the list of choices.

12. **Which of the following is true regarding WordArt?**
    a. WordArt is a shape.
    b. Cell references to WordArt can be used in formulas.
    c. Spelling errors in WordArt can be detected by the spell checker.
    d. Cells containing WordArt can be sorted.

13. **Descriptive text that appears above a data marker is called a:**
    a. Data label.   c. High point.
    b. Data series.   d. Period.

14. **A chart's scale:**
    a. Always has a maximum of 80000.   c. Always has a minimum of 0.
    b. Can be adjusted.   d. Always appears in units of 10.

15. **Which Chart Tools tab is used to format the axes of a chart?**
    a. Layout   c. Insert
    b. Design   d. Format

16. **What is a data table?**
    a. The data used to create a chart, displayed in a grid
    b. A customized data series
    c. A grid with chart data displayed above a chart
    d. A three-dimensional arrangement of data on the y-axis

Skills Review

1. **Customize a data series.**
   a. Start Excel, open the file EX J-2.xlsx from the drive and folder where you save your Data Files, then save it as **EX J-Pastry Sales**.
   b. With the Sales sheet active, select the range A2:D6.
   c. Create a 3-D column chart using the selected data. (*Hint*: Do not choose the 3-D clustered column chart.)
   d. Move and resize the chart to fit in the range A8:G20.
   e. Change the color of the January data series to a light blue color in the Standard Colors group.
   f. Save the workbook.

2. **Change a data source and add data labels.**
   a. Add the April, May, and June data to the chart.
   b. Change the chart view by exchanging the row and column data.
   c. Resize the chart to fill the range A8:J28 to display the new data.
   d. Change the chart view back to show the months in the legend by exchanging the row and column data. Add data labels to your chart. Delete the data labels for all but the June series. (*Hint*: Click one of the data labels in the series, then press [Delete].) Move any June data labels that are difficult to view.
   e. Save the workbook.

3. **Format the axes of a chart.**
   a. Change the vertical axis major unit to 1000. (*Hint*: Use the Format Axis dialog box to set the Major unit to a fixed value of 1000.)
   b. Change the display of the vertical axis values to Thousands, then move the Thousands label lower along the axis so it appears centered between $2 and $4.
   c. Set the value axis maximum to 5000.
   d. Add a horizontal axis title below the chart. Label the axis **Products**.
   e. Move the horizontal axis title so it appears between the Cookies and Brownies axis labels.
   f. Save the workbook.

Skills Review (continued)

4. Add a data table to a chart.

   a. Move the chart to its own sheet named **Sales Chart**.

   b. Add a data table with legend keys.

   c. Move the horizontal axis title up to a location above the data table between the Cookies and Brownies axis labels.

   d. Format the data table to change the border color to the standard color purple.

   e. Save the workbook, then compare your screen to Figure J-19.

5. Rotate a chart.

   a. Remove the data table and adjust the axes titles as necessary.

   b. Set the X: rotation to 70 degrees.

   c. Set the Y: rotation to 20 degrees.

   d. Change the depth to 180% of the base.

   e. Adjust the axes titles. Add a white fill to the June data labels to make them visible. Save the workbook.

6. Enhance a chart with WordArt and pictures.

   a. Add a chart title of **Pastry Sales** to the top of the chart. Format the chart title with WordArt Fill – None, Outline - Accent 2 (the second style on the first line).

   b. Position the new title approximately half way across the top of the chart and closer to the chart.

   c. Select the legend. Format the legend with the picture cookie.gif from the drive and folder where you store your Data Files.

   d. Increase the size of the legend to show the picture of the cookie. Compare your chart to Figure J-20.

   e. Add your name to the chart footer, then save the workbook.

7. Add Sparklines to a worksheet.

   a. On the Sales worksheet, add a Line sparkline to cell H3 that represents the data in the range B3:G3.

   b. Copy the sparkline in cell H3 into the range H4:H6.

   c. Change the sparklines to columns.

   d. Change the Sparkline color to Blue-Gray, Accent 6 (the last color in the top row of Theme colors).

   e. Save the workbook.

8. Identify data trends.

   a. Create a 2-D line chart using the data in the range A2:G6, then move and resize the chart to fit in the range A8:G20.

   b. Add a linear trendline to the Muffins data series.

   c. Change the trendline color to red and the line style to Square Dot.

   d. Set the forward option to six periods to view the future trend, increase the width of the chart to the border between columns J and K, deselect the chart, then compare your screen to Figure J-21.

FIGURE J-19

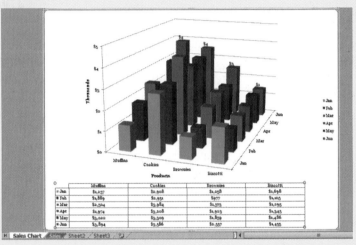

FIGURE J-20

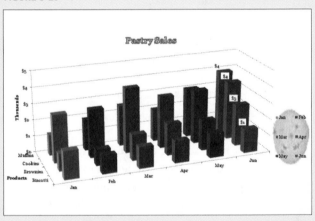

FIGURE J-21

Skills Review (continued)

e. Add your name to the center footer section, save the workbook, preview the worksheet, close the workbook, then submit the workbook to your instructor.

f. Exit Excel.

Independent Challenge 1

You are the assistant to the vice president of marketing at the Metro-West Philharmonic located outside of Boston. The vice president has asked you to chart some information from a recent survey of the Philharmonic's customers. Your administrative assistant has entered the survey data in an Excel worksheet, which you will use to create two charts.

a. Start Excel, open the file titled EX J-3.xlsx from the drive and folder where you store your Data Files, then save it as **EX J-Customer Demographics**.

b. Using the data in A2:B7 of the Education Data worksheet, create a 3-D pie chart (the first chart in the 3-D Pie group) on the worksheet.

c. Move the chart to a separate sheet named **Education Chart**. Format the chart using chart Style 34.

d. Add a title of **Education Data** above the chart. Format the title using WordArt Gradient Fill – Dark Red, Accent 1 (fourth style in the third row). Change the chart title font to a size of 28, and center it over the chart.

e. Add data labels to the outside end of the data points. Format the legend text in a 14-point font. (*Hint*: Use the font options on the Home tab or the Mini toolbar.)

f. Select the Bachelor's degree pie slice by clicking the chart, then clicking the Bachelor's degree slice. Change the slice color to the standard color of Olive Green, Accent 3 from the Theme colors. (*Hint*: On the Chart Tools Format tab, click the Format Selection button in the Current Selection group and use the Format Data Point dialog box.) Compare your chart to Figure J-22.

FIGURE J-22

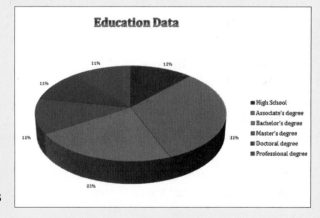

g. On the Income Data worksheet, use the data in A2:B6 to create a standard clustered column (the first chart in the 2-D Column group) chart.

h. Delete the legend. (*Hint*: Select the legend and press [Delete].)

i. Place the chart on a new sheet named **Income Chart**. Format the chart using chart Style 7.

j. Add a chart title of **Income Data** above the chart, and format the title using WordArt Style Gradient Fill - Blue, Accent 4, Reflection.

k. Title the category axis **Income**. Format the category axis title in 18-point bold. (*Hint*: Use the font options on the Home tab or use the Mini toolbar.)

l. Enter your name in the center sections of the footers of the Income Chart and Education Chart sheets.

m. Save the workbook, preview the Income Chart and the Education Chart sheets.

n. Close the workbook, submit the workbook to your instructor, and exit Excel.

Independent Challenge 2   *Homework A10 due Wed. Nov. 13*

You manage the Chicago Athletic Club, which offers memberships for swimming, tennis, and fitness. You also offer a full membership that includes all of the activities at the club. The club owner has asked you to assemble a brief presentation on the membership data over the past 4 years while it has been under your management. You decide to include a chart showing the memberships in each category as well as an analysis of trends in memberships.

a. Start Excel, open the file titled EX J-4.xlsx from the drive and folder where you store your Data Files, then save it as **EX J-Memberships**.

Independent Challenge 2 (continued)

b. Create a clustered bar chart (the first chart in the 2-D Bar group) on the worksheet, comparing the membership enrollments in the four types of memberships. Format the chart using chart Style 7.

c. Change the row and column data so the years are shown in the legend.

d. Add a chart title of **Membership Data** above the chart, and format it using WordArt Style Gradient Fill – Green, Accent 4, Reflection.

e. Add Line sparklines to cells F4:F7 showing the membership trend from 2010 to 2013, moving the chart as necessary.

f. Format the sparklines using Sparkline Style Accent 5 (no dark or light).

g. Add a new membership type of **Family** in row 8 of the worksheet with the following data:

Year	Membership
2010	1445
2011	1877
2012	1925
2013	2557

h. Add the new data to the bar chart. Copy the sparklines into cell F8.

i. Move the chart to a sheet named **Membership Chart**.

j. Add a horizontal axis title of **Number of Memberships**, and format the title in 18-point bold font.

k. Add a data table with legend keys to the chart. Delete the legend on the right side of the chart. Format the data table lines to be displayed in Tan, Accent 6 (the last Theme color in the top row). Compare your chart to Figure J-23.

FIGURE J-23

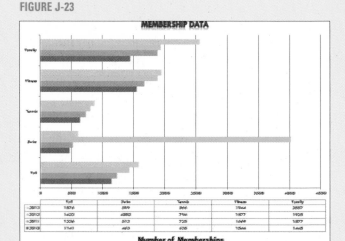

Advanced Challenge Exercise

- Use the Format Data Series dialog box to add a border color of Tan Accent 6, Darker 50% to the bars that represent the year 2010 in the chart.
- Add a top circle bevel of width 10 pt. to the bars that represent the year 2013 in the chart.
- Add a border to the plot area of the chart with the color of Gold, Accent 5.

l. Enter your name in the center section of the Membership Chart sheet footer, save the workbook, then preview the sheet.

m. Close the workbook, submit the workbook to your instructor, then exit Excel.

Independent Challenge 3

You manage the Pine Hills Pro Shop. You meet twice a year with the store owner to discuss store sales trends. You decide to use a chart to represent the sales trends for the department's product categories. You begin by charting the sales for the first 5 months of the year. Then you add data to the chart and analyze the sales trend using a trendline. Lastly, you enhance the chart by adding a data table, titles, and a picture.

a. Start Excel, open the file EX J-5.xlsx from the drive and folder where you store your Data Files, then save the workbook as **EX J-Golf Sales**.

b. Create a 3-D column chart on the worksheet showing the May through July sales information. Move the upper-left corner of the chart to cell A8 on the worksheet.

c. Format the May data series using the color yellow on the standard colors.

d. Add the Aug, Sep, and Oct data to the chart.

e. Move the chart to its own sheet named **May - Oct**.

Independent Challenge 3 (continued)

f. Rotate the chart with an X:Rotation of 40 degrees, a Y Rotation of 50 degrees, a perspective of 15 and the Depth (% of base) of 200.

g. Add a chart title of **May - October Sales** above the chart. Format the chart title using the WordArt Style Gradient Fill – Green, Accent1.

h. Add a rotated title of **Sales** in 20-point bold to the vertical axis.

i. Change the value axis scale to a maximum of **4000**.

j. Insert the golfball.gif picture from the drive and folder where your Data Files are stored into the legend area of the chart. Move the legend lower in the chart area and increase its width. Compare your chart to Figure J-24.

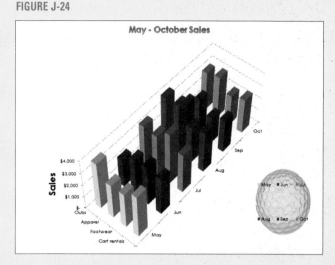

Advanced Challenge Exercise

- Move the legend to the upper-left side of the chart.
- Change the value axis scale to increment by 500.
- Remove the primary horizontal gridlines. Add a gradient fill of your choice to the plot area.

k. Enter your name in the center footer section of the chart sheet, save the workbook, then preview the chart.

l. Close the workbook, submit the workbook to your instructor, then exit Excel.

Real Life Independent Challenge *Do this for class*

This Independent Challenge requires an Internet connection.

Stock charts are used to graph a stock's high, low, and closing prices. You will create a stock chart using 4 weeks of high, low, and close prices for a stock that you are interested in tracking.

a. Start Excel, save a new workbook as **EX J-Stock Chart** in the drive and folder where you store your Data Files.

b. Use your Web browser to research the weekly high, low, and close prices for a stock over the past 4 weeks. (*Hint*: You may need to search for historical prices.)

c. Create a worksheet with the data from your chart. Enter the column labels **Date**, **High**, **Low**, and **Close** in columns A, B, C, and D. In the Date column, enter the Friday dates for the past 4 weeks starting with the oldest date. In columns B, C, and D, enter the high, low, and closing prices for your stock. Apply a document theme and formatting of your choice.

d. Create a High-Low-Close stock chart using your worksheet data. (*Hint*: To find the stock charts, click the Other Charts button.)

e. Format the horizontal axis to change the major unit to 7 days.

f. Change the color of the high-low lines to the standard color of red.

g. Add a rotated vertical axis title of **Stock Price**. Format the title in 14-point bold.

h. Format the Close data series in a color of purple from the standard colors and a size of 5. (*Hint*: You can change the size using the Marker Options in the Format Data Series dialog box.)

i. Add a chart title with your stock name above the chart. Format the title with a WordArt style of your choice from the WordArt Styles gallery. Change the vertical axis minimum and maximum values as necessary to view the chart lines.

j. Format the chart area using a gradient fill and transparency of your choice. Move the chart so it is below the worksheet data, leaving a couple of empty worksheet rows between the data and the chart.

k. Add Line sparklines to the cell below the Closing prices in the worksheet to show the trend of the stock over the past month. Format the sparklines in a color of your choice.

l. Enter your name in the center footer section of the worksheet, save the workbook, then preview the worksheet.

m. Close the workbook, submit the workbook to your instructor, then exit Excel.

Visual Workshop

Open the file EX J-6.xlsx from the drive and folder where you store your Data Files, and create the custom chart shown in Figure J-25. Save the workbook as **EX J-Organic Sales**. Study the chart and worksheet carefully to make sure you select the displayed chart type with all the enhancements shown. Enter your name in the center section of the worksheet footer, then preview the worksheet in landscape orientation on one page. Submit the workbook to your instructor.

FIGURE J-25

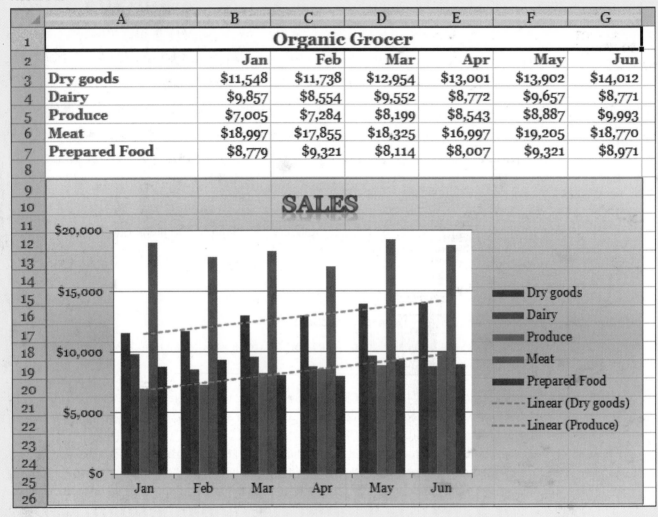

Using What-if Analysis

Each time you use a worksheet to explore different outcomes for Excel formulas, you are performing a **what-if analysis**. For example, what would happen to a firm's overall expense budget if company travel expenses decreased by 30 percent? Using Excel, you can perform a what-if analysis in many ways. In this unit, you learn to track what-if scenarios and generate summary reports using the Excel Scenario Manager. You design and manipulate data tables to project outcomes. Also, you use the Goal Seek feature to solve a what-if analysis. Finally, you use Solver to perform a complex what-if analysis involving multiple variables and use the Analysis ToolPak to generate descriptive statistics about your data. Kate Morgan, the vice president of sales at Quest, is meeting with the U.S. region manager to discuss sales projections for the first half of the year. Kate asks you to help analyze the U.S. sales data in preparation for her meeting.

OBJECTIVES

Define a what-if analysis

Track a what-if analysis with Scenario Manager

Generate a scenario summary

Project figures using a data table

Use Goal Seek

Set up a complex what-if analysis with Solver

Run Solver and summarize results

Analyze data using the Analysis ToolPak

Defining a What-if Analysis

By performing a what-if analysis in a worksheet, you can get immediate answers to questions such as "What happens to profits if we sell 25 percent more of a certain product?" or "What happens to monthly payments if interest rates rise or fall?". A worksheet you use to produce a what-if analysis is often called a **model** because it acts as the basis for multiple outcomes or sets of results. To perform a what-if analysis in a worksheet, you change the value in one or more **input cells** (cells that contain data rather than formulas), then observe the effects on dependent cells. A **dependent cell** usually contains a formula whose resulting value changes depending on the values in the input cells. A dependent cell can be located either in the same worksheet as the changing input value or in another worksheet. Kate Morgan has received projected sales data from regional managers. She has created a worksheet model to perform an initial what-if analysis, as shown in Figure K-1. She thinks the U.S. sales projections for the months of February, March, and April should be higher. You first review the guidelines for performing a what-if analysis.

DETAILS

When performing a what-if analysis, use the following guidelines:

- **Understand and state the purpose of the worksheet model**
  Identify what you want to accomplish with the model. What problem are you trying to solve? What questions do you want the model to answer for you? Kate's Quest worksheet model is designed to total Quest sales projections for the first half of the year and to calculate the percentage of total sales for each Quest region. It also calculates the totals and percentages of total sales for each month.

- **Determine the data input value(s) that, if changed, affect the dependent cell results**
  In a what-if analysis, changes in the content of the data input cells produces varying results in the output cells. You will use the model to work with three data input values: the February, March, and April values for the U.S. region, in cells C3, D3, and E3, respectively.

- **Identify the dependent cell(s) that will contain results**
  The dependent cells usually contain formulas, and the formula results adjust as you enter different values in the input cells. The results of two dependent cell formulas (labeled Total and Percent of Total Sales) appear in cells H3 and I3, respectively. The totals for the months of February, March, and April in cells C7, D7, and E7 are also dependent cells, as are the percentages for these months in cells C8, D8, and E8.

- **Formulate questions you want the what-if analysis to answer**
  It is important that you know the questions you want your model to answer. In the Quest model, you want to answer the following questions: (1) What happens to the U.S. regional percentage if the sales for the months of February, March, and April are each increased by $5000? (2) What happens to the U.S. regional percentage if the sales for the months of February, March, and April are each increased by $10,000?

- **Perform the what-if analysis**
  When you perform the what-if analysis, you explore the relationships between the input values and the dependent cell formulas. In the Quest worksheet model, you want to see what effect a $5000 increase in sales for February, March, and April has on the dependent cell formulas containing totals and percentages. Because the sales amounts for these months are located in cells C3, D3, and E3, any formula that references the cells is directly affected by a change in these sales amounts—in this case, the total formulas in cells H3, C7, D7, and E7. Because the formula in cell I3 references cell H3, a change in the sales amounts affects this cell as well. The percentage formulas in cells C8, D8, and E8 will also change because they reference the total formulas in cells C7, D7, and E7. Figure K-2 shows the result of the what-if analysis described in this example.

FIGURE K-1: Worksheet model for a what-if analysis

	A	B	C	D	E	F	G	H	I
1	**2014 Projected Sales**								
2		Jan	Feb	Mar	Apr	May	Jun	Total	Percent of Total Sales
3	U.S.	$91,473	$65,189	$67,423	$62,564	$102,926	$91,244	$480,819	30.32%
4	Canada	$65,068	$72,326	$76,244	$71,353	$68,015	$69,388	$422,394	26.64%
5	U.K.	$61,373	$65,756	$64,241	$72,716	$62,191	$42,334	$368,611	23.25%
6	Australia	$36,843	$55,657	$61,552	$59,708	$46,868	$53,224	$313,852	19.79%
7	Total	$254,757	$258,928	$269,460	$266,341	$280,000	$256,190	$1,585,676	
8	Percent of Total Sales	16.07%	16.33%	16.99%	16.80%	17.66%	16.16%		
9									
10									

Data input values

Dependent cell formulas

FIGURE K-2: Changed input values and dependent formula results

A1   *fx*   2014 Projected Sales

	A	B	C	D	E	F	G	H	I
1	**2014 Projected Sales**								
2		Jan	Feb	Mar	Apr	May	Jun	Total	Percent of Total Sales
3	U.S.	$91,473	$70,189	$72,423	$67,564	$102,926	$91,244	$495,819	30.98%
4	Canada	$65,068	$72,326	$76,244	$71,353	$68,015	$69,388	$422,394	26.39%
5	U.K.	$61,373	$65,756	$64,241	$72,716	$62,191	$42,334	$368,611	23.03%
6	Australia	$36,843	$55,657	$61,552	$59,708	$46,868	$53,224	$313,852	19.61%
7	Total	$254,757	$263,928	$274,460	$271,341	$280,000	$256,190	$1,600,676	
8	Percent of Total Sales	15.92%	16.49%	17.15%	16.95%	17.49%	16.01%		
9									

Changed input values

Changed formula results

Tracking a What-if Analysis with Scenario Manager

A **scenario** is a set of values you use to observe different worksheet results. For example, you might plan to sell 100 of a particular item, at a price of $5 per item, producing sales results of $500. But what if you reduced the price to $4 or increased it to $6? Each of these price scenarios would produce different sales results. A changing value, such as the price in this example, is called a **variable**. The Excel Scenario Manager simplifies the process of what-if analysis by allowing you to name and save multiple scenarios with variable values in a worksheet. ▰▰▰ Kate asks you to use Scenario Manager to create scenarios showing how a U.S. sales increase can affect total Quest sales over the 3-month period of February through April.

STEPS

1. **Start Excel, open the file EX K-1.xlsx from the drive and folder where you store your Data Files, then save it as EX K-Sales**

   The first step in defining a scenario is choosing the changing cells. **Changing cells** are those that will vary in the different scenarios.

2. **With the Projected Sales sheet active, select range C3:E3, click the Data tab, click the What-If Analysis button in the Data Tools group, then click Scenario Manager**

   The Scenario Manager dialog box opens with the following message: No Scenarios defined. Choose Add to add scenarios. You decide to create three scenarios. You want to be able to easily return to your original worksheets values, so your first scenario contains those figures.

3. **Click Add, drag the Add Scenario dialog box to the right if necessary until columns A and B are visible, then type Original Sales Figures in the Scenario name text box**

   The range in the Changing cells box shows the range you selected, as shown in Figure K-3.

4. **Click OK to confirm the scenario range**

   The Scenario Values dialog box opens, as shown in Figure K-4. The existing values appear in the changing cell boxes. Because you want this scenario to reflect the current worksheet values, you leave these unchanged.

QUICK TIP
You can delete a scenario by selecting it in the Scenario Manager dialog box and clicking Delete.

5. **Click OK**

   The Scenario Manager dialog box reappears with the new scenario, named Original Sales Figures, listed in the Scenarios box. You want to create a second scenario that will show the effects of increasing sales by $5,000.

6. **Click Add; in the Scenario name text box type Increase Feb, Mar, Apr by 5000; verify that the Changing cells text box reads C3:E3, then click OK; in the Scenario Values dialog box, change the value in the $C$3 text box to 70189, change the value in the $D$3 text box to 72423, change the value in the $E$3 text box to 67564, then click Add**

   You are ready to create a third scenario. It will show the effects of increasing sales by $10,000.

7. **In the Scenario name text box, type Increase Feb, Mar, Apr by 10000 and click OK; in the Scenario Values dialog box, change the value in the $C$3 text box to 75189, change the value in the $D$3 text box to 77423, change the value in the $E$3 text box to 72564, then click OK**

   The Scenario Manager dialog box reappears, as shown in Figure K-5. You are ready to display the results of your scenarios in the worksheet.

QUICK TIP
To edit a scenario, select it in the Scenario Manager dialog box, click the Edit button, then edit the Scenario.

8. **Make sure the Increase Feb, Mar, Apr by 10000 scenario is still selected, click Show, notice that the percent of U.S. sales in cell I3 changes from 30.32% to 31.62%; click Increase Feb, Mar, Apr by 5000, click Show, notice that the U.S. sales percent is now 30.98%; click Original Sales Figures, click Show to return to the original values, then click Close**

9. **Save the workbook**

FIGURE K-3: **Add Scenario dialog box**

Cell range containing value that you will change

Your user name and date will be different

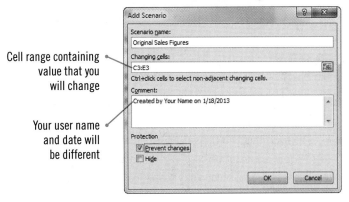

FIGURE K-4: **Scenario Values dialog box**

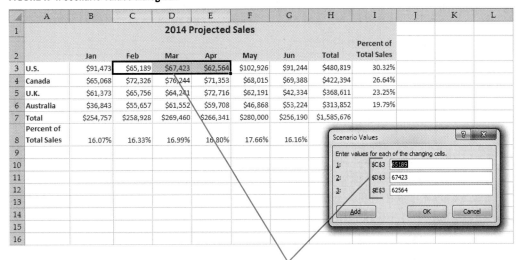

Changing cell boxes with original values

FIGURE K-5: **Scenario Manager dialog box with three scenarios listed**

Scenarios

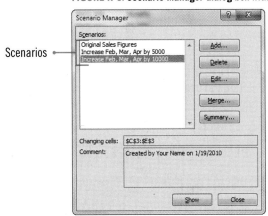

Merging scenarios

Excel stores scenarios in the workbook and on the worksheet in which you created them. To apply scenarios from another worksheet or workbook into the current worksheet, click the Merge button in the Scenario Manager dialog box. The Merge Scenarios dialog box opens, letting you select scenarios from other locations. When you click a sheet name in the sheet list, the text under the sheet list tells you how many scenarios exist on that sheet. To merge scenarios from another workbook, such as those sent to you in a workbook by a coworker, open the other workbook file, click the Book list arrow in the Merge Scenarios dialog box, then click the workbook name. When you merge workbook scenarios, it's best if the workbooks have the same structure, so that there is no confusion of cell values.

Generating a Scenario Summary

Although it may be useful to display the different scenario outcomes when analyzing data, it can be difficult to keep track of them. In most cases, you will want to refer to a single report that summarizes the results of all the scenarios in a worksheet. A **scenario summary** is an Excel table that compiles data from the changing cells and corresponding result cells for each scenario. For example, you might use a scenario summary to illustrate the best, worst, and most likely scenarios for a particular set of circumstances. Using cell naming makes the summary easier to read because the names, not the cell references, appear in the report. ▓▓▓▓ Now that you have defined Kate's scenarios, she needs you to generate and print a scenario summary report. You begin by creating names for the cells in row 2 based on the labels in row 1, so that the report will be easier to read.

STEPS

1. **Select the range B2:I3, click the Formulas tab, click the Create from Selection button in the Defined Names group, click the Top row check box to select it if necessary, then click OK**
   Excel creates the names for the data in row 3 based on the labels in row 2. You decide to review them.

QUICK TIP
You can also click the Name box list arrow on the formula bar to view cell names.

2. **Click the Name Manager button in the Defined Names group**
   The eight labels appear, along with other workbook names, in the Name Manager dialog box, confirming that they were created, as shown in Figure K-6. Now you are ready to generate the scenario summary report.

3. **Click Close to close the Name Manager dialog box, click the Data tab, click the What-If Analysis button in the Data Tools group, click Scenario Manager, then click Summary in the Scenario Manager dialog box**
   Excel needs to know the location of the cells that contain the formula results that you want to see in the report. You want to see the results for U.S. total and percentage of sales, and on overall Quest sales.

4. **With the Result cells text box selected, click cell H3 on the worksheet, type , (a comma), click cell I3, type , (a comma), then click cell H7**
   With the report type and result cells specified, as shown in Figure K-7, you are now ready to generate the report.

QUICK TIP
To see the Comments for each scenario, which by default contain the creator name and creation date, click the plus sign to the left of row 3.

5. **Click OK**
   A summary of the worksheet's scenarios appears on a new sheet titled Scenario Summary. The report shows outline buttons to the left of and above the worksheet so that you can hide or show report details. Because the Current Values column shows the same values as the Original Sales Figures column, you decide to delete column D.

6. **Right-click the column D heading, then click Delete in the shortcut menu**
   Next, you notice that the notes at the bottom of the report refer to the column that no longer exists. You also want to make the report title and labels for the result cells more descriptive.

7. **Select the range B13:B15, press [Delete], select cell B2, edit its contents to read Scenario Summary for U.S. Sales, click cell C10, then edit its contents to read Total U.S. Sales**

QUICK TIP
The scenario summary is not linked to the worksheet. If you change the values in the worksheet, you must generate a new scenario summary.

8. **Click cell C11, edit its contents to read Percent U.S. Sales, click cell C12, edit its contents to read Total Quest Sales, then click cell A1**
   The completed scenario summary is shown in Figure K-8.

9. **Add your name to the center section of the Scenario Summary sheet footer, change the page orientation to landscape, then save the workbook and preview the worksheet**

FIGURE K-6: **Name Manager dialog box displaying new names**

Newly created names

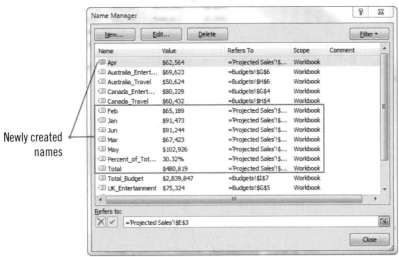

FIGURE K-7: **Scenario Summary dialog box**

Default report type

Cells to be recalculated when a new scenario is applied

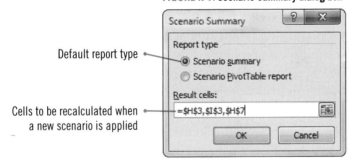

FIGURE K-8: **Completed Scenario Summary report**

Report is in outline format

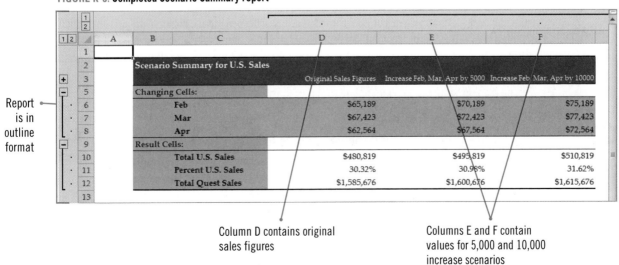

Column D contains original sales figures

Columns E and F contain values for 5,000 and 10,000 increase scenarios

Projecting Figures Using a Data Table

Another way to answer what-if questions in a worksheet is by using a data table. A **data table** is a range of cells that simultaneously shows the varying resulting values when one or more input values is changed in a formula. For example, you could use a data table to display your monthly mortgage payment based on several different interest rates. A **one-input data table** is a table that shows the result of varying one input value, such as the interest rate. ▆▆▆▆ Now that you have completed Kate's analysis, she wants you to find out how the U.S. sales percentage would change as U.S. total sales increased.

STEPS

1. **Click the Projected Sales sheet tab, enter Total U.S. Sales in cell K1, widen column K to fit the label, in cell K2 enter 480819, in cell K3 enter 530819, select the range K2:K3, drag the fill handle to select the range K4:K6, then format the values using the Accounting number format with zero decimal places**

   You begin setting up your data table by entering the total U.S. sales from cell H3 and then increasing the amount by increments of $50,000. These are the **input values** in the data table. With the varying input values listed in column K, you enter a formula reference to cell I3 that you want Excel to use in calculating the resulting percentages (the **output values**) in column L, based on the possible sales levels in column K.

2. **Click cell L1, type =, click cell I3, click the Enter button ☑ on the formula bar, then format the value in cell L1 using the Percentage format with two decimal places**

   The value in cell I3, 30.32%, appears in cell L1, and the cell name =Percent_of_Total_Sales appears in the formula bar, as shown in Figure K-9. Because it isn't necessary for users of the data table to see the value in cell L1, you want to hide the cell's contents from view.

3. **With cell L1 selected, click the Home tab, click the Format button in the Cells group, click Format Cells, click the Number tab in the Format Cells dialog box if necessary, click Custom under Category, select any characters in the Type box, type ;;; (three semicolons), then click OK**

   The three semicolons hide the values in a cell. With the table structure in place, you can now generate the data table showing percentages for the varying sales amounts.

4. **Select the range K1:L6, click the Data tab, click the What-If Analysis button in the Data Tools group, then click Data Table**

   You have highlighted the range that makes up the table structure. The Data Table dialog box opens, as shown in Figure K-10. This is where you indicate in which worksheet cell you want the varying input values (the sales figures in column K) to be substituted. Because the percentage formula in cell I3 (which you just referenced in cell L1) uses the total sales in cell H3 as input, you enter a reference to cell H3. You place this reference in the Column input cell text box, rather than in the Row input cell text box, because the varying input values are arranged in a column in your data table structure.

TROUBLE
If you receive the message "Selection not valid", repeat Step 4, taking care to select the entire range K1:L6.

5. **Click the Column input cell text box, click cell H3, then click OK**

   Excel completes the data table by calculating percentages for each sales amount.

6. **Format the range L2:L6 with the Percentage format with two decimal places, then click cell A1**

   The formatted data table is shown in Figure K-11. It shows the sales percentages for each of the possible levels of U.S. sales. By looking at the data table, Kate determines that if she can increase total U.S. sales to over $700,000, the U.S. division will then comprise about 40% of total Quest sales for the first half of 2014.

QUICK TIP
You cannot delete individual output values in a data table; you must delete all output values.

7. **Add your name to the center section of the worksheet footer, change the worksheet orientation to landscape, then save the workbook and preview the worksheet**

FIGURE K-9: One-input data table structure

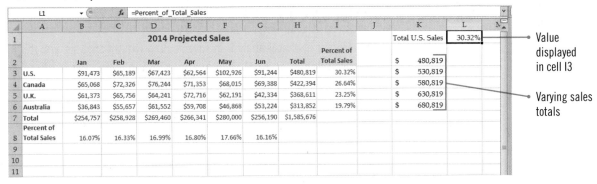

Value displayed in cell I3

Varying sales totals

FIGURE K-10: Data Table dialog box

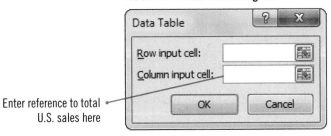

Enter reference to total U.S. sales here

FIGURE K-11: Completed data table with resulting values

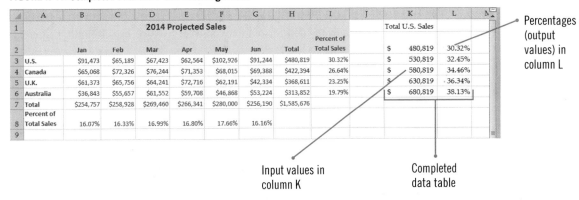

Percentages (output values) in column L

Input values in column K

Completed data table

Creating a two-input data table

A **two-input data table** shows the resulting values when two differ-ent input values are varied in a formula. You could, for example, use a two-input data table to calculate your monthly car payment based on varying interest rates and varying loan terms, as shown in Figure K-12. In a two-input data table, different values of one input cell appear across the top row of the table, while different values of the second input cell are listed down the left column. You create a two-input data table the same way that you created a one-input data table, except you enter both a row and a column input cell. In the example shown in Figure K-12, the two-input data table struc-ture was created by first entering the number of payments in the range B6:D6 and rates in the range A7:A19. Then the data table val-ues were created by first selecting the range A6:D19, clicking the Data tab, clicking the What-If Analysis button in the Data Tools group, then clicking Data Table. In the Data Table dialog box, the row input value is the term in cell C2. The column input value is the

interest rate in cell B2. You can check the accuracy of these values by cross-referencing the values in the data table with those in row 2 where you can see that an interest rate of 7% for 36 months has a monthly payment of $617.54.

FIGURE K-12: Two-input data table

	A	B	C	D
1	Loan Amount	Interest Rate	# Payments	Monthly Payment
2	$ 20,000.00	7.00%	36	$617.54
3				
4		Car Payment for $20,000 Loan		
5			Term	
6		36	48	60
7	6.48%	$612.80	$474.11	$391.14
8	6.61%	$613.98	$475.31	$392.35
9	6.74%	$615.17	$476.52	$393.58
10	6.87%	$616.35	$477.72	$394.80
11	7.00%	$617.54	$478.92	$396.02
12	7.13%	$618.73	$480.13	$397.25
13	7.26%	$619.92	$481.34	$398.48
14	7.39%	$621.11	$482.55	$399.71
15	7.52%	$622.31	$483.76	$400.95
16	7.65%	$623.50	$484.98	$402.19
17	7.78%	$624.70	$486.20	$403.43
18	7.91%	$625.90	$487.41	$404.67
19	8.04%	$627.10	$488.63	$405.91

Using Goal Seek

You can think of goal seeking as a what-if analysis in reverse. In a what-if analysis, you might try many sets of values to achieve a certain solution. To **goal seek**, you specify a solution, then ask Excel to find the input value that produces the answer you want. "Backing into" a solution in this way, sometimes referred to as **backsolving**, can save a significant amount of time. For example, you can use Goal Seek to determine how many units must be sold to reach a particular sales goal or to determine what expense levels are necessary to meet a budget target. ▓▓▓▓ After reviewing her data table, Kate has a follow-up question: What January U.S. sales target is required to bring the January Quest sales percentage to 17%, assuming the sales for the other regions don't change? You use Goal Seek to answer her question.

STEPS

1. **Click cell B8**

   The first step in using Goal Seek is to select a goal cell. A **goal cell** contains a formula in which you can substitute values to find a specific value, or goal. You use cell B8 as the goal cell because it contains the percent formula.

2. **Click the Data tab, click the What-If Analysis button in the Data Tools group, then click Goal Seek**

   The Goal Seek dialog box opens. The Set cell text box contains a reference to cell B8, the percent formula cell you selected in Step 1. You need to indicate that the figure in cell B8 should equal 17%.

3. **Click the To value text box, then type 17%**

   The value 17% represents the desired solution you want to reach by substituting different values in the By changing cell.

4. **Click the By changing cell text box, then click cell B3**

   You have specified that you want cell B3, the U.S. January amount, to change to reach the 17% solution, as shown in Figure K-13.

5. **Click OK**

   The Goal Seek Status dialog box opens with the following message: "Goal Seeking with Cell B8 found a solution." By changing the sales amount in cell B3 to $109,232, Goal Seek achieves a January percentage of 17.

QUICK TIP

Before you select another command, you can return the worksheet to its status prior to the Goal Seek by pressing [Ctrl][Z].

6. **Click OK, then click cell A1**

   Changing the sales amount in cell B3 changes the other dependent values in the worksheet (B7, H3, I3, and H7) as shown in Figure K-14.

7. **Save the workbook, then preview the worksheet**

FIGURE K-13: **Completed Goal Seek dialog box**

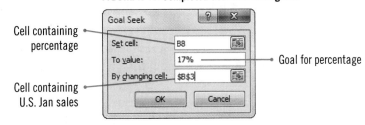

Cell containing percentage → Set cell: B8

To value: 17% ← Goal for percentage

Cell containing U.S. Jan sales → By changing cell: $B$3

FIGURE K-14: **Worksheet with new dependent values**

	A	B	C	D	E	F	G	H	I	J
1				2014 Projected Sales						
2		Jan	Feb	Mar	Apr	May	Jun	Total	Percent of Total Sales	
3	U.S.	$109,232	$65,189	$67,423	$62,564	$102,926	$91,244	$498,578	31.09%	
4	Canada	$65,068	$72,326	$76,244	$71,353	$68,015	$69,388	$422,394	26.34%	
5	U.K.	$61,373	$65,756	$64,241	$72,716	$62,191	$42,334	$368,611	22.99%	
6	Australia	$36,843	$55,657	$61,552	$59,708	$46,868	$53,224	$313,852	19.57%	
7	Total	$272,516	$258,928	$269,460	$266,341	$280,000	$256,190	$1,603,435		
8	Percent of Total Sales	17.00%	16.15%	16.81%	16.61%	17.46%	15.98%			
9										
10										
11										

New target values calculated by Goal Seek

New dependent values

Setting up a Complex What-if Analysis with Solver

The Excel Solver is an **add-in** program that provides optional features. It must be installed before you can use it. Solver finds the best solution to a problem that has several inputs. The cell containing the formula is called the **target cell**, or **objective**. As you learned earlier, cells containing the values that vary are called "changing cells." Solver is helpful when you need to perform a complex what-if analysis involving multiple input values or when the input values must conform to specific limitations or restrictions called **constraints**. 🎬🎬🎬 Kate decides to fund each region with the same amount, $757,500, to cover expenses. She adjusts the travel and entertainment allocations to keep expenditures to the allocated amount of $757,500. You use Solver to help Kate find the best possible allocation.

STEPS

TROUBLE
If Solver is not on your Data tab, click the File tab, click Options, click Add-Ins, in the list of Add-ins click Solver Add-in, click Go, in the Add-Ins dialog box click the Solver Add-in check box to select it, then click OK.

1. **Click the Budgets sheet tab**

   This worksheet is designed to calculate the travel, entertainment, and other budgets for each region. It assumes fixed costs for communications, equipment, advertising, salaries, and rent. You use Solver to change the entertainment and travel amounts in cells G3:H6 (the changing cells) to achieve your target of a total budget of $3,030,000 in cell I7 (the target cell). You want your solution to include a constraint on cells G3:H6 specifying that each region is funded $757,500. Based on past budgets, you know there are two other constraints: the travel budgets must include at least $80,000, and the entertainment budgets must include at least $93,000. It is a good idea to enter constraints on the worksheet for documentation purposes, as shown in Figure K-15.

2. **Click the Data tab, then click the Solver button in the Analysis group**

   In the Solver Parameters dialog box opens, you indicate the target cell with its objective, the changing cells, and the constraints under which you want Solver to work. You begin by entering your total budget objective.

TROUBLE
If your Solver Parameters dialog box has entries in the By Changing Cells box or in the Subject to the Constraints box, click Reset All, click OK, then continue with Step 3.

3. **With the insertion point in the Set Objective text box, click cell I7 in the worksheet, click the Value Of option button, double-click the Value Of text box, then type 3,030,000**

   You have specified an objective of $3,030,000 for the total budget. In typing the total budget figure, be sure to type the commas.

4. **Click the By Changing Variable Cells text box, then select the range G3:H6 on the worksheet**

   You have told Excel which cells to vary to reach the goal of $3,030,000 total budget. You need to specify the constraints on the worksheet values to restrict the Solver's answer to realistic values.

5. **Click Add, with the insertion point in the Cell Reference text box in the Add Constraint dialog box, select the range I3:I6 in the worksheet, click the list arrow in the dialog box, click =, then with the insertion point in the Constraint text box click cell C9**

   As shown in Figure K-16, the Add Constraint dialog box specifies that cells in the range I3:I6, the total region budget amounts, should be equal to the value in cell C9. Next, you need to add the constraint that the budgeted entertainment amounts should be at least $93,000.

QUICK TIP
If your solution needs to be an integer, you can select it in the Add Constraint dialog box.

6. **Click Add, with the insertion point in the Cell Reference text box select the range G3:G6 in the worksheet, click the list arrow, select >=, with the insertion point in the Constraint text box click cell C11**

   Next, you need to specify that the budgeted travel amounts should be greater than or equal to $80,000.

7. **Click Add, with the insertion point in the Cell Reference text box select the range H3:H6, select >=, with the insertion point in the Constraint text box click cell C10, then click OK**

   The Solver Parameters dialog box opens with the constraints listed, as shown in Figure K-17. In the next lesson, you run Solver and generate solutions to the budget constraints.

Using What-if Analysis

FIGURE K-15: Worksheet set up for a complex what-if analysis

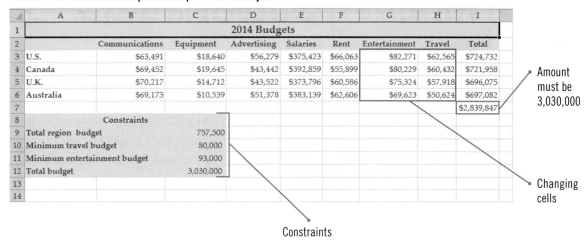

Amount must be 3,030,000

Changing cells

Constraints

FIGURE K-16: Adding constraints

Cells containing region budget amounts

Value in cell C9 should be 757,500

FIGURE K-17: Completed Solver Parameters dialog box

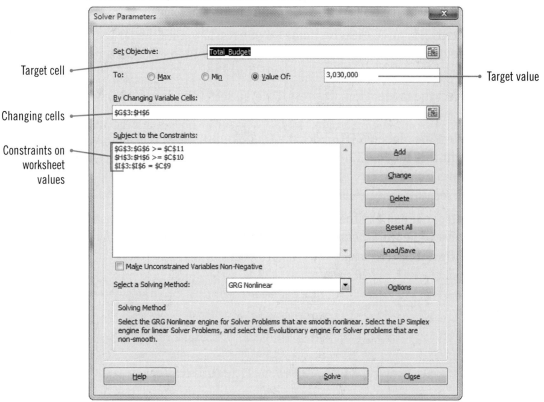

Target cell

Changing cells

Constraints on worksheet values

Target value

Running Solver and Summarizing Results

After entering all the parameters in the Solver Parameters dialog box, you can run Solver to find a solution. In some cases, Solver may not be able to find a solution that meets all of your constraints. Then you would need to enter new constraints and try again. Once Solver finds a solution, you can choose to create a summary of the solution or a special report displaying the solution. You have finished entering the parameters in the Solver Parameters dialog box. Kate wants you to run Solver and create a summary of the solution on a separate worksheet.

STEPS

1. **Make sure your Solver Parameters dialog box matches Figure K-17 in the previous lesson**

2. **Click Solve**

   The Solver Results dialog box opens, indicating that Solver has found a solution, as shown in Figure K-18. The solution values appear in the worksheet, but you decide to save the solution values in a summary worksheet and display the original values in the worksheet.

3. **Click Save Scenario, enter Adjusted Budgets in the Scenario Name text box, click OK, in the Solver Results dialog box click the Restore Original Values option button, then click OK to close the Solver Results dialog box**

   The Solver Results dialog box closes, and the original values appear in the worksheet. You will display the Solver solution values on a separate sheet.

4. **Click the What-If Analysis button in the Data Tools group, click Scenario Manager, with the Adjusted Budgets scenario selected in the Scenario Manager dialog box click Summary, then click OK**

   The Solver results appear on the Scenario Summary 2 worksheet, as shown in Figure K-19. To keep the budget at $3,030,000 and equally fund each region, the travel and entertainment budget allocations are calculated in column E labeled Adjusted Budgets. You want to format the solution values on the worksheet.

5. **Select Column A, click the Home tab if necessary, click the Delete button in the Cells group, right-click the Scenario Summary 2 sheet tab, click Rename on the shortcut menu, type Adjusted Budgets, then press [Enter]**

6. **Select the range A16:A18, press [Delete], select the range A2:D3, click the Fill Color list arrow, then click Blue, Accent 2**

7. **Select the range A5:D15, click the Fill Color list arrow, click Blue, Accent 2, Lighter 80%, right-click the row 1 header to select the row, click Delete, select cell A1, then enter Solver Solution**

   The formatted Solver solution is shown in Figure K-20.

8. **Enter your name in the center section of the worksheet footer, save the workbook, then preview the worksheet**

   You have successfully found the best budget allocations using Solver.

FIGURE K-18: **Solver Results dialog box**

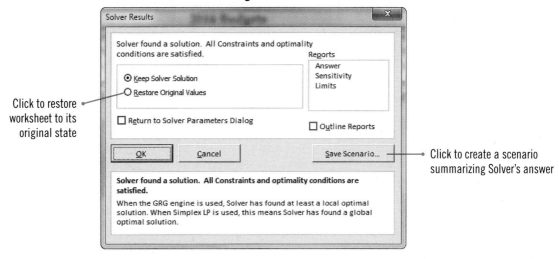

Click to restore worksheet to its original state

Click to create a scenario summarizing Solver's answer

FIGURE K-19: **Solver Summary**

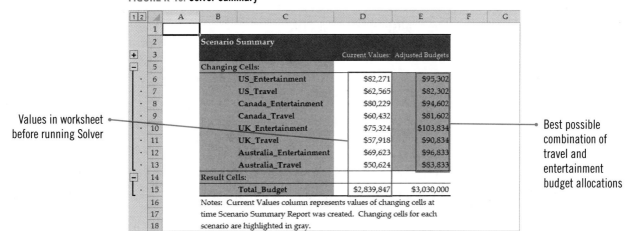

Values in worksheet before running Solver

Best possible combination of travel and entertainment budget allocations

FIGURE K-20: **Formatted Solver Summary**

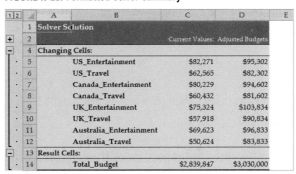

Understanding Answer Reports

Instead of saving Solver results as a scenario, you can select from three types of answer reports in the Solver Results window. One of the most useful is the Answer Report, which compares the original values with the Solver's final values. The report has three sections. The top section has the target cell information; it compares the original value of the target cell with the final value. The middle section of the report contains information about the adjustable cells. It lists the original and final values for all cells that were changed to reach the target value. The last report section has information about the constraints. Each constraint that was added into Solver is listed in the Formula column along with the cell address and a description of the cell data. The Cell Value column contains the Solver solution values for the cells. These values will be different from your worksheet values if you restored the original values to your worksheet rather than keeping Solver's solution. The Status column contains information on whether the constraints were binding or not binding in reaching the solution. If a solution is not binding, the slack—or how far the result is from the constraint value—is provided. Frequently, the answer report shows equality constraints as nonbinding with a slack of zero.

Analyzing Data Using the Analysis ToolPak

The Analysis ToolPak is an Excel add-in that contains many statistical analysis tools. The Descriptive Analysis tool in the Data Analysis dialog box generates a statistical report including mean, median, mode, minimum, maximum, and sum for an input range you specify on your worksheet. After reviewing the projected sales figures for the Quest regions, Kate decides to statistically analyze the projected regional sales totals submitted by the managers. You use the Analysis ToolPak to help her generate the sales statistics.

STEPS

1. **Click the Projected Sales sheet tab, click the Data tab, then click the Data Analysis button in the Analysis group**

   The Data Analysis dialog box opens, listing the available analysis tools.

2. **Click Descriptive Statistics, then click OK**

   The Descriptive Statistics dialog box opens, as shown in Figure K-21.

3. **With the insertion point in the Input Range text box, select the range H3:H6 on the worksheet**

   You have told Excel to use the total projected sales cells in the statistical analysis. You need to specify that the data is grouped in a column and the results should be placed on a new worksheet named Region Statistics.

4. **Click the Columns option button in the Grouped By: area if necessary, click the New Worksheet Ply option button in the Output options section if necessary, then type Region Statistics in the text box**

   You want to add the summary statistics to the new worksheet.

5. **Click the Summary statistics check box to select it, then click OK**

   The statistics are generated and placed on the new worksheet named Region Statistics. Table K-1 describes some of the statistical values provided in the worksheet. Column A is not wide enough to view the labels, and the worksheet needs a descriptive title.

6. **Widen column A to display the row labels, then edit the contents of cell A1 to read Total Projected Sales Jan – Jun**

7. **Enter your name in the center section of the Region Statistics footer, preview the report, save the workbook, close the workbook, then exit Excel**

8. **Submit the workbook to your instructor**

   The completed report is shown in Figure K-22.

Choosing the right tool for your data analysis

The Analysis ToolPak offers 19 options for data analysis. ANOVA, or the analysis of variance, can be applied to one or more samples of data. The regression option creates a table of statistics from a least-squares regression. The correlation choice measures how strong of a linear relationship exists between two random variables. A moving average is often calculated for stock prices or any other data that is time sensitive. Moving averages display long-term trends by smoothing out short-term changes. The Random Number Generation creates a set of random numbers between values that you specify. The Rank and Percentile option creates a report of the ranking and percentile distribution.

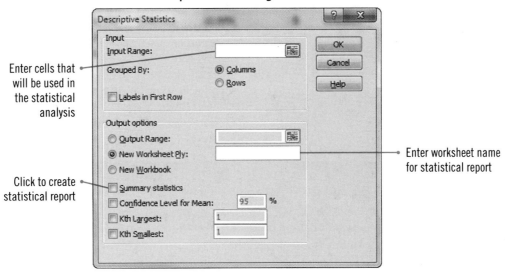

FIGURE K-21: **Descriptive Statistics dialog box**

Enter cells that will be used in the statistical analysis

Enter worksheet name for statistical report

Click to create statistical report

FIGURE K-22: **Completed Report**

Total Projected Sales Jan - Jun

Mean	400858.7
Standard Error	39394.23
Median	395502.5
Mode	#N/A
Standard Deviation	78788.46
Sample Variance	6.21E+09
Kurtosis	-0.54301
Skewness	0.342022
Range	184725.8
Minimum	313852
Maximum	498577.8
Sum	1603435
Count	4

TABLE K-1: **Descriptive statistics**

statistic	definition
Mean	The average of a set of numbers
Median	The middle value of a set of numbers
Mode	The most common value in a set of numbers
Standard Deviation	The measure of how widely spread the values in a set of numbers are; if the values are all close to the mean, the standard deviation is close to zero
Range	The difference between the largest and smallest values in a set of numbers
Minimum	The smallest value in a set of numbers
Maximum	The largest value in a set of numbers
Sum	The total of the values in a set of numbers
Count	The number of values in a set of numbers
Skewness	The measure of the asymmetry of the values in a set of numbers
Sample Variance	The measure of how scattered the values in a set of numbers are from an expected value
Kurtosis	The measure of the peakedness or flatness of a distribution of data

Practice

For current SAM information, including versions and content details, visit SAM Central (http://www.cengage.com/samcentral). If you have a SAM user profile, you may have access to hands-on instruction, practice, and assessment of the skills covered in this unit. Since various versions of SAM are supported throughout the life of this text, check with your instructor for the correct instructions and URL/Web site for accessing assignments.

Concepts Review

FIGURE K-23

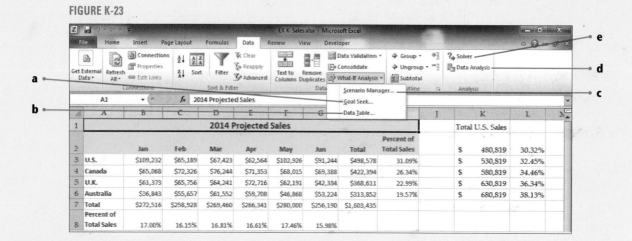

1. Which element do you click to perform a statistical analysis on worksheet data?
2. Which element do you click to create a range of cells showing the resulting values with varied formula input?
3. Which element do you click to perform a what-if analysis involving multiple input values with constraints?
4. Which element do you click to name and save different sets of values to forecast worksheet results?
5. Which element do you click to find the input values that produce a specified result?

Match each term with the statement that best describes it.

6. One-input data table
7. Solver
8. Goal Seek
9. Scenario summary
10. Two-input data table

a. Add-in that helps you solve complex what-if scenarios with multiple input values
b. Separate sheet with results from the worksheet's scenarios
c. Generates values resulting from varying two sets of changing values in a formula
d. Helps you backsolve what-if scenarios
e. Generates values resulting from varying one set of changing values in a formula

Select the best answer from the list of choices.

11. To hide the contents of a cell from view, you can use the custom number format:
    a. ;;;
    b. —
    c. Blank
    d. " "
12. The _____ button in the Scenario Manager dialog box allows you to bring scenarios from another workbook into the current workbook.
    a. Combine
    b. Add
    c. Import
    d. Merge

Using What-if Analysis

13. **When you use Goal Seek, you specify a _____, then find the values that produce it.**
   - **a.** Row input cell
   - **b.** Column input cell
   - **c.** Solution
   - **d.** Changing value

14. **In Solver, the cell containing the formula is called the:**
   - **a.** Changing cell.
   - **b.** Target cell.
   - **c.** Input cell.
   - **d.** Output cell.

15. **Which of the following Excel add-ins can be used to generate a statistical summary of worksheet data?**
   - **a.** Solver
   - **b.** Lookup Wizard
   - **c.** Analysis ToolPak
   - **d.** Conditional Sum

Skills Review

1. **Define a what-if analysis.**
   - **a.** Start Excel, open the file EX K-2.xlsx from the drive and folder where you store your Data Files, then save it as **EX K-Repair**.
   - **b.** Examine the Auto Repair worksheet to determine the purpose of the worksheet model.
   - **c.** Locate the data input cells.
   - **d.** Locate any dependent cells.
   - **e.** Examine the worksheet to determine problems the worksheet model can solve.

2. **Track a what-if analysis with Scenario Manager.**
   - **a.** On the Auto Repair worksheet, select the range B3:B5, then use the Scenario Manager to set up a scenario called **Most Likely** with the current data input values.
   - **b.** Add a scenario called **Best Case** using the same changing cells, but change the Labor cost per hour in the $B$3 text box to **80**, change the Parts cost per job in the $B$4 text box to **65**, then change the Hours per job value in cell $B$5 to **1.5**.
   - **c.** Add a scenario called **Worst Case**. For this scenario, change the Labor cost per hour in the $B$3 text box to **95**, change the Parts cost per job in the $B$4 text box to **80**, then change the Hours per job in the $B$5 text box to **3**.
   - **d.** If necessary, drag the Scenario Manager dialog box to the right until columns A and B are visible.
   - **e.** Show the Worst Case scenario results, and view the total job cost.
   - **f.** Show the Best Case scenario results, and observe the job cost. Finally, display the Most Likely scenario results.
   - **.g.** Close the Scenario Manager dialog box.
   - **h.** Save the workbook.

3. **Generate a scenario summary.**
   - **a.** Create names for the input value cells and the dependent cell using the range A3:B7.
   - **b.** Verify that the names were created.
   - **c.** Create a scenario summary report, using the Cost to complete job value in cell B7 as the result cell.
   - **d.** Edit the title of the Summary report in cell B2 to read **Scenario Summary for Auto Repair**.
   - **e.** Delete the Current Values column.
   - **f.** Delete the notes beginning in cell B11. Compare your worksheet to Figure K-24.
   - **g.** Return to cell A1, enter your name in the center section of the Scenario Summary sheet footer, save the workbook, then preview the Scenario Summary sheet.

FIGURE K-24

	A	B	C	D	E	F
1						
2		Scenario Summary for Auto Repair				
3				Most Likely	Best Case	Worst Case
5		Changing Cells:				
6			Labor_cost_per_hour	$90.00	$80.00	$95.00
7			Parts_cost_per_job	$70.00	$65.00	$80.00
8			Hours_per_job	2.00	1.50	3.00
9		Result Cells:				
10			Cost_to_complete_job	$250.00	$185.00	$365.00

Skills Review (continued)

4. Project figures using a data table.

a. Click the Auto Repair sheet tab.

b. Enter the label **Labor $** in cell D3.

c. Format the label so that it is boldfaced and right-aligned.

d. In cell D4, enter **75**; then in cell D5, enter **80**.

e. Select the range D4:D5, then use the fill handle to extend the series to cell D8.

f. In cell E3, reference the job cost formula by entering **=B7**.

g. Format the contents of cell E3 as hidden, using the ;;; Custom formatting type on the Number tab of the Format Cells dialog box.

h. Generate the new job costs based on the varying labor costs. Select the range D3:E8 and create a data table. In the Data Table dialog box, make cell B3 (the labor cost) the column input cell.

i. Format the range E4:E8 as currency with two decimal places. Compare your worksheet to Figure K-25.

j. Enter your name in the center section of the worksheet footer, save the workbook, then preview the worksheet.

5. Use Goal Seek.

FIGURE K-25

▲	A	B	C	D	E
1	Auto Repair Model				
2					
3	Labor cost per hour	$90.00		Labor $	
4	Parts cost per job	$70.00		75	$220.00
5	Hours per job	2.00		80	$230.00
6				85	$240.00
7	Cost to complete job:	$250.00		90	$250.00
8				95	$260.00
9					

a. Click cell B7, and open the Goal Seek dialog box.

b. Assuming the labor rate and the hours remain the same, determine what the parts would have to cost so that the cost to complete the job is $220. (*Hint*: Enter a job cost of **220** as the To value, and enter **B4** (the Parts cost) as the By changing cell. Write down the parts cost that Goal Seek finds.

c. Click OK, then use [Ctrl][Z] to reset the parts cost to its original value.

d. Enter the cost of the parts in cell A14.

e. Assuming the parts cost and hours remain the same, determine the fee for the labor so that the cost to complete the job is $175. Use [Ctrl][Z] to reset the labor cost to its original value. Enter the labor cost in cell A15.

f. Save the workbook, then preview the worksheet.

6. Set up a complex what-if analysis with Solver.

a. With the Brake Repair sheet active, open the Solver Parameters dialog box.

b. Make B14 (the total repair costs) the objective cell, with a target value of 15,000.

c. Use cells B6:D6 (the number of scheduled repairs) as the changing cells.

d. Specify that cells B6:D6 must be integers. (*Hint*: Select int in the Add Constraint dialog box.)

e. Specify a constraint that cells B6:D6 must be greater than or equal to 10.

7. Run Solver and summarize results.

a. Use Solver to find a solution.

b. Save the solution as a scenario named **Repair Solution**, and restore the original values to the worksheet.

c. Create a scenario summary using the Repair Solution scenario, delete the notes at the bottom of the solution, and rename the worksheet Repair Solution. Compare your worksheet to Figure K-26.

d. Enter your name in the center section of the worksheet footer, save the workbook, then preview the worksheet.

FIGURE K-26

▲	A	B	C	D	E
1					
2		Scenario Summary			
3				Current Values:	Repair Solution
5		Changing Cells:			
6		$B$6		25	20
7		$C$6		35	31
8		$D$6		15	12
9		Result Cells:			
10		$B$14		$17,950.00	$15,000.00

Skills Review (continued)

8. **Analyze data using the Analysis ToolPak.**

   a. With the Brake Repair sheet active, generate summary descriptive statistics for the repair cost per model, using cells B10:D10 as the input range. (*Hint*: The input is grouped in a row.) Place the new statistics on a worksheet named **Repair Cost Statistics**.

   b. Widen columns as necessary to view the statistics.

   c. Change the contents of cell A1 to **Repair Cost Per Model**. Delete row 9 containing the kurtosis error information. (This was generated because you only have three data values.) Compare your worksheet to Figure K-27.

   d. Add your name to the center section of the worksheet footer, then preview the worksheet.

   e. Save and close the workbook, submit the workbook to your instructor, then exit Excel.

FIGURE K-27

	A	B
1	Repair Cost Per Model	
2		
3	Mean	5983.333333
4	Standard Error	1626.238844
5	Median	7125
6	Mode	#N/A
7	Standard Deviation	2816.728303
8	Sample Variance	7933958.333
9	Skewness	-1.524287472
10	Range	5275
11	Minimum	2775
12	Maximum	8050
13	Sum	17950
14	Count	3
15		

Independent Challenge 1

You are the manager for Smith & Weston, an environmental consulting firm based in Chicago. You are planning a computer hardware upgrade for the engineers in the company. The vice president of finance at the company has asked you to research the monthly cost for a $100,000 equipment loan to purchase the new computers. You will create a worksheet model to determine the monthly payments based on several different interest rates and loan terms, using data from the company's bank. Using Scenario Manager, you will create the following three scenarios: a 4-year loan at 7.5 percent; a 3-year loan at 6.75 percent; and a 2-year loan at 6.5 percent. You will also prepare a scenario summary report outlining the payment details.

a. Start Excel, open the file EX K-3.xlsx from the drive and folder where you store your Data Files, then save it as **EX K-Equipment Loan**.

b. Create cell names for the cells B4:B11 based on the labels in cells A4:A11, using the Create Names from Selection dialog box.

c. Use Scenario Manager to create scenarios that calculate the monthly payment on a $100,000 loan under the three sets of loan possibilities listed below. (*Hint*: Create three scenarios using cells B5:B6 as the changing cells.)

Scenario Name	Interest Rate	Term
7.5% 4 Yr	.075	48
6.75% 3 Yr	.0675	36
6.5% 2 Yr	.065	24

d. Show each scenario to make sure it performs as intended, then display the 7.5% 4 Yr scenario.

e. Generate a scenario summary titled **Scenario Summary for $100,000 Hardware Purchase**. Use cells B9:B11 as the Result cells.

f. Delete the Current Values column in the report, and delete the notes at the bottom of the report.

g. Enter your name in the center section of the Scenario Summary sheet footer. Save the workbook, then preview the scenario summary.

Advanced Challenge Exercise

- Copy the range A1:B11 from the Loan sheet, and paste it on Sheet2. Widen the columns as necessary. Rename Sheet2 to **My Loan**.
- Create a new scenario in the copied sheet called **Local**, using an interest rate and term available at a local lending institution. Test the new scenario by displaying the local values in the worksheet.
- Return to the Loan sheet and merge the scenario from the My Loan sheet into the Loan sheet. (*Hint*: Use the Merge option in the Scenario Manager dialog box.)
- Verify that the Local scenario appears in the Scenario Manager dialog box of the Loan sheet, then generate a scenario summary titled **Advanced Scenario Summary**, using cells B9:B11 as the Result cells. Delete the Current Values column in the report and the notes at the bottom.

Independent Challenge 1 (continued)

- Enter your name in the center section of the Scenario Summary 2 sheet footer, save the workbook, then preview the Advanced Scenario Summary.

h. Close the workbook, exit Excel, then submit the workbook to your instructor.

Independent Challenge 2

You are a CFO at Northern Interactive, an interactive media consulting company based in Minneapolis. The company president has asked you to prepare a loan summary report for a business expansion. You need to develop a model to show what the monthly payments would be for a $500,000 loan with a range of interest rates. You will create a one-input data table that shows the results of varying interest rates in 0.2% increments, then you will use Goal Seek to specify a total payment amount for this loan application.

a. Start Excel, open the file EX K-4.xlsx from the drive and folder where you store your Data Files, then save it as **EX K-Capital Loan Payment Model**.

b. Reference the monthly payment amount from cell B9 in cell E4, and format the contents of cell E4 as hidden.

c. Using cells D4:E13, create a one-input data table structure with varying interest rates for a 5-year loan. Use cells D5:D13 for the interest rates, with 9% as the lowest possible rate and 10.6% as the highest. Vary the rates in between by 0.2%. Use Figure K-28 as a guide.

FIGURE K-28

	A	B	C	D
1	Northern Interactive			
2				
3				
4	Loan Amount	$500,000.00		Interest Rate
5	Annual Interest Rate	9.80%		9.00%
6	Term in Months	60		9.20%
7				9.40%
8				9.60%
9	Monthly Payment:	$10,574.39		9.80%
10	Total Payments:	$634,463.11		10.00%
11	Total Interest:	$134,463.11		10.20%
12				10.40%
13				10.60%
14				

d. Generate the data table that shows the effect of varying interest rates on the monthly payments. Use cell B5, the Annual Interest Rate, as the column input cell. Format the range E5:E13 as currency with two decimal places.

e. Select cell B10 and use Goal Seek to find the interest rate necessary for a total payment amount of $600,000. Use cell B5, the Annual Interest Rate, as the By changing cell. Accept the solution found by Goal Seek.

Advanced Challenge Exercise

- Reference the monthly payment amount from cell B9 in cell A13, and format the contents of cell A13 as hidden.
- Using cells A13:C22, create a two-input data table structure with varying interest rates for 10- and 15-year terms. Use Figure K-29 as a guide.
- Generate the data table that shows the effect of varying interest rates and loan terms on the monthly payments. (*Hint*: Use cell B6, Term in Months, as the row input cell, and cell B5, the Annual Interest Rate, as the column input cell.)
- Format the range B14:C22 as currency with two decimal places.

FIGURE K-29

	A	B	C	D	E	F
1	Northern Interactive					
2						
3						
4	Loan Amount	$500,000.00		Interest Rate		
5	Annual Interest Rate	7.42%		9.00%	$10,379.18	
6	Term in Months	60		9.20%	$10,427.78	
7				9.40%	$10,476.51	
8				9.60%	$10,525.38	
9	Monthly Payment:	$10,000.00		9.80%	$10,574.39	
10	Total Payments:	$600,000.00		10.00%	$10,623.52	
11	Total Interest:	$100,000.00		10.20%	$10,672.79	
12				10.40%	$10,722.20	
13			120	180	10.60%	$10,771.74
14	7.00%					
15	7.25%					
16	7.50%					
17	7.75%					
18	8.00%					
19	8.25%					
20	8.50%					
21	8.75%					
22	9.00%					
23						

f. Enter your name in the center section of the worksheet footer, save the workbook, then preview the worksheet.

g. Close the workbook, exit Excel, then submit the workbook to your instructor.

Independent Challenge 3

You are the owner of Home Health, a home medical products company based in Boston. You are considering adding local delivery service to your business. You decide on a plan to purchase a combination of vans, sedans, and compact cars that can deliver a total of 1500 cubic feet of products. You want to first look at how the interest rate affects the monthly payments for each vehicle type you are considering purchasing. To do this, you use Goal Seek. You need to keep the total monthly payments for all of the vehicles at or below $6,000. You use Solver to help find the best possible combination of vehicles.

a. Start Excel, open the file EX K-5.xlsx from the drive and folder where you store your Data Files, then save it as **EX K-Vehicle Purchase**.

b. Use Goal Seek to find the interest rate that produces a monthly payment for the van purchase of $1,650, and write down the interest rate that Goal Seek finds. Record the interest rate in cell A19, enter **Interest rate for $1650 van payment** in cell B19, then reset the interest rate to its original value.

c. Use Goal Seek to find the interest rate that produces a monthly payment for the sedan purchase of $950. Record the interest rate in cell A20, enter **Interest rate for $950 sedan payment** in cell B20, then reset the interest rate to its original value of 6.75%.

d. Use Goal Seek to find the interest rate that produces a monthly payment for the compact purchase of $790. Record the interest rate in cell A21, enter **Interest rate for $790 compact payment** in cell B21, then reset the interest rate to its original value.

e. Assign cell B8 the name **Quantity_Van**, name cell C8 **Quantity_Sedan**, name cell D8 **Quantity_Compact**, and name cell B15 **Total_Monthly_Payments**. Use Solver to set the total delivery capacity of all vehicles to 1500. Use the quantity to purchase, cells B8:D8, as the changing cells. Specify that cells B8:D8 must be integers. Make sure that the total monthly payments amount in cell B15 is less than or equal to $6,000.

f. Generate a scenario named **Delivery Solution** with the Solver values, and restore the original values in the worksheet. Create a scenario summary using the Delivery Solution scenario, delete the notes at the bottom of the solution, and edit cell B2 to contain **Solver Solution**.

g. Enter your name in the center footer section of both worksheets. Preview both worksheets, then save the workbook.

h. Close the workbook, then submit the workbook to your instructor.

Real Life Independent Challenge   *All Klapperich T   Due Wed 11/20 Ex-K6*

You decide to take out a loan for a new car. You haven't decided whether to finance the car for 3, 4, or 5 years. You will create scenarios for car loans with the different terms, using interest rates at your local lending institution. You will summarize the scenarios to make them easy to compare.

a. Start Excel, open the file EX K-6.xlsx from the drive and folder where you store your Data Files, then save it as **EX K-Car Payment**.

b. Research the interest rates for 3-year, 4-year, and 5-year auto loans at your local lending institution. Record your 48-month interest rate in cell B3 of the worksheet. Change the data in cell B2 to the price of a car you would like to purchase, then widen columns as necessary.

c. Create cell names for the cells B2:B9 based on the labels in cells A2:A9.

d. Create a scenario named **48 months** to calculate the monthly payment for your loan amount, using the 48-month term and the corresponding interest rate at your lending institution.

e. Create a scenario named **36 months** to calculate the monthly payment for your loan amount, using the 36-month term and the corresponding interest rate at your lending institution.

f. Create a scenario named **60 months** to calculate the monthly payment for your loan amount, using the 60-month term and the corresponding interest rate at your lending institution.

g. Generate a scenario summary titled **Scenario Summary for Car Purchase** that summarizes the payment information in cells B7:B9 for the varying interest rates and terms. Delete the Current Values column in the report and the notes at the bottom of the report.

h. Enter your name in the center section of the scenario summary footer, then preview the scenario summary.

i. Enter your name in the center section of the Loan sheet footer, then preview the Loan sheet.

j. Save the workbook, close the workbook, then exit Excel and submit the workbook to your instructor.

Visual Workshop

Open the file EX K-7.xlsx from the drive and folder where you save your Data Files, then save it as **EX K-Atlanta Manufacturing**. Create the worksheet shown in Figure K-30. (*Hint*: Use Goal Seek to find the Hourly labor cost to reach the total profit in cell H11 in the figure and accept the solution.) Then generate descriptive statistics for the products' total profits on a worksheet named **Manufacturing Profits**, as shown in Figure K-31. Add your name to the center footer section of each sheet, change the orientation of the Profit sheet to landscape, then preview and print both worksheets.

FIGURE K-30

	A	B	C	D	E	F	G	H
1	Atlanta Manufacturing							
2	January Production							
3	Hourly Labor Cost	$61.18						
4								
5								
6	Product Number	Hours	Parts Cost	Cost to Produce	Retail Price	Unit Profit	Units Produced	Total Profit
7	NA1547	8	$452	$ 941.43	$1,695.00	$ 753.57	327	$ 246,417.12
8	CB5877	10	$214	$ 825.79	$1,588.00	$ 762.21	407	$ 310,220.07
9	QW5287	15	$384	$1,301.68	$1,995.00	$ 693.32	321	$ 222,554.82
10	TY8894	17	$610	$1,650.04	$2,544.00	$ 893.96	247	$ 220,807.99
11	Total Profit							$ 1,000,000.00
12								

FIGURE K-31

	A	B
1	*Profit Statistics*	
2		
3	Mean	250000
4	Standard Error	20905.95
5	Median	234486
6	Mode	#N/A
7	Standard Deviation	41811.9
8	Sample Variance	1.75E+09
9	Kurtosis	2.254124
10	Skewness	1.575897
11	Range	89412.07
12	Minimum	220808
13	Maximum	310220.1
14	Sum	1000000
15	Count	4
16		

Glossary

Add-in An extra program, such as Solver and the Analysis ToolPak, that provides optional Excel features. To activate an add-in, click the File tab, click Options, click Add-Ins, then select or deselect add-ins from the list.

And condition A filtering feature that searches for records by specifying that all entered criteria must be matched.

Ascending order In sorting an Excel field (column), the order that begins with the letter A or the lowest number of the values in the field.

AutoFilter A table feature that lets you click a list arrow and select criteria by which to display certain types of records; *also called* filter.

AutoFilter list arrows *See* Filter List arrows.

Backsolving A problem-solving method in which you specify a solution and then find the input value that produces the answer you want; sometimes described as a what-if analysis in reverse. In Excel, the Goal Seek feature performs backsolving.

Backward-compatible Software feature that enables documents saved in an older version of a program to be opened in a newer version of the program.

Calculated columns In a table, a column that automatically fills in cells with formula results, using a formula entered in only one other cell in the same column.

Category axis Horizontal axis in a chart, usually containing the names of data categories; in a 2-dimensional chart, also known as the x-axis.

Changing cells In what-if analysis, cells that contain the values that change in order to produce multiple sets of results.

Color scale In conditional formatting, a formatting scheme that uses a set of two, three, or four fill colors to convey relative values of data.

Comments Notes you've written about a workbook that appear when you place the pointer over a cell.

Constraints Limitations or restrictions on input data in what-if analysis.

Criteria range In advanced filtering, a cell range containing one row of labels (usually a copy of column labels) and at least one additional row underneath it that contains the criteria you want to match.

Data entry area The unlocked portion of a worksheet where users are able to enter and change data.

Data label Descriptive text that appears above a data marker in a chart.

Data table A range of cells that shows the resulting values when one or more input values are varied in a formula; when one input value is changed, the table is called a one-input data table, and when two input values are changed, it is called a two-input data table. In a chart, it is a grid containing the chart data.

Dependent cell A cell, usually containing a formula, whose value changes depending on the values in the input cells. For example, a payment formula or function that depends on an input cell containing changing interest rates is a dependent cell.

Descending order In sorting an Excel field (column), the order that begins with the letter Z or the highest number of the values in the field.

Dynamic page breaks In a larger workbook, horizontal or vertical dashed lines that represent the place where pages print separately. They also adjust automatically when you insert or delete rows or columns, or change column widths or row heights.

Extract To place a copy of a filtered table in a range you specify in the Advanced Filter dialog box.

Field In a table (an Excel database), a column that describes a characteristic about records, such as first name or city.

Field name A column label that describes a field.

Filter To display data in an Excel table that meet specified criteria. *See also* AutoFilter.

Filter list arrows List arrows that appear next to field names in an Excel table; used to display portions of your data. *Also called* AutoFilter list arrows.

Freeze To hold in place selected columns or rows when scrolling in a worksheet that is divided in panes. *See also* Panes.

Goal cell In backsolving, a cell containing a formula in which you can substitute values to find a specific value, or goal.

Goal Seek A problem-solving method in which you specify a solution and then find the input value that produces the answer you want; sometimes described as a what-if analysis in reverse; *also called* backsolving.

Header row In a table, the first row that contains the field names.

HTML (Hypertext Markup Language) The format of pages that a Web browser can read.

Hyperlink An object (a filename, a word, a phrase, or a graphic) in a worksheet that, when clicked, displays another worksheet or a Web page called the target. *See also* Target.

Icon sets In conditional formatting, groups of images that are used to visually communicate relative cell values based on the values they contain.

Input cells Spreadsheet cells that contain data instead of formulas and that act as input to a what-if analysis; input values often change to produce different results. Examples include interest rates, prices, or other data.

Input values In a data table, the variable values that are substituted in the table's formula to obtain varying results, such as interest rates.

Instance A worksheet in its own workbook window.

Intranet An internal network site used by a group of people who work together.

Keywords Terms added to a workbook's Document Properties that help locate the file in a search.

Linear trendline In an Excel chart, a straight line representing an overall trend in a data series.

List arrows See Filter list arrows.

Lock To secure a row, column, or sheet so that data in that location cannot be changed.

Logical conditions Using the operators And and Or to narrow a custom filter criteria.

Macros Programmed instructions that perform tasks in a workbook.

Metadata Information that describes data and is used in Microsoft Windows document searches.

Model A worksheet used to produce a what-if analysis that acts as the basis for multiple outcomes.

Mode In dialog boxes, a state that offers a limited set of possible choices.

Modeless Describes dialog boxes that, when opened, allow you to select other elements on a chart or worksheet to change the dialog box options and format, or otherwise alter the selected elements.

Module In Visual Basic, a module is stored in a workbook and contains macro procedures.

Multilevel sort A reordering of table data using more than one column at a time.

Objective *See* Target cell.

One-input data table A range of cells that shows resulting values when one input value in a formula is changed.

Or condition The records in a search must match only one of the criterion.

Output values In a data table, the calculated results that appear in the body of the table.

Panes Sections into which you can divide a worksheet when you want to work on separate parts of the worksheet at the same time; one pane freezes, or remains in place, while you scroll in another pane until you see the desired information.

Personal macro workbook A workbook that can contain macros that are available to any open workbook. By default, the personal macro workbook is hidden.

Plot area In a chart, the area inside the horizontal and vertical axes.

Print area A portion of a worksheet that you can define using the Print Area button on the Page Layout tab; after you select and define a print area, the Quick Print feature prints only that worksheet area.

Print title In a table that spans more than one page, the field names that print at the top of every printed page.

Program code Macro instructions, written in the Visual Basic for Applications (VBA) programming language.

Properties File characteristics, such as the author's name, keywords, or the title, that help others understand, identify, and locate the file.

Publish To place an Excel workbook or worksheet on a Web site or an intranet in HTML format so that others can access it using their Web browsers.

Read-only format Data that users can view but not change.

Record In a table (an Excel database), data that relates to an object or a person.

Regression analysis A way of representing data with a mathematically-calculated trendline showing the overall trend represented by the data.

Relative cell reference In a formula, a cell address that refers to a cell's location in relation to the cell containing the formula and that automatically changes to reflect the new location when the formula is copied or moved; default type of referencing used in Excel worksheets. *See also* Absolute cell reference.

Run To play, as a macro.

Scenario A set of values you use to forecast results; the Excel Scenario Manager lets you store and manage different scenarios.

Scenario summary An Excel table that compiles data from various scenarios so that you can view the scenario results next to each other for easy comparison.

Search criterion In a workbook or table search, the text you are searching for.

Shared workbook An Excel workbook that several users can open and modify.

Single-file Web page A Web page that integrates all of the worksheets and graphical elements from a workbook into a single file in the MHTML file format, making it easier to publish to the Web.

Sparkline A quick, simple chart located within a cell that serves as a visual indicator of data trends.

Structured reference Allows table formulas to refer to table columns by names that are automatically generated when the table is created.

Table An organized collection of rows and columns of similarly structured data on a worksheet.

Table styles Predesigned formatting that can be applied to a range of cells or even to an entire worksheet; especially useful for those ranges with labels in the left column and top row, and totals in the bottom row or right column. *See also* Table.

Table total row A row you can add to the bottom of a table for calculations using the data in the table columns.

Target The location that a hyperlink displays after the user clicks it.

Target cell In what-if analysis (specifically, in Excel Solver), the cell containing the formula; *also called* objective.

Toggle A button with two settings, on and off.

Track To identify and keep a record of who makes which changes to a workbook.

Trendline A series of data points on a line that shows data values that represent the general direction of the data.

Two-input data table A range of cells that shows resulting values when two input values in a formula are changed.

Value axis In a chart, the axis that contains numerical values; in a 2-dimensional chart, also known as the y-axis.

Variable In the Visual Basic programming language, an area in memory in which you can temporarily store an item of information; variables are often declared in Dim statements such as *DimNameAsString*. In an Excel scenario or what-if analysis, a changing input value, such as price or interest rate, that affects a calculated result.

VBA *See* Visual Basic for Applications.

View A set of display or print settings that you can name and save for access at another time. You can save multiple views of a worksheet.

Virus Destructive software that can damage your computer files.

Visual Basic Editor A program that lets you display and edit macro code.

Visual Basic for Applications (VBA) A programming language used to create macros in Excel.

Watermark A translucent background design on a worksheet that is displayed when the worksheet is printed. Watermarks are graphic files that are inserted into the document header.

What-if analysis A decision-making tool in which data is changed and formulas are recalculated in order to predict various possible outcomes.

Wildcard A special symbol that substitutes for unknown characters in defining search criteria in the Find and Replace dialog box. The most common types of wildcards are the question mark (?), which stands for any single character, and the asterisk (*), which represents any group of characters.

WordArt Specially formatted text, created using the WordArt button on the Drawing toolbar.

Workspace An Excel file with an .xlw extension containing information about the identity, view, and placement of a set of open workbooks. Rather than opening each workbook individually, you can open the workspace file instead.

Index